LAST LETTERS *to*
Christian

The Workmanship of God in Our Salvation

DOUGLAS A. WEIGENT

WESTBOW
PRESS®
A DIVISION OF THOMAS NELSON
& ZONDERVAN

WestBow Press books may be ordered through booksellers or by contacting:

WestBow Press
A Division of Thomas Nelson & Zondervan
1663 Liberty Drive
Bloomington, IN 47403
www.westbowpress.com
844-714-3454

ISBN: 978-1-6642-7817-2 (sc)
ISBN: 978-1-6642-7819-6 (hc)
ISBN: 978-1-6642-7818-9 (e)

Library of Congress Control Number: 2022916943

Print information available on the last page.

WestBow Press rev. date: 10/19/2022

Contents

Acknowledgements

I acknowledge the help of previous Christian authors, whose writings on occasion have provided hints and guided my thoughts. They confirm my spiritual journey. Helpful authors included Thomas Brooks, Watchman Nee, Stephen Charnock, Arthur Pink, and Charles Spurgeon. The most helpful has been The Whole Bible Commentary by Matthew Henry. Some books have been consulted and these are listed in the back as selected references for additional reading. Most scripture quotations in this book are from The New American Standard Bible (The Open Bible, 1977). A few scripture quotations are from the King James version of the Bible. I have written from my memory and previous lessons taught in Sunday School and for the Jails. I share my understanding and experience in the Lord over the past 60 years. I acknowledge the generous support of my wife, Diane, my daughter, Rachel and my grandson, Christian. I gratefully acknowledge many friends, that over the years have been important pieces of my life. I gratefully acknowledge my wife for editorial assistance, and the publisher for help in the preparation of this book. The most important acknowledgement I have, is for the lovingkindness of God. I believe I have been led and blessed by the Lord. To God be the glory. Amen.

Introduction

Dear Reader,

After I retired from work, I planned on writing one book about Jesus to my grandson. That book, entitled "Letters to Christian," was about the grace of God in the battle for the future of his soul. The letters described how to equip and protect the soul against temptation and sin with His armor of truth. After I finished the book, I was surprised by the feeling of being lonely and empty. It turned out that I missed being with the Lord in worship, and reading and writing about the Bible. The blessing of being with the Lord spurred me onto writing a second book entitled "More Letters to Christian." The second book described the gifts that God provides for our souls that establish us in Jesus, help us grow in grace and delight in our Christian experience. The gifts of God become an experiential truth. We are His workmanship (Eph. 2:10). The Lord works out our journey into His heart. We have been blessed, and God is the reason and the source of amazing grace. Again, the time spent with the Lord was the stimulus to write another book. This one I have entitled "Last Letters to Christian". I think this book will be my final written words. God has been faithful and good to me with His presence and grace to accomplish this task. If you read them and are spiritually nourished in Jesus, I will consider my effort a great reward.

In part of my journey as a Christian, I found the experience to be a battle. I spent some time struggling with my responsibility for salvation. I knew I was a sinner and that holiness was important, but I was weak and never had a peace about where I was at. At the same time, I failed to understand and appreciate the meaning or role of God's sovereignty in salvation. Today, I know that human responsibility and God's sovereignty are both important and true for salvation. Early on, I knew about the Bible, but I never read it in any kind of detail where it helped me. I think the world, my flesh and the Devil combined their effort to keep me ignorant. I knew the Bible said "you shall know the truth, and the truth shall make you free" (John 8:32), but I was not free. Eventually, God sent me deeper into the Gospel of John, the book of Ephesians and finally Romans; by the grace of God, I woke up. Bible study has been an indispensable part for me to understand my salvation and to know the Lord. Thank you, Jesus.

There are at least two passages in the Bible that have meant a lot to me in writing books. The first is, "For by grace you have been saved through faith and not of yourselves, it is a gift of God; not as a result of works, that no one should boast. For we are His workmanship, created in Christ Jesus for good works, which God prepared beforehand, that we should walk in them" (Eph. 2:8-10). The second passage is "work out your salvation with fear and trembling; for it is God who is at work in you, both to will and to work for His good pleasure" (Phil. 2:12-13). The two scripture passages cited above highlight the importance of God's gifts and work, and our part for salvation. Jesus Himself said, "This is the work of God, that you believe in Him who He has sent" (John 6:29). God requires that we believe in Jesus. The only work that God accepts is faith in His Son (Acts 16:31). The natural man does not have the heart or mind to come to Jesus, he must be drawn by God. "No one can come to Me, unless the Father who sent Me draws him" (John 6:44). To be drawn by Christ is for us to believe in Christ. In believing in Christ, we come to Jesus as Savior. In this way, we are born again and made spiritually alive (John 3:3). We become a new creation (2 Cor. 5:17), and a partaker of the Divine nature (2 Pet. 1:4). "It is the Spirit who gives life" (John 6:63). The convicting power of the Holy Spirit works in our heart to lay hold of Jesus for salvation. With the heart, man believes that God raised Jesus from the dead, resulting in righteousness (Rom. 10:9-10). By the grace of God, the convicting power of the Spirit is the source of the gifts of faith, repentance and eternal life in Christ Jesus our Lord (Rom. 6:23). In believing, we receive in our heart a motive for holy living and walking by faith in freedom. We come to know and behold the work of God in our heart, soul, mind and strength. Amen.

The Bible tells us that, "In the exercise of His will He brought us forth by the word of truth so that we might be, as it were, the first fruits among His creatures" (James 1:18). Peter tells us, "You have been born again not of seed which is perishable but imperishable, that is, through the living and abiding word of God" (1 Pet. 1:23). Christ is the Savior appointed by God, and faith in Him is what God approves and accepts for salvation. We must only accept the work already done by Christ, and not try to be saved by ourselves. Believe and then see. It becomes our responsibility to discover what God has already built up into us, by fear and trembling, after we were born again. We must read the Bible to know God, because this is where He has chosen to reveal Himself. The Bible tells us that "God hast magnified Thy word according to all Thy name" (Ps. 138:2). In the Bible, we learn about God's attributes and His workmanship to save us from the penalty of sin. In the Bible, we learn about Jesus and that God is good. Amen.

In His goodness, He chose to save us and make us holy children through the Gospel or Word of truth. God acted in love according to His own good pleasure. He made us (Job 33:4) and fashions within us a new heart (Ps. 33:15, Ezek. 11:19). He works for us (Eph. 3:20, Phil. 1:6, 2:13, Ps. 57:2). He accomplishes the work that concerns us and causes all things to work together for good (Rom. 8:28). From the new birth we are brought forth in character, by the grace of God, as first fruits, consecrated to God and holy to the Lord. Grace is the first-fruit of glory begun. We have groans within ourselves, as evidence of life as a first fruit waiting for our adoption (Rom. 8:23). As God's first fruits, we are to bear fruit for Him. God's goal for us is to be conformed to the image of His Son (Rom. 8:29). The fruit of the Spirit are characteristics Jesus displayed that appear in the life of a believer through the power of the Holy Spirit. Some attributes of God are considered "communicable"; that is, they are qualities that both God and man can possess though only God possesses them perfectly. Some of the communicable qualities include wisdom, faithfulness, goodness, patience, mercy, lovingkindness and holiness. This book is about the attributes of God that He communicates to us as fruit of the Holy Spirit. They reflect His image and bless our lives. God works to give you a desire for His word, a holy life and a service life for His glory. God works to adopt you into His family and give you eternal life in a way that will survive His presence with great joy.

The fruit of the Spirit is produced in us by the Spirit, and not by the Christian. As we grow in grace, the characteristics of Christ become manifested in our lives. The Holy Spirit works to rid our lives of the sinful nature (Gal. 5:19) and display His fruit. Our responsibility is to work out our salvation with fear and trembling (Phil. 2:12). God plants the seed and it is our responsibility to work out what God has planted into us. The growth in grace is accomplished by the Holy Spirit as we read the Bible, pray and follow after Jesus. There is a reproducing of the life of Christ in us. We experience a kind of transfiguration. It is a manifestation of His presence in and through the believer (2 Cor. 3:18). It is not an imitation or a fixing of the old man, but a new creation (2 Cor. 5:17). God works in man by His truth, Spirit, and grace "both to will and to work for His good pleasure" (Phil. 2:13). The graces of the Spirit of God wrought into our hearts by God are the evidence of our salvation. God gives the desire, but the choice is still ours. Our work is an attitude of fear and trembling, or humility and vigilance, carrying out the actions of Bible study, prayer and striving against sin. This "work" is not a work to be saved, but a work of discovery where we come to fear sin and dishonoring God. The Lord says, "To this one I will look, to him who is humble and contrite of spirit, and who trembles at My word" (Isa. 66:2). We are to present our bodies as a living and holy sacrifice to God (Rom. 12:1), and "cleanse ourselves from all defilement of flesh and spirit, perfecting holiness in the fear of God" (2 Cor. 7:1). The fear of the Lord is the beginning of wisdom or wise living (Prov. 9:10, Eccl. 12:13). Fear is both an awe of the greatness of God and a dread of His discipline (Heb. 12:6). The fear is about our diligence (Heb. 4:1). We are to distrust the ways of the flesh, the world and the Devil, and trust Jesus. By the grace of God, we grow into a place of trembling before God. We tremble because we have become serious about following Jesus with an obedience of faith. It is not a trembling because you might lose your soul, but a reminder that we are acting against His love and in need of discipline (Heb. 12:5, 10:31). We are to work from a tender conscience and avoid areas of temptation to sin that would discredit the Lord Jesus. The work will be difficult, but God's decrees will be carried on in hope with diligence and His grace. The rewards will be spiritual riches because they will disclose more of Jesus in your heart. The trembling at God's word shows that your heart is in awe of God's majesty and purity, and has become a living temple where God dwells. We have a promise of growing up, until we are made perfect to enter His rest in glory (Phil. 1:6, Heb. 4:1). We are to do our utmost with fear, and then, by the grace of God, we gain a rest in our conscience. It is like heaven on earth. To God be the glory.

Our working depends upon His working. We cannot act without God's grace. Only because of the merits of Jesus, can we gain back spiritual life and be changed back into the image of the heavenly (1 Cor. 15:45-49). By the grace of God, we are "predestined to become conformed to the image of His Son, that He might become the first-fruits among many brethren" (Rom. 8:29). We are "renewed to a true knowledge according to the image of the One who created him" (Col. 3:10). We are being transformed into His Bride, that will mirror the holy and beautiful character of God. When we read the word, it reads us and we can see our true self. God's word does not return to Himself void (Isa. 55:11). When a man reads the word of God and turns to the Lord, the veil of blindness is taken away and he sees the glory of the Lord. With an unveiled face, beholding Him, we are transformed into the same image from glory to glory (2 Cor. 3:16-18). The proof of faith in your heart is a gift from God's heart (1 Pet. 1:3-7). The proof of salvation is in your reflection of His image. His good will in us is the strength that enables us to work, so all the merit and glory belong to God. We are stewards of God's grace. God gives us the evidence of His loving presence through the fruit we have from the Holy Spirit. The fruit that God gives is the grace to be holy, and serve Him in gladness. The love of God for us is great. He blesses us with spiritual gifts from the Spirit, that mirror, in many ways His own attributes and image. We shall grow slowly and eventually be like Him (1 John 3:2). We are to use the spiritual gifts to worship and serve God, and serve other people with the strength that God supplies (1 Pet. 4:10-11).

The purpose of this book is to share the great work that God does in our souls to insure our forgiveness of sin and acceptance as His children for eternal life. We were originally made in His image (Gen. 1:26). Though we lost it in the Garden of Eden, He brings it back for us. We are always on a journey, outlined and empowered by the love of God. He provides the spiritual fountain we drink from to be like Christ. For the new creation, we are transformed into the image of Jesus. For the new creation, God builds into our lives the fruit of His own Spirit. The discussion of God's attributes in these letters, allows the comparison to be made between the transfiguration of our hearts, and the reflection of His image. We are not gods, but we can be godly. The approach I have taken includes letters on God's power, wisdom and providence, proving that only God is able to do this work. Next, I included letters on the fruit of the Spirit for patience, goodness and faithfulness, proving we can know that God is doing a saving work in us. Finally, I included letters on the heart, freedom and holiness, further establishing our reflection of God's handiwork. Though each letter is different and can stand by itself, I want you to read the whole book. Some aspects of the fruit of the Spirit, such as love, joy and peace, have been woven into these letters where appropriate. In God's time and way, He brings us to places in our lives where we experience and better understand His goodness. His work of grace in our soul, is our greatest blessing. I thank the Lord for giving me a heart to read His word and spend time with Him writing three books. To God be the glory. "Let the words of my mouth and the meditation of my heart be acceptable in Thy sight, O Lord, my rock and my redeemer" (Ps. 19:14). Amen.

Power

> "I pray that the eyes of your heart may be enlightened so that you may know what is the hope of His calling, what are the riches of the glory of His inheritance in the saints, and what is the surpassing greatness of His power toward us who believe. These are in accordance with the working of the strength of His might. Which He brought about in Christ Jesus when He raised Him from the dead" (Eph. 1:18-20).

Dear Christian,

Many years ago, a verse of the scripture that got my attention and made me think about God was in Romans. It said, "For from Him and through Him and to Him are all things. To Him be the glory forever. Amen" (Rom. 11:36). This made me think that the whole of my life was known to God. Not only my life, Christian, but that everyone's life was inside the purpose of God. God is in charge of the beginning, the middle and the end of our lives. Amen. By God's wisdom, goodness and power, all things are being governed by Him. God is the all-sufficient cause of everything. God is the source of our lives, our thoughts, our will and the workings in our conscience. He brings about our salvation through a regenerated will and gives and sustains our ability to believe and persevere. From the power in His mercy, He "has caused us to be born again to a living hope through the resurrection of

Jesus Christ from the dead, to obtain an inheritance reserved in heaven" (1 Pet. 1:3-4). "We are protected by the power of God through faith for a salvation ready to be revealed at the last time" (1 Pet. 1:5). The scheme of redemption was designed by God. God poured the wealth of His nature into Jesus Christ to bless us for a reconciliation with Himself. God sustains us by the work and power of the Holy Spirit, and when He is done, we will enter into His presence. He deserves all the glory forever. In all these things, Christian, the sovereignty, providence and power of God will be necessary and evident for our salvation and joy. God's glory will be in our beginning and for the conclusion of our earthly lives. His power in grace will be working for us forever (Rom.1:20). Amen.

The power of God, which created the universe and saves our soul, is the essence of God. He is a Creator and a Savior. "For by Him all things were created, both in the heavens and on earth, visible and invisible, whether thrones or dominions or rulers or authorities, all things have been created by Him and for Him" (Col. 1:16). Glorious things are said here of the Christ, our Redeemer. He is the image of the invisible God, and in Him all things hold together. He is the head of the body, which means, He is the foundation and the cornerstone of the church (Col. 1:15-18). He was before all things, before He was born of the virgin. "In the beginning was the Word, and the Word was with God, and the Word was God" (John 1:1). He is the principle of our resurrection. "Our God is in the heavens; He does whatever He pleases" (Ps. 115:3). Incomprehensible in essence, absolute in will and infinite in power (Eph. 1:19).

Man cannot understand God's power. We have a little portion or a taste of "this treasure in earthen vessels, that the surpassing greatness of the power may be of God and not from ourselves" (2 Cor. 4:7). The grace of God, by the illumination of the Spirit, creates a light in our soul that enlightens the mind. It cleanses the conscience, rejoices the heart and converts us to the gospel. This power is from God, Christian, and not ourselves or other men. "The word of God is living and active and sharper than any two-edged sword, and piercing as far as the division of soul and spirit, of both joints and marrow, and able to judge the thoughts and intentions of the heart" (Heb. 4:12). The gospel is empowered by God. Amen. It changes your heart in a way that you know something has happened that you do not fully understand, but you more easily welcome the gospel into your heart. In addition, you are convinced that the change was not because of something you did or what someone else said. Exactly how the power of God works is a mystery, but the fact a work has been done in your heart cannot be disputed. The Bible, church, prayer and holiness bring forth, by the power of God, a more sincere priority for spiritual life in Jesus.

I am convinced "there is but one God, the Father, from whom are all things, and we exist for Him; and one Lord, Jesus Christ, by whom are all things, and we exist through Him" (1 Cor. 8:6). Not all men experience this change or conversion in the same way, and some men do not show any change in attitudes about God. Some men do not understand it, or desire more of it, and some sneer and rage against it. The grace of God is His grace to give. No one and nothing can thwart or hinder the eternal purposes of God. "So shall My word be which goes forth from My mouth; It shall not return to Me empty, without accomplishing what I desire, and without succeeding in the matter for which I sent it" (Isa. 55:11). My own human power, Christian, is severely limited. I have had trouble even breaking free from bad habits. How could I really ever understand how God's word moves my heart to be like Jesus. The gospel will not be proclaimed in vain. The death of Jesus will not be in vain. The power and faithfulness of God for our salvation, and much more, will shine in His glory. "He who began a good work in you will perfect it until the day of Jesus Christ (Phil. 1:6). I want you to give God more chances to demonstrate the power of His love for you in the gospel. I want you to behold your salvation growing deeper and deeper in your heart. Amen.

"Not by might nor by power, but by My Spirit, says the Lord of hosts" (Zech. 4:6). This is found in a passage of the scripture from Zechariah, the prophet, to Zerubbabel, the leader of the first group of folks returning to Israel from the Babylonian exile.

They were words of encouragement to a small number of people to keep their vision of a restored Jerusalem. It applies to us today. "If God be for us, who is against us?" (Rom. 8:31). If we only rely on our own human power and might, the road will be long and challenging and too difficult to traverse. If we rely on the certainty of the power of Jesus within us, that is, His Spirit, we will succeed. The weapons of our warfare are not carnal for the pulling down of strongholds, but spiritual weapons which include the word of God, prayer, love, the armor of God and the power of God's Spirit working in our lives (2 Cor. 10:4). Amen. The work of grace in our soul is a new creation, a new man, and is called regeneration. The power to accomplish this transformation is from God. We become children of God "who believe in His name, who were born not of blood, nor of the will of the flesh, nor of the will of man, but of God" (John 1:12-13). The gift of faith in our hearts with power, Christian, is a work of grace by God to believe in Jesus for salvation. The Spirit of grace causes us to abound in the exercise of grace unto the obedience of faith. To God be all the glory for this powerful action of love that delivers us peacefully and safely into His kingdom. Finally, my brethren, be strong in the Lord, and the power of His might" (Eph. 6:10). The treasure we have in our earthen vessel is very important. It is the supernatural power that the Lord provides for us and wants us to operate through against temptation, and fight all the spiritual battles against our souls. When we surrendered to Jesus and received Him into our hearts, this new strength became available to us through the Holy Spirit working in our lives. Nothing is impossible for the strength of God to carry out (Luke 1:37). Only the power of God brings about the salvation of lost sinners. Amen.

In the Book of Ephesians, Paul prayed "that the eyes of your heart may be enlightened, so that you may know what is the hope of His calling, what are the riches of the glory of His inheritance in the saints, and what is the surpassing greatness of His power toward us who believe. These are in accordance with the working of the strength of His might" (Eph.1:8-9). He continues by describing the demonstration of God's power in the raising of Jesus from the dead, and seating Him at His right hand far above all authority and power. Further, He put all things in subjection under His feet and gave Him as head over the church which is His body (Eph. 1:20-22). So, because we are in Christ and He is in us, we have resurrection power. Paul tells us, Christian, "that the gift of God's grace given to him as a minister was according to the working of His power" (Eph. 3:7). Paul's hope and desire was to know Jesus, "and the power of His resurrection" (Phil. 3:10). God has bestowed on believers a kind of strength that becomes inherent, called "might". We rely on this "might" when we walk with and serve Jesus. I know this "might" or strength in my soul is from God. I know this strength by my interest and renewed conviction to follow Jesus. I know this "might", Christian, from an obedience of faith, as a fact. I know this "might" by my determination to be found loving the Lord's presence (Mark 12:30). To God be the glory. I know this "might" when I go to jails and exercise the gift of encouragement. His presence goes before us and with us and follows up to complete the work of His word, which does not return to Him void (Isa. 55:11). I have known this "might" when I found myself standing against my sin. Thank you, Jesus.

We conquer through Him who loved us (Rom. 8:37). "Put on the full armor of God, that you may be able to stand firm against the schemes of the devil" (Eph. 6:11). Remember, God's armor is spiritual and the power it releases in the soul is from the truth against a lie. The power that the truth of God releases, protects the soul against spiritual wickedness and schemes of the devil. Each piece of armor is rich in doctrine, and is the spiritual knowledge and power of God that protects a specific portion of your soul. For example, the breastplate of righteousness protects your heart. It reminds you that your righteousness is as a filthy rag (Isa. 64:6), but the righteousness of Jesus removes guilt and completely secures your acceptance with God. When the shield of faith is lifted, it calls out for the Lord's help. The helmet of salvation reminds you that you are saved by grace and not works. The truth has power, by the grace of God, that sets you free. The devil wants you to be ignorant of truth, and to trust yourself and not the Lord. I wrote a lot about this in my first book entitled "Letters to Christian". God is all-powerful, and the power of the Lord is reflected from a new man in Jesus. Amen.

God's presence and power is experienced in hearing and or reading the words of God. "So, faith comes by hearing, and hearing by the word of Christ" (Rom. 10:17). The Lord made the hearing ear and the seeing eye (Prov. 20:12). "Now faith is the assurance of things hoped for, the conviction of things not seen (Heb. 11:1). "Without faith it is impossible to please Him, for he who comes to God must believe that He is, and that He is a rewarder of those who seek Him" (Heb. 11:6). "For by grace you have been saved through faith; and that not of yourselves, it is the gift of God" (Eph. 2:8). God is rich in mercy and grace and takes us through the experiences of the gift of a maturing faith. Amen. God's grace opens our soul, we become alive in Jesus, and then live a life of sanctification from faith to faith in Jesus. The gospel is the power of God unto salvation. Our justification, acceptance and reconciliation are revealed as the righteousness of God (Rom. 1;16-17). The just shall live by faith (Hab. 2:4) and live to know the faithfulness of God (1 Cor. 10:13, 1 John 1:9). Amen. We are set apart, separated and sanctified for salvation and service for the gospel and glory of God (Rom 1:1). The word of God has the power to separate the believer from sin (John 17:17). God the Father has the power to sanctify your spirit, soul and body and preserve you completely, without blame at the coming of our Lord Jesus Christ (1 Thess. 5:23). God the Son has the power to separate the believer unto a righteousness with no spot or wrinkle (Eph. 5:24-27). God the Holy Spirit has the power to separate the believer unto salvation and service (2 Thess. 2:13).

The rewards are great, and when you know and realize this, by the power of God's grace, you do not repent of all the pain and struggle you experienced in seeking after the Lord. We are difficult cases, but God is patient, not willing that any should perish but for all to come to repentance (2 Pet. 3:9). Yes, you had to be diligent and patient and seek Him with all your heart. Yes, you had to wake up and be sincere and find the knees of your heart. Yes, you had to learn faith and become active and earnest. Yes, you had to read the word, and gain some knowledge of God and the gospel. Yes, you had to show obedience of faith, giving and serving the Lord. The reward is Jesus in your heart. Amen. The power for change is from God, and the responsibility is yours to discover and receive His goodness. You find Jesus and God's will. You find that the scripture is alive and that understanding it is a gift of God. You hear the voice of the Holy Spirit guiding you into paths of righteousness. You know the power of God for salvation and rejoice in Jesus. You are not ashamed of the gospel, because it is the power of God for salvation (Rom. 1:16). You want more of Jesus in your life, and more of Jesus in the life of your family members and friends.

God's word is powerful and informative. It answers a lot of questions about life. It is the truth about life, and as such, it sets us free of ignorance. God's word is a place where we wake up spiritually, and gain strength and power to live for Jesus. It tells us about sin. Sin is lawlessness (1 John 3:4) and unrighteousness (1 John 5:17) and disobedience of God's law. The source of sin is the devil (John 8:44). Satan and his angels rebelled against God before man was created (Jude 6, 2 Pet. 2:4). When Adam and Eve first appeared, Satan was present to tempt them to sin and disobey God (Gen. 3). As a result, Satan is called the tempter (1 Thess. 3:5), the ruler of this world (John 14:30) and "The god of this world who blinds the minds of the unbelieving, that they might not see the light of the gospel of the glory of Christ, who is the image of God" (2 Cor. 4:4). As a result of the fall of man, he died spiritually and became only a natural man, unable to accept the things of the Spirit of God (1 Cor. 2:14). He became powerless to know God. The source of man's sin became his own heart (Matt. 15:19-20, Mark 7:21-23). "Each one is tempted when he is carried away and enticed by his own lust. Then when lust has conceived, it gives birth to sin, and when sin is accomplished, it brings forth death" (James 1:14-15). "For all have sinned and fall short of the glory of God" (Rom. 3:23). "For the wages of sin is death, but the free gift of God is eternal life in Christ Jesus our Lord (Rom. 6:23).

Since the source of sin was Satan's lies, and he and his minions could not repent, Hades was created for the devil and his angels to experience eternity (Matt. 25:41). Satan was not more powerful than God. In lovingkindness, God chose to be merciful with man and devised a plan to save him by grace through faith (Eph. 2:8). To honor God's holiness and justice, Christian, the penalty for our sin had to be paid. "For God so loved the world, that He gave His only begotten Son, that whoever believes in Him should not perish, but have eternal life" (John 3:16). God showed us mercy and love. While we were yet sinners, Christ died for us (Rom. 5:8), and we were saved from the wrath of God, because Jesus paid the penalty for our sin (Rom. 5:9). Amen.

Sin is powerful. Look at all the trouble and problems that have plagued man throughout his history. Look at all the wars, jealousies and greed of man that have wrought havoc and unkindness on human nature. Look at all the addictions, broken families, selfish behaviors, and wickedness that have broken out upon the earth in every generation. The power of lust is in your heart, Christian, not in your flesh, but your body is dishonored by sin (Rom. 1:24). God wants your body to be an "instrument of righteousness" (Rom. 6:13). Sin came through Adam but not from him. Eve was deceived but Adam knew better (1 Tim. 2:14). Sin entered the world through one man, and death through sin, and so death spread to all men (Rom. 5:12). "Through one man's disobedience the many were made sinners, even so through the obedience of the One that many will be made righteous" (Rom. 6:19). Amen. The free gift of salvation, Christian, is God showing the powerful grace of love and patience that reigns through righteousness to eternal life through Jesus Christ. Grace is the love and mercy of God in action. We were dead in sin, but God was rich with mercy, and in love sent His Son to die and bear our sins in His body on the cross (John 3:16). He used His power for our good. God makes us alive in Christ, and seats us in the heavenly places in Christ Jesus (Eph. 2:1-6). Why would He do this? "In order that in the ages to come He might show the surpassing riches of His grace in kindness toward us in Christ Jesus" (Eph. 2:7). God's grace is more powerful than our sin. Amen.

God's word, Christian, tells us a lot about God. We are unable to know everything about God because of our limited nature, but the Bible tells us enough to trust and follow Jesus, who was God (John 10:30-33, Col. 2:9). We know that God is love and has divine compassion (1 John 4:8). We know that God is light and in Him there is no darkness (1 John 1:5). We know that God is a consuming fire and has divine holiness (Heb. 12:29). We know that God is spirit in His divine essence (John 4:24). God's nature, Christian, is a mystery. It is a fact though, that God chose to reveal that He is relational. There is a union of three persons; Father, Son and the Holy Spirit in one Godhead. The three persons are coequal, co-eternal and in agreement. He is one God in three persons having the same nature and attributes, and worthy of the same worship, confidence and obedience. It is one God, not three forms of God or three pieces of God. All three persons are called God in the Bible; the Father is called God (Gal 1:1), the Son is called God (John 20:28) and the Holy Spirit is called God (Acts 5:3-4). We call this concept of God the Trinity and speak of God as a Tri-unity of God or the Triune God. The nature of God is omnipotent.

The word Trinity is not actually found in the Bible. The word was apparently used the first time by a fellow named Tertullian in the late second century. The word Trinity did not find a more formal place in the church until the fourth century. Around this time, the people demanded understanding and action from their church leaders about the nature of God, based on what they were believing from the scriptures. The doctrine makes three affirmations: first, there is one God; second, the Father, Son and Spirit is God; and third, that the Father, Son and the Spirit were each a distinct person. There are passages in the Old Testament where God, His Word, and Spirit are brought together suggesting a three-fold source (Gen. 1:2-3, 1:26; Num. 6:24, 11:25; Isa. 7:14,9:6, 11:2, 42:1, 48:16, 63:8-10). In the New Testament, the Trinity is more clearly suggested in the incarnation of God the Son and the outpouring of the Holy Spirit (Luke 1:35, Acts 2: 32-33). At the baptism of Christ, the three persons can be distinguished: the Son being baptized, the Father speaking from heaven, and the

Spirit descending as a dove (Matt. 3: 16-17). From the teachings of Jesus, we know that the Father sent Him and that the Spirit is the One that the Father and the Son work through (John 14:6-9, 16-26). In the commission given by Christ before His ascension, He made a reference that baptism should be done in the name of the Father, the Son and the Holy Spirit (Matt. 28:19). In the Trinity, there is a perfect equality in nature, honor and dignity between the three Persons. In the functions ascribed to each of the Persons in the Godhead, it appears that there are differences in relation though not in nature. Thus, the Father works through the Son by the Spirit. The Son was sent by the Father and the Spirit was sent by the Son with permission from the Father (John 14: 16,26). The Son revealed the Father and the Spirit reveals the Son (John 14:9, 16:14, Heb.1:3). The early believers knew that they were reconciled to the Father by the atoning work of the Son, and that this was mediated to them by the work of the Holy Spirit. Amen.

It is a mystery exactly how God is relational, but it is not a mystery that He desires to be in a relationship with us. We are invited to come to Jesus, to be saved and reconciled to God (2 Cor. 5:17-18). He sends the Holy Spirit to comfort, teach, guide and strengthen us in the truth (John 14:16-17,26;16:7-13). Jesus is glorified in our hearts by the power of the Holy Spirit (John 16:14). Amen. We were made in His image (Gen. 1:26). By His power and authority, He takes us up and works on us with His own hands, and makes us flesh and spirit and soul. The immortal soul bears God's image with intelligence, will, power and dominion, and holiness. God created both the male and the female and blessed the couple to be fruitful and multiply (Gen. 1: 26-28). God desires His children to live upon the earth as families in their respective cultures, and come to know Him with the help of the church. He desires them to have loving relationships, make their living at work according to His will, with the gifts He gives them. God wants them to live and walk by faith, be kind and generous, and receive Jesus as Savior and Lord.

Life is ascribed to God (John 5:26). All knowledge is ascribed to God (Ps. 147:5). All power is ascribed to God (Rev. 19:6). God is everywhere, but He is not in everything (Ps. 139:1-10). He who has the Son has the life; he who does not have the Son of God does not have the life (1 John 5:12). He who has the Son has eternal life by the grace of God. He who does not have the Son lives under the condemnation of the law and provokes God to deliver him over to death. Without the Son of God, he must pay his own penalty for sin, which he will always be unable to do. The only price for sin that God accepts is the shed blood of the perfect Son of God. Thus, we are invited to come to Jesus to be saved. We must receive Jesus into our hearts and believe that God raised Him from the dead, and confess with our mouth Jesus as Lord to be saved (Rom. 10:9-10). We must be born again (John 3:5). We must have a new heart and spirit, and the presence of the Holy Spirit to know the power required for salvation. This is the miracle of God's work for us; He alone has the power to bring about our true conversion (Ezek. 36:26-27, John 1:12-13). There is mercy in the power of God. What we could not or cannot do, He does for us. Amen. It is a work of power we come to know in our life, that we know we do not have the strength to do. Amen. The gospel is an important and strong call from an all-powerful God. God's work for us, Christian, is made clear to us, because of the spiritual power that God exercises in and for our soul (John 6:29).

God sends you into His word to grow in grace and knowledge. God sends you into His word to know Jesus, and to know you have eternal life (1 John 5:13). God speaks to us through His Son (Heb. 1:2). God sends us into His word for strength to believe that Jesus is the Christ, the Son of the living God. God wants you to know that you have been made the righteousness of God, you are a child of God (1 John 3;2). God cannot lie (Heb. 618). God's word is scientifically and historically accurate. God has the power to keep His word. "Heaven and earth will pass away, but My words shall not pass away" (Matt. 24:35). "All authority has been given to Me in heaven and on earth (Matt. 28:18). God has highly exalted Jesus, Christian, "that at the name of Jesus every knee shall bow, and every tongue confess that Jesus Christ is Lord, to the glory of the Father (Phil. 2: 9-11). He promises faith when we take time to attend to His word. God wants you to know His purpose for your life, and wants you to experience a full assurance of hope in Jesus. The word of God has power to change your life, and convict you about sin, righteousness and judgment (John 16:8). The word of God has power to guide you into a holy life, without which, you will not see the Lord (Heb. 12:14).

I do not know everything that is going to happen after we die, but I believe that not having Jesus standing by you will be an unimaginable horror that will release your greatest eternal regret. Please, do not reject the love of God. Do not let your desire to sin and seeking the enjoyments for this life deter you from being too humble to come to Him. "I'm not ashamed of the gospel, for it is the power of God for salvation, for in it the righteousness of God is revealed from faith to faith" (Rom. 1:16-17). Amen. God's word answers questions about creation of the world and man, salvation, and what happens after we die. All scripture is inspired by God for training in righteousness (2 Tim. 3:16). God is omnipotent in creation (Ps. 33:6), salvation (Phil. 1:6), understanding and power (Job 37:23) and for our resurrection (Rom. 6:4). Our new heart allows us to walk in newness of life. Old things have passed away and all things have become new. The new life is a full life and a blessed life. A life that yields to a man's heart the blessing of the possibility of doing God's will with God's helping power. We walk with the Lord in His victory in this world, and then pass into the new world to worship and serve Him in eternity. By the power of God, we are always going to be found with Him. Amen.

The three Persons of the Trinity at times work together. For example; in creation (Gen. 1:26), at similar tasks like intercession (Rom. 8: 26-27; John 17:1-26), to achieve God's purpose. I have no doubt that the purpose of God will always be completed in love and unity. God is spirit (John 4:24). God does not have a wife or a family as we experience them on earth. I think the picture of God as a father and Jesus as a son, may be showing us the importance of unity and love in our family relationships. We learn about love and submission growing up in our families, and we learn about love and submission growing up with God. Jesus said, "I do nothing on My own initiative, but I speak these things as the Father taught Me" (John 8:28). The Father sent Jesus into the world (John 17:18). The Holy Spirit never leads the Son or the Father, but rather follows their leadership (John 15:26). There is a perfect order in God's work that works together for us with perfect unity. Although the spirit world is largely mysterious to us from this life, in the future we will have greater understanding as well as appreciation for the relationships of God. The Triunity is God. Amen.

God is Almighty. "Power belongs to God" (Ps. 62:11). The firm belief in God's power, Christian, is important in religion. My faith, in part, is stronger because I believe that "nothing is impossible for God" (Luke 1:37). In the Old Testament, the power of God was shown in the creation of the world (Ps. 148:5) and the sustaining of the world (Ps. 65:5-8). He calls beasts and they hear (Dan. 6:22), and makes iron float (2 Kings 6:6). In one case, God intervened with miracles to demonstrate His power in giving the Hebrew people freedom from the Egyptians, and the land of Israel (Ex. 15:6, Ps. 111:6). In the New Testament, Jesus came to His ministry in the power of the Spirit (Luke 4:14) with healing miracles (Luke 5:17) and mighty works (Matt. 11:20). In the book of Acts, we see the power of the Spirit operating in the life of the church (Acts 1:8, 4:33, 6:8,10:38). Paul sees the evidence of God's power in the resurrection of Jesus (Eph. 1:19-20) and the power of the gospel working in men's lives (Rom. 1:16, 1 Cor. 1:18). Paul had a strong taste of God's power on the road to Damascus (Acts 9). He ended up in life wanting to know more about Jesus, and the power of His resurrection (Phil. 3:10).

The convincing nature of the power of God acting in our own life to save our souls, supports our faith, trust and confidence that He can do what He says. Because God is love, Christian, and invites us to attend at His throne of grace (Heb. 4:16), we are greatly encouraged to seek His help. It is good for us to be at the throne of grace to receive mercy. We need grace to pardon all our sins and grace to purify our souls. This is a work that God calls for us to do as our duty and interest before Him in worship. Besides our daily dependence and hopes, Christian, we come for help against temptation. We come before this powerful God with Jesus as the ground of our confidence. In Jesus, we come with a humble freedom, godly fear and liberty of spirit and speech. We are welcome to enter into His presence, because we have been reconciled by the blood of Jesus, and with a spirit of adoption as His children. We have a perfect High Priest in Jesus (Heb. 4:14, 6:20). Amen. Faith grows into a knowledge that God will visit with us, and then an ambition grows from the heart for help to further grow in grace for sanctification. We need God's mercies every day, Christian, that only God has the power to supply. I surrender to His wisdom and power. To be in the hands of God and near His heart is as good and secure as life gets. Amen.

The power of God is clearly manifested throughout the Bible. The members of the Trinity are co-equal and co-eternal but also appear to have different roles or functions in the Godhead. They each are in full cooperation. The Father creates, the Son redeems and the Holy Spirit sets apart. The Father is the creator, but the Son and the Spirit were involved (-17, Gen. 1:2). The Son is the redeemer, but the Father and the Spirit are described in sending the Son (1 John 4:14, Luke 1:35). The Holy Spirit is the Sanctifier, but the Father and the Son participate in sending the Spirit for this work (John 14:26, 15:26). There is cooperation and order in the works of God within the Godhead. Some folks think that the Son and the Holy Spirit may have had different roles in eternity past; but in our history, the Son became Jesus and the Holy Spirit became the Spirit of Christ. The power of God was manifested: in miracles (Luke 4:36, 11:20), in creation (Jer. 51:15, John 1: 3,10), in regeneration (John 5:21, Eph. 1:19), in Christ's resurrection (Rom. 1:4, 2 Cor. 13:4), in believer's resurrection (John 5:28-29, 1 Cor. 6:14), in salvation (Heb. 7:25), in sanctification (Heb.2:18, 2 Cor. 12:9, Phil. 2:13), Christ's birth (Luke 1:35), in comfort and teaching (John 14), the return of Jesus (Matt. 24:30) and much more. The power of Christ is described as power by God (John 17:2), derived from the Spirit (Luke 4:14), and determined by Christ (John 10:18). The Son "upholds all things by the word of His power" (Heb. 1:3). By the Son, God made the old creation and the new creation, and by the Son, He rules and upholds all things by the word of His power. By the Son, all the actions of Divine providence are unceasing, as well as being governed for all events to His own glory. This includes simple and complicated aspects of nature, world history and personal circumstances. "He speaks and it is done (Gen. 1-2).

"All authority has been given to Me in heaven and on earth" (Matt. 28:18). The King James Bible in this verse uses the word "power" in place of the word "authority". He has all power and authority. Amen. As God, and equal with the Father, all power was originally His; but as God-man, all power was given Him, that is, Jesus. In humbling Himself, He purchased it. He has authority to forgive sins (Matt. 9:6), teach (Luke 4:32), lay down His own life (John 10:18), give sonship (John 1:12), promise eternal life (John 17:2, 1 John 2:25), put into service (1 Tim. 1:12, 2 Tim. 4:17) and give strength (Phil. 4:13). He has the power of intercession with His Father (Rom. 8:34). The power is in the hands of Jesus, Christian, and this is my great comfort and peace. He said, "All things have been handed over to Me by My Father" (Matt. 11:27). The Son has the power to reveal God the Father to us (Matt. 11:27).

Jesus is the One who has the power to give you rest for your soul (Matt. 11:29). By the sacrifice of His atonement, He has the power and authority to deal with us for our salvation and reconciliation. If we chose the world and/or our sinful pleasures, we will be powerless. We lose the sense of assurance in Jesus, the comforts of doing God's will, and your testimony for the gospel will be ineffective. "God is not mocked; for whatever a man sows, this he will also reap" (Gal. 6:7). With faith, there will be compliance with God, and with unbelief, there is opposition to God. God's power in His mind always knows where we are, Christian, and He can intercede for the saints according to the will of God (Rom. 8:26-27). We learn to do well by the patience, love and grace of God. "Humble yourself, therefore under the mighty hand of God, that He may exalt you at the proper time" (1 Pet. 5:6). The consideration of the omnipotent hand of God, Christian, will make you humble and prepare the way for help and mercy. Never forget His lovingkindness, "He cares for you" (1 Pet. 5:7).

Remember "The word of the Lord to Zerubbabel saying, not by might nor by power, but by My Spirit, says the Lord of hosts" (Zech. 4:6). It takes God's power to live by God's power. Only God's power is mighty enough to get into your conscience, convict you, and pull down the strongholds. "The fear of the Lord is a fountain of life" (Prov. 14:27). "Whenever a man turns to the Lord, the veil is taken away. Now the Lord is the Spirit; and where the Spirit of the Lord is, there is liberty" (2 Cor. 3:16-17). There is liberty and power to be an effectual doer, and not just a forgetful hearer, of the word (James 1:25). "The word of God is living and active and sharper than two-edged sword, and piercing as far as the division of soul and spirit, of both joints and marrow, and able to judge the thoughts and intentions of the heart" (Heb. 4:12). These verses clearly describe the spiritual power of God.

We are born the first time as a natural man, not understanding or accepting the things of the spirit of God (1Cor. 2:14). We must be born again of the water and the Spirit to see the kingdom of God (John 3:5). Although somewhat controversial, the new birth, I believe, is by the word of God, which is likened to water, because it cleanses (Ps. 119:9, John 15:3, Eph. 5:26). Some think that the water mentioned here is from baptism. "This is my comfort in my affliction, that Thy word has revived me" (Ps. 119:50). The KJV of the Bible uses the word "quickened" for "revived". The new birth is being born of the water and the Spirit (John 3:5). "That which is born of the Spirit is spirit" (John 3:6) and "It is the Spirit who gives life" (John 6:63). The KJV of the Bible uses the word "quickened" for the phrase "who gives life" in the New American Standard Bible. The new birth, Christian, is when we receive a new spiritual nature from God. We become "partakers of the divine nature" (2 Pet. 1:4). It is not the reformation of the outward man, it is not the education of the natural man, it is not the purification of the old man, but it is the creation of a new man. My favorite Old Testament scripture on this topic is Ezekiel 36:25-27. What is involved is a new heart, a new spirit, a heart of flesh and God's

Spirit being placed within us to help us be careful to walk in God's statutes. A powerful miracle takes place and a veil that was covering our heart has been removed. The veil was unbelief, ignorance, prejudice and self-righteousness. The veil permitted the love of sin and the world and the pride of life to keep us from seeing a salvation in Jesus. The veil is blindness and requires God's power to have it removed. We do not save ourselves and see God, but God removes the veil and we can more clearly see God in Jesus. Amen.

By the grace of God, we turn to the Lord Jesus who has sovereign power and supreme authority to forgive us of our sin and save us from the wrath of God. The turning occurs at a moment in God's time, by the grace of God, once and for all time, and is a choice of your will. It is God who has been at work in you, both to will and to work for His good pleasure (Phil. 2:13). Amen. With an unveiled face, we behold as in a mirror the glory (gospel) of the Lord. We are being transformed into the same image from glory to glory, just as from the Lord, the Spirit (2 Cor. 3:18). It is in this framework that we learn liberty and experience the power of God at work for our freedom. The removal of guilt and bondage, the law and the fear of death frees us to live in the liberty of holiness. "The law of the Lord is perfect, restoring the soul" (Ps. 19:7). The KJV of the Bible, in place of "restoring the soul", uses the phrase of "converting the soul". The law means the doctrine or manner of instruction to the Christian, which includes the gospel wisdom and hope which really opens your heart to receive forgiveness and salvation. Our hearts are hard and cannot be broken without God's power to incline us to Christ. The practical effect of hearing and reading the word of God, because it is alive, is to move the soul to turn to God about ourself and holiness. To God be the glory.

The spiritual understanding of Jesus is available, Christian, for a person who expresses genuine repentance and belief in Christ (Rom. 10:9-10, Acts 4:12, 16:31). The answer is in the grace of God. Unless God does this work, you will never see the surpassing greatness of Jesus in the gospel. When we come to believe, the veil has already been removed by God, the gospel has become clear and the understanding of forgiveness and eternal life in Jesus is flooding your soul. To turn to Jesus is to have turned to the light of the world (John 8:12). The light in your soul is the beginning of true spiritual power that will transfigure you into His likeness. Amazing grace is the experience of the believer from the Holy Spirit that does not go away, but stays to complete the work (Phil.1:6). The mystery of God's sovereignty and your responsibility has met.

The spirit of Christ turns your life around with repentance and faith in the direction of Jesus, the Christ, the Savior, the Lord forevermore. The encounter may not be as dramatic as Paul's on the road to Damascus (Acts 9:3-5), but it is in every way just as important to you. You mind is transforming and your life is headed into a new and different direction. Your conscience is clear and your heart is filled with a different kind of joy. The ideas of the meaning and purpose of life take on a new perspective. A heart of flesh appears that reflects being generous and merciful. The person of Jesus becomes great in your thoughts. He Himself bore your sins in His body on the cross that you might die to sin and live to righteousness. By His wounds you were healed (Isa. 53:5-6). The healing, dear Christian, is spiritual and not physical, but God can heal bodies also. We strayed like sheep, but by the grace of God, "we have returned to the Shepherd and Guardian of our souls" (1 Pet. 2:25). "Turn to Me, and be saved, all the ends of the earth; for I am God, and there is no other" (Isa. 45:22). I have felt the reality of Jesus burning in My heart, Christian, like the disciples on the Road to Emmaus (Luke 24:32). I have not seen Jesus with my eyes, but I have an inward sense of His presence, that I believe is a deep spiritual reality that He brought to my life. I did not earn or deserve it, for sure, but I cannot deny the powerful work and blessing of the gospel in my mind and heart. It draws me forward to seek more of His presence, with a desire to live for Jesus and contribute to His glory. Amen.

"You have been born again not of seed which is perishable but imperishable, that is, through the living and abiding word of God" (1 Pet. 1:23). The word of God is alive (Heb. 4:12). The evidence of His presence and power is that He is within you. Amen. "The Spirit bears witness with our spirit that we are children of God:

(Rom. 8: 16). The work of the Holy Spirit is both as a Sanctifier and a Comforter. God knows we need this kind of support for the assurance of our salvation. My mind knows the weakness, sorrow, and grief in my heart because of sin. At the same time, my conscience bears me witness of the Holy Spirit (Rom. 9:1). I'm not perfect, Christian, but my changes are in the direction for Jesus and heaven. I'm His child. He stirs me to pray and study the Bible and draws me to works of love. I used to chase after sin, but today, sin chases me and by the grace of God I stand against it and for my Father in heaven. God's power can only be experienced and explained by the grace of God. "In the exercise of His will He brought us forth by the word of truth, so that we might be, as it were, the first fruits among His creatures" (James 1:18). The spiritual power exhibited in the removing of the veil, receiving a new birth, abiding in Jesus and see all this take place in your life, is the love of God in action. It is the Father, the Son, and the Holy Spirit's words of grace, gospel, truth and power that will abide forever (Matt. 24:35). It is the living power in the living word that brings forth spiritual life to one that was spiritually dead. Amen. The word of God has promised that "the gospel of the kingdom shall be preached in the whole world for a witness to all nations and then the end will come" (Matt. 24:14). To those called by God (Rom. 8:28), Christ is the power of God and wisdom of God (1 Cor. 1:24) for salvation to everyone who believes (Rom. 1:16). "Our faith should not rest on the wisdom of men, but on the power of God" (1 Cor. 2:5). The kingdom of God is coming in power (Mark 9:1). To those children who believe, God gives secret assurances of the greatness of His power (Eph. 1:19) and the gift of trusting in the strength of His might (Eph. 6:10). Amen. My heart reflects God's power.

"I am; and you shall see the Son of Man sitting at the right hand of power, and coming with the clouds of heaven" (Mark 14:62). This verse of scripture, Christian, is the reply of Jesus to the high priest who wanted to know if Jesus was the Christ. The right hand of God is the right hand of power. Since God is a lot more than I can think, His power is a lot more than I can conceive.

He is infinite in nature or essence, and therefore infinite in ability and strength. Jesus declared Himself to be the Messiah. He will be exalted to the throne of God. He will return with power to judge and rule over the earth (Ps. 96:13). Since God is love (1 John 4:8), His power naturally and actively comes forth in mercy with promises that bear this truth out. "He is able to do exceedingly abundantly beyond all that we ask or think, according to the power that works within us" (Eph. 3:20). That is, the resurrection power of Christ working in our lives in the inner man, according to God's grace. Paul prayed, "that God would grant you, according to the riches of His glory, to be strengthened with power through the Spirit in the inner man" (Eph. 3:16). God is omnipotent in reaching into our inner man leading us into paths of righteousness, for His name's sake (Ps.23:3). God cannot die (1 Tim. 3:16), lie (Heb. 6:18) or deny Himself because of His faithfulness (2 Tim. 2:13). "But our God is in the heavens; He does whatever He pleases" (Ps. 115:3). The throne of God will never be shaken, Christian, and His providence and will, will be done. He rules with infinite power. When human history is over, I believe the sovereignty and providence of God will be more fully known and understood. We will see the surpassing riches of His grace in kindness, patience, faithfulness, goodness, love, holiness and power toward us in Christ Jesus (Eph.2:7). Amen. I gladly yield my will to Jesus.

The power of God can be seen in Creation, Providence and our redemption. "Worthy art Thou, our Lord and our God, to receive glory and honor and power: for Thou didst create all things, and because of Thy will they existed, and were created" (Rev. 4:11). "He upholds all things by the word of His power" (Heb. 1:3). All God's works of nature are miracles. In the beginning God created the heavens, the earth, water and light, all on the first day (Gen. 1:1-5). God always has authority, Christian, and in creation, He showed a strength to act which signifies great power. "For I am the Lord: I will speak, and the word that I shall speak shall come to pass" (Ezek. 12:25). God spoke the world into existence out of nothing (Ps. 33:6), which speaks of infinite power, of which I cannot imagine. In the first day, God made light (Gen. 1:3). The source of this light may have been special, since the sun was not made and set in place yet to give light upon the earth. Some folks think that the sun was created on day one but the light did not strike the earth until day four. Some think that God made the sun, moon and stars before day one, and then made them visible from earth on day four. There may have been sufficient light to allow vegetation to sprout on day three. The sun was not the origin of life and an object for worship. I do not know what exactly happened. What I do know is that the Bible is true and God is light (1 John 1:5). The rest of creation, throughout the first week may have proceeded from the substances that God may have laid into the earth. This would include; vegetation, creatures in the water, birds, creeping things, beasts and man (Gen. 1: 11, 20, 25, 27; 2:19). God brought forth a tremendous variety. He had no tools or help, but He had a will. The power in creation was a work of God. We were made in His image (Gen. 1:26).

As God decreed the creation of things in time, He decreed the details and ends of creatures by the power expressed in His providence. Though we do have some violent storms, the earth is preserved. The conditions for life and the maintenance of life, is a powerful action of God's creative abilities. "In Him we live and move and exist (Acts 17:28). By the same powerful Person that we were created, our lives are maintained. The power of God moves everything. "Thou hast also performed all our works" (Isa. 26:12). God is a sustaining power. He holds up our nature, that is, our hearts and brains, muscles and bones, and the lung, stomach and all organs. The human body is an amazing creation. He holds up nature, that is, all the plants and animals. He holds up the nature of governments and restrains the malice of the devil and the corruptions of men. "The mind of man plans his way, but the Lord directs his steps" (Prov. 16:9). "The king's heart is in the hand of the Lord" (Pro. 21:1). God is great, Christian, in power, for both the important things as well as the small and seemingly insignificant things. No detail has been overlooked. Amen.

The power of God appeared in our redemption. Christ Himself is called the power of God and the wisdom of God (1 Cor. 1:24).

In redemption, God created a new world with life from a broken world with sin. The power and love of God brought forth Christ to redeem us. Jesus Christ was conceived by the Holy Spirit in the womb of a virgin (Luke 1:35). The third Person of the Trinity overshadowed the virgin Mary, and by a miracle of grace brought together the humanity of Christ united to God. It became a natural birth but the conception was supernatural. The union of two natures, Christian, was not only an act of wisdom but an act of power. God's thoughts become creative and are not like our thoughts; His turn into action, while ours have no creative ability. God and man in one Person (Rom. 1:3-4, John 1:14). The blood of His human nature was called the blood of God (Acts 20:28). He was fully God and fully man with two natures that were not mixed. The Deity did not become a humanity and the humanity did not become deity. The construct of Christ was a miracle of God. Man is further distant from God, than man from nothing (Charnock). Divine power by Christ was shown in the miracles He performed. Divine power by Christ was shown in His patience for the contradiction of sinners against Himself. The power of God was present in Christ, in the fact that He was found without sin (Heb. 4:15). Amen.

Divine power was evident in His resurrection. The power of God rescued Jonah from the whale (Jonah 2:10), Daniel from the lion's den (Dan. 6:22), and the Hebrew people from the Egyptians (Ex. 14:13-28), as types of resurrection power. God has power over every natural force. The restoring of a dead body to life requires an infinite power, that to man is impossible and unimaginable. In His lifetime, Jesus raised Lazarus from the dead (John 11:43-44). Jesus Himself was raised from the dead through the glory of the Father (Rom. 6:4). The restoring of a dead body alone reveals infinite power, but what about restoring the soul and spirit of a man, of which we have no clue. The exceeding greatness of this power (Eph. 1:19) is beyond understanding and expression. Man's reasonings cannot discover a God who has chosen to reveal Himself by gifts of love and faith. The gospel has triumphed in man's world by the power of God, which the natural man cannot see or understand (1 Cor. 2:14). This reminds me of the story of Elisha and his servant, when they were surrounded by the chariots and army of the King of Aram, and the servant was alarmed. Elisha prayed that the Lord would open the eyes of the servant. When the Lord opened his eyes, he saw the mountain was full of horses and chariots of fire all around Elisha (2 Kings 6:15-17). The opening of the eyes of faith, Christian, will silence your doubts and fears. God is always all around us. When you know that the Lord is with you, and you see the sovereignty and power of heaven, the less you will fear the calamities of this earth. Amen.

The power of God for our redemption appears in our souls by the grace of God. This is a personal miracle. You know it came with power, because it gives you victory over sins that you could not get rid of with your most determined resolutions. You know it came with power, because you have a peace that passes your understanding. You know it came with power, because you are being transformed into the image of a person that you have never met. You know it came with power, because the Bible and fellow believers take you to a place of agreement and peace. You know it came with power, because the fear of death, and the presence of guilt, are not something that control your life. You know it came with power, because the miracle has not left you. I have frequent thoughts about the goodness of God, and strong desires to hear the Holy Spirit about living and serving Jesus with my life. "For by grace you have been saved by faith, and that not of yourselves, it is the gift of God" (Eph. 2:8). It is the infinite wisdom and efficacy in the grace of God, Christian, that is completely necessary and powerful enough for the experience of salvation. The miracle of faith that grows in our lives becomes our greatest interest, because it pertains to our peace in eternal life. It is by "His divine power that everything pertaining to life and godliness has been granted to us" (2 Pet. 1:3). Saving faith is a precious grace. It is precious. because it is priceless, personal and a gift from God. We were fashioned by the Spirit of God that raised up Jesus from the dead. It bears witness of Jesus, and has a great value to us, because it leads and guides us into paths of righteousness. Those who partake of the gospel of Christ, Christian, carry the Spirit of God as a powerful close friend, a comforter and helper. Jesus is the Savior of all men in the world that believe (1 Tim. 4:10).

A Christian becomes renewed in the spirit of his mind, after the image of God, in knowledge, righteousness and holiness. They are freed from the bondage of sin and blessed with liberty as the children of God. The Christian will know the rod of God's strength (Ps. 110:2). The Christian will volunteer freely in the day of God's power (Ps. 110:3) and know the experience of a spiritual resurrection. The turning of your heart against your desire to sin is a strength that grows out from conversion. You have been changed; you are much more aware of holiness and spiritual warfare in your heart. God's power loosens up your stiff neck and carnal heart. God's power, pictured as a strong arm (Ex. 6:6, Jer. 27:5, Isa.30:30), not only defeats your passions for sin, but chases the devil away. The power of temptation, in many cases wanes, to the point you no longer consider it or are overcome by it. The power of God, Christian, works this miracle in your heart and you will be glad you received this strength. The practice of sin is a thorn in your heart. The devil wants you to suffer and believe you are a hypocrite. You know the battle of two natures (Rom. 7:14-24). God's power constrains your will, without forcing it, and drags it away from sin at times, when you may be a little reluctant, but willing. God's grace will always be sufficient for you. His power is perfected in weakness (2 Cor. 12:9). Our thorns may be trials, tribulations and/or temptations. Either way, we may learn to pray and/or be more patient. We know God's will towards us is always good, therefore we will be strengthened and God will be glorified. Amen.

God inclines the will to good and then enables you to act on it, according to the new principles in your new nature. "It is God who is at work in you, both to will and to work for His good pleasure (Phil. 2:13). This is the power of God's grace and mercy, acting for our redemption and resurrection on the path to becoming a more complete new creation. It is being drawn to God with cords of love (John 6:44, Hosea 11:4). "I have loved you with an everlasting love; therefore, I have drawn you with lovingkindness" (Jer. 31:3). We are overcome and surrender into God's lovingkindness for forgiveness of sin and eternal life. It is a strong everlasting love that cannot fail. It is a love that nothing can separate us from (Rom. 8:38-39). At one time in my life, I did not know that this kind of love was available, until God's power acted upon me. He found me when I was blind and brought me home. I was like the blind man who could now see (John 9:25), and the Prodigal son when he came to his senses and went home (Luke 15: 17-20). I was drawn into the gospel covenant, and given understanding to believe it, by the powerful influences of the Holy Spirit upon my soul. Thank you, Jesus.

The preservation of grace required to keep us in a state of regeneration is also a demonstration of the power of God. The grace of God is a powerful spiritual force that initially establishes us in a state of justification with God. The Spirit of God is released for us to accomplish the work of sanctification in our souls. What God foreknew, He predestinated, called, justified and glorified (Rom. 8:29-30). The power of God for our being glorified, by necessity, includes our sanctification. The result of justification is sanctification (Rom. 5: 1-5). "His divine power has granted to us everything pertaining to life and godliness" (2 Pet. 1). It is the power of God that defeats the power of Satan. It is the power of God, Christian, that weakens and eventually eliminates the power of our temptations to sin. It is our responsibility to cooperate with the Spirit of God. My mind can wander and my behavior weak for the Lord at times, but the continuing grace of God sustains me. The grace of God teaches us to confess our sins for forgiveness and cleansing (1 John 1:9). I cannot be snatched out of the Father's hand (John 10: 29). God delivers us from the domain of darkness (Col. 1:13) in His way at His time. He knows our hearts and what it takes to build sincerity and a pure heart. He establishes our hope and diligence. Amen.

Our precious faith, obtained as a gift from God through the Spirit, is a powerful gift of grace. Faith keeps us united to Christ, and growing in grace and knowledge from our experiences with sin, tribulation and the kindness of the Lord. God's power sometimes is delivered to our hearts in reading God's promises to us from the scripture. Faith comes by hearing (Rom. 10:17). My prayer for you is Paul's prayer for you. "That God may count you worthy of your calling, and fulfill every desire for goodness, and the work of faith with power" (2 Thess. 1:11). "For the Lord God is my strength and song, and He has become my salvation" (Isa. 12:2). God's work in our lives becomes so great to us, we dare not forget it. I've been changed, forgiven, comforted, and strengthened. He saved me by the power of His grace. Amen. "Therefore, you will joyously draw water from the springs of salvation" (Isa. 12:3). God, in His power, gives me assurances of His love and comforts by His grace that greatly encourage my faith. God's promises are wells of salvation. "I will never desert you, nor will I ever forsake you" (Heb. 13:5).

Sin is a powerful taskmaster, and in spite of our close walk with the Lord, sometimes we stumble into sin. "There is not a righteous man on earth who continually does good and who never sins" (Eccl. 7:20). "If we say that we have no sin, we are deceiving ourselves, and the truth is not in us" (1 John 1:8). We have a God-given conscience that is a light for our sensibilities. The sense of sin in your heart is a very despairing condition. When we sin against our knowledge and relationship with Jesus, it hurts and takes away our comfort and joy. Sin breaks a Christian's heart, that only the power of God can heal. David stumbled badly and left us Psalm 51 as a guide to instruct us about forgiveness. David, convicted of his sin, poured out his soul to God for mercy and grace. He confessed his sin and prayed for cleansing. It takes the love and power of God to reach deep into ourselves, to clean our "house" and create a pure heart (Ps.73:1, Ps. 51:10). To clean your conscience of guilt requires a merciful and powerful God. To be reconciled to God requires the willingness and the power of God. "I create the fruit of the lips; peace" (Isa. 57:19). God created the fruit of Christ's lips for preaching and our lips for praying and praise.

To restore the joy of salvation to us after we sin is an act of sovereign power (Ps. 51:12). I have a favorite verse of scripture on the topic on confession and God's power that applies here.

"If we confess our sins, He is faithful and righteous to forgive us our sins and to cleanse us of all unrighteousness" (1 John 1:9). God is faithful to the gospel covenant in Jesus He has made with you, Christian, where He has promised forgiveness to penitent believers. He is just to Himself, His Son and His glory, by keeping His promise to forgive those who come to Him on the account of Jesus. There is forgiveness for the penitent believing confessors and the contrite confessor. If we are already saved, then our confession confirms we still desire and want His continuing forgiveness. We still need cleansing from all unrighteousness. This is God's way of renewing our hearts for His will in our lives. We still need God's cleansing grace and power to restore the deep sense of forgiveness and reconciliation. The cleansing grace of God is precious to us; it quickly chases away the sense of being defiled and allows the acceptance and comfort of being God's child to return. Amen. Sin defiles our hearts, but true confession of sin restores our fellowship by God's grace. We are reminded of our weakness when we choose self over our God, who loved us and died for our salvation. We are reminded that we are a new man, and not what we used to be because of the goodness of God. Being selfish with God leaves a pain that hurts and makes us feel insincere with the Lord. We are reminded that His grace has brought me this far, and His grace will see me through. In due time, we are delivered from the power and practice of sin. The Lord teaches us the precious value of being faithful, Thank you, Jesus. Amen.

God is great and all powerful. By the grace of God, we learn a lot with a desire to want to know more. We learn what is important, that is, how to be saved. We learn the Bible and experience His presence with us to help us grow in grace and knowledge. The all-powerful and all-knowing God has found that what we do learn and know is sufficient. God has chosen to save us by faith (Eph. 2:8). We grow in the assurance of things hoped for. We grow in the conviction for things not seen. God has chosen to save you by His grace. God has chosen to go to work in your life and draw your soul, by love, to Himself. This is the plan of God who has not, cannot and will not, ever make a mistake. "You did not choose Me, but I chose you, and appointed you, that you should go and bear fruit, and that your fruit should remain, that whatever you ask of the Father in My name, He may give it to you" (John 15:16). He sought us when we were lost and in misery. He had compassion on us when we did not know how to call upon Him. "He chose us in Him before the foundation of the world, that we should be holy and blameless before Him in love. He predestined us to adoption as sons through Jesus Christ to Himself, according to the kind intention of His will, to the praise of the glory of His grace, which He freely bestowed on us in the Beloved" (Eph. 1:4-6). We had no power before we were formed, and nothing desirable after we appeared, to recommend us for salvation. He always was working with great power to prepare us to be the bride of Christ. The God who brought us out to be alive from nothing, surely has the power to complete the work He started. It is great comfort, Christian, that He has chosen us. We were chosen and appointed to go and bear fruit. This refers to the fruit of the Spirit (Gal.5:22-23) as our lives are transformed into the image of Christ (2 Cor. 3:18). We are also appointed to go into the world and bear fruit (Matt. 28:19). We are to labor and reflect the image of Christ in the church. The fruit from this labor will not be in vain, because it will be accompanied with power according to the will of God. Whatever you may need and pray for, the Lord will give comfort and confidence to pray, believing in Jesus name that God will be glorified.

"Behold, these are the fringes of His ways; and how faint a word we hear of Him! but His mighty thunder, who can understand?" (Job 26:14). What God has revealed about Himself are but parts of His ways. We know God is light (1 John 1:5) and love (1 John 4:8) and spirit (John 4:24). We know God is faithful (1 Cor. 10:13), gracious and righteous (Ps. 116:5). We know God is a creator (Gen. 1:1) and a Savior (John 3:16). We know God is a Wonderful Counselor, Eternal Father and Prince of Peace (Isa. 9:6). From the gospel of John, we know that God is the bread of life (John 6:35), light of the world (John 8:12), the door (John 10:9), good shepherd (John 10:11), the resurrection and the life (John 11:25), the way the truth and the life (John 14:6), and the true vine (John 15:1). God is omnipotent (Rev. 19:6), Omniscient (1 John 3:20) and Omnipresent (Jer. 23:24). What we do know about God, we clearly adore and admire. What we know about our salvation and God, is worthy of worship. Amen. Thank you, Lord, for what we do know. Thank you, Lord, for what we will know in the future. Thank you, Lord, for what we do not know. God is infinite in wisdom and power. "Oh, the depth of the riches both of the wisdom and knowledge of God! How unsearchable are His judgments and unfathomable His ways!" (Rom. 11:33). The depths of God's power working for our salvation and His love for our souls is unsearchable. We have glimpses of the glory of God. God's plans for our future will be vast, powerful and profound, reaching well beyond our present visions and understanding. May your constant desire be, to God be the glory. We will be alive in the unspeakable privilege of praising God, by the powerful grace of God, to eternity. Amen.

Wisdom

"But by His doing you are in Christ Jesus, who became to us wisdom from God, and righteousness and sanctification, and redemption" (1 Cor. 1:30).

Dear Christian,

It becomes your wisdom to know God's wisdom. The wisdom of God is revealed to us in the design of the gospel covenant in Jesus. The wisdom of God is revealed in us by the Holy Spirit. He reveals kindness and sincerity and love for the future of our souls. In His wisdom and power, "we become His people, and He becomes our God" (Jer. 32:38). "I will give them one heart and one way, that they may fear Me always, for their own good, and for the good of their children" (Jer. 32:39). God makes an everlasting covenant with us, Christian, and promises that He will not turn away and will give us a heart of fear, so that we will not turn away. He promises to never leave us or desert us and to rejoice over us (Jer. 32:40-41). God's words of wisdom combined with God's power are a security that His grace will always be sufficient (2 Cor. 12:9). God's grace will not be defeated. It is unimaginable to me that God would or could be disgraced in His own wisdom and power. It is unimaginable to me that God's workmanship in believers, for faith and repentance, could be defeated by a foe that He could not understand. The gospel is called the manifold wisdom of God (Eph. 3:10). Amen. "O, the depth of the riches both of the wisdom and knowledge of God! How unsearchable are His judgments and unfathomable His ways!" (Rom. 11:33). The things of this world are shallow. The Lord's judgments are a great deep (Ps. 36:6). The forgiveness we have in Jesus is a great deep, it fills our hearts with fear and worship. Our thinking is weak and short-sighted, and for the reason of darkness, we do not know how or what to think. The riches of God's wisdom in love can be seen and felt, contemplated and humbling. "Blessed are the poor in spirit, for theirs is the kingdom of heaven" (Matt. 5:3).

The wisdom in God's providence is inscrutable, and His love for us is infinite. God's dealings with us for redemption can be pondered and appreciated, though not always understood. God's dealings with us can be trusted, because He is always righteous and perfect in wisdom. He has reasons for His ways with us, which our weak and foolish minds will not always understand. "God has chosen the foolish things of the world to shame the wise, and God has chosen the weak things of the world to shame the things which are strong" (1 Cor. 1: 27). No man will be boasting about himself before God. "God sees not as man sees, for man looks at the outward appearance, but the Lord looks at the heart" (1 Sam. 16:7). A man's brain or his physical attributes do not help him see His wisdom; he needs to be born again and gain a new heart (John 3:5). The way to God is clear; it is through or by His wisdom, that is, Jesus. The true knowledge and the wisdom of God for salvation is not hidden from us, but offered to us in Jesus Christ. All the treasures of God's knowledge and wisdom that is offered to human beings is made available to us through Him. "He is the radiance of His glory and the exact representation of His nature, and upholds all things by the word of His power" (Heb. 1:3). In Him, God's wisdom was embodied and made possible to see and be comprehended by man. We are saved in Him, by grace through faith, which is God's way and not a man's way, that we cannot boast (Eph. 2:8-9). It is in Jesus that God makes it possible for man to be made alive spiritually or born again. It is because of the sacrifice of Jesus, that we can receive, understand, believe and follow after the wisdom of God. "To those who are called, Christ becomes the power and the wisdom of God" (1 Cor. 1:24). This wisdom, as the truth of God, becomes a light in the mind and a fire in the heart of believers for forgiveness of sin and salvation. To those unwilling to come to Jesus and receive Him as God's way to eternal life is not wisdom, but foolishness.

Wisdom is the ability to judge correctly and to follow the best course of action. Wisdom refers to a true insight and is based on correct knowledge and understanding. Wisdom is the proper use of knowledge. The most important, and best wisdom, is revealed to us by God. True wisdom is a divine revelation and a gift of God (Prov. 2:6). Wisdom as a gift from God, reflects God's wisdom in us about Jesus, and our salvation. God's wisdom in the soul of a believer appears righteous, a magnificent truth, satisfying and complete. The world's wisdom appears shallow, weak, unsatisfying and incomplete. The Bible tells us that the wisdom of God is revealed in the Person named Jesus. The Bible tells us that the most important wisdom from God we can know is that Jesus is the Savior for fallen man. The word of God is living (Heb. 4:12) and "causes men to be born again to a living hope through the resurrection of Jesus Christ from the dead" (1 Pet. 1:3). The Bible is the place of wisdom where God has chosen to speak faith into men hearts. The Bible is where the assurance of things hoped for and the conviction of things not seen, that is faith, comes by hearing the word of Christ (Rom. 10:17). We cannot understand anything about God's wisdom unless He reveals it to us, and He does this from His word. The wisdom of God is called manifold (Eph. 3:10), which means it is marked by infinite diversity.

The transformation of one man by Christ into a new man, and the unification of all new persons in Christ, is an awesome display of the wisdom of God. All the pieces of the providence of God in our life, being woven together to bring us to Christ, and then, to build His church with believers is a magnificent display of God's wisdom and power. Even angels long to comprehend more of the mystery in the saving of the souls of men (1 Pet. 1:12). God's plans and purpose for our souls in the future, reveal a complex wisdom and a great love for our souls to be saved. He is worthy of our worship and praise. We can be certain that God wants us to be wise, just as we are sure that He wants us not to sin (R. C. Sproul). The greatest wisdom on this earth is holiness (William S. Plumer). Amen. The manifold wisdom of God brought forth the church. The church is alive, composed of living people, through which Christ is Lord. The church functions under the leadership of the Holy Spirit. The knowledge of Christ, that is called God's mystery (Col. 2:2), is a gift of faith by the grace of God (Eph. 2:8). We must receive Christ into our hearts and be born again to be able to receive spiritual treasures of wisdom and knowledge from God (Col. 2:3). Amen.

Spiritual wisdom is godly wisdom. We get answers to questions about life and death, holiness and sin, being saved and lost, God and man, the purpose of life, heaven and Hades and eternal life. The answers to these questions from God bring a peace that passes our understanding, and become the treasures of our lives. We learn that the greatest treasure is Jesus in our heart, and that He is all we will ever need. "The word of the cross is to those who are perishing foolishness, but to us who are being saved it is the power of God" (1 Cor.1:18). The Bible says that, "God will destroy the wisdom of the wise, and the cleverness of the clever I will set aside" (1 Cor. 1:19). To those who are called, Jesus Christ is the power of God and the wisdom of God. "By His doing you are in Christ Jesus, who became to us wisdom from God, and righteousness and sanctification, and redemption" (1 Cor. 1:30). The revelation of Jesus as God in your soul is the most important knowledge and wisdom you will ever have. The grace to change and become holy, obedient and a new man (2 Cor. 5:17) will be the most profound and important behaviors you will experience in this life. You will have lived out of the wisdom and providence of God. You will know the blessing and you will know you have been changed. It was by a wisdom that you never knew existed, until you received Jesus into your heart.

The Bible speaks about the truth of being saved by Jesus in

the gospel message, as a mystery and hidden wisdom, "which God predestined before the ages to our glory" (1 Cor. 2:7). God's secret wisdom was about the cross of Jesus, and how His death would pay the penalty for our debt of sin and at the same time serve the justice of God's holiness. A mystery is a secret that man cannot penetrate with his intelligence; he needs revelation from God. God's wisdom is spiritually perceived and received by the gift of faith from God. God's Spirit must aid man in the steps to receive Christ (John 1:12-13). "God saved us, and called us with a holy calling, not according to our works, but according to His own purpose and grace which was granted us in Christ Jesus from all eternity" (2 Tim. 1:9). The gospel was a mystery kept secret for long ages past, but is now manifested by the commandment of the eternal God, and made known to all nations, leading to the obedience of faith (Rom. 16:25-26). Paul was an apostle of Jesus Christ, "for the faith of those chosen of God and the knowledge of the truth which is according to godliness, in the hope of eternal life, which God, who cannot lie, promised long ages ago" (Titus 1:1-2). The spirit of the gospel, agreed to between the Father and the Son, was from eternity. The creation of the world took place in order that the gospel could be manifested to man. The wisdom of God revealed in the gospel was first made known in the garden of Eden (Gen. 3:15), but was veiled by the smoke of sacrifices and the Law. The gospel was not fully realized until the death of the Redeemer. The infinite wisdom of God brought forth for us a covenant of grace. "God demonstrates His own love toward us, in that while we were yet sinners, Christ died for us" (Rom. 5:8). He died to save us from our sins. Amen. Without question, Christian, this demonstrates the goodness and rich mercies of God. Without question, Christ has been exalted. He died to save us and now lives to make intercession for us (Heb. 7:25). Christ is alive, Christian; we have been called and justified, we are being changed into His image and have peace with God. We are saved by an exalted Jesus. The Holy Spirit has been sent to help us in Jesus' name (John 14:16, 26). We are adopted into the family of God to obtain an undefiled inheritance. We are forever protected by the wisdom and power of

God. Let us worship and bow down before our Lord and Savior. Amen.

All three members of the Godhead covenanted together to save sinners on the basis of faith in Jesus. The Father can be thought of as the Originator of salvation and the Son, through His sacrifice, thought of as the Executor of salvation. The Holy Spirit can be thought of as the Applier of salvation by awakening our hearts and bringing knowledge through the new birth to become children of God. It is a mystery to us, but not to God. In our finite condition, we are unable to see the full picture and understand many details. What we do know is that the saving truth about Jesus, by the grace of God, is not being hidden from us. We are being transformed by faith in Jesus. Amen. God's truth, wisdom and power, we must admit, is at a depth too profound for us to fully fathom. To understand Jesus and the gospel, we must admit we needed to be born again from above by the grace of God (John 3:5). Sin clouded and impaired our mental and spiritual faculties, and we needed a miracle of God's wisdom and grace to wake up to hear His call for us. The natural man (1 Cor. 2:14) must be created into a new man, with a new heart and spirit, before he will be able to understand the truth of God in a mystery. God, in His wisdom, ordained that the preaching and hearing of His word, would be the means by which men would be drawn to trust Christ. It is "by grace you have been saved through faith; and that not of yourselves, it is the gift of God; not as a result of works, that no one should boast" (Eph. 2:8-9). God's word is alive (Heb. 4:12), and when God's word is preached, heard or taught, it is able to pierce through the darkness in a man's heart and mind. In His wisdom, God knows how to open a man's heart so he can see truth. The man sees the truth about himself, the truth about God, Jesus and the Bible. He sees the truth about the future. "And there is no creature hidden from His sight, but all things are open and laid bare to the eyes of Him with whom we have to do" (Heb. 4:13). This is the wisdom and power and the love of God at work to save a soul. God's eyelids test the sons of men (Ps. 11:4). The word lets us see sin and unbelief in our heart. In the word, we see God, and we see how God sees us. We will give an account of ourselves to God (Rom. 14:12). "Fear God and keep His commandments, because this applies to every person. For God will bring every act to judgment, everything which is hidden, whether it is good or evil" (Eccl. 12:13-14). Amen.

"To the only wise God, through Jesus Christ, be the glory forever. Amen" (Rom. 16:27). Wisdom is something that most people think is a good thing to have. Biblical wisdom is the ability to judge correctly, but it has also a much larger practical connotation. It is to live and learn by experiencing the godly ways of the Lord. God is the source of this quality of wisdom. God is holy, righteous and just. His wisdom is expressed through omniscience and omnipotence and love to guide a man to live a moral and ethical life (Pro. 2:6, 1 Cor. 1:24, Isa. 40:28). The Son of God, who is wisdom (1 Cor. 1:24), "becomes to us wisdom from God and righteousness and sanctification and redemption" (1 Cor. 1:30). The gospel from God places us in Jesus Christ, who becomes to us wisdom from God. When God saves us, Christian, He equips us with the Holy Spirit to lead and guide us, and make available His wisdom for our hearts. Our being in Jesus is necessary for how God wanted us to grow in grace and knowledge, be godly and serve Him in this life. We need His wisdom and power to be spiritually healed. By His stripes we are healed (Isa. 53:5). It is knowing God in your troubles and failures, and in the good times, and in Bible study that His presence and wisdom are experienced. God's wisdom will be seen in your creation as a new man and in His kindly providences throughout your life. To God be the glory forever. All things are working together for good (Rom. 8:28). The result of God's wisdom and perfect patience with us is ultimately reflected by our obedience, holiness, faithfulness, joy, peace, patience, love, and goodness. The wisdom of God is alive and working in you. The wisdom of God nurses you to live and walk and work by His Spirit. Amen.

"The fear of the Lord is the beginning of wisdom: A good understanding have all those who do His commandments; His praise endures forever" (Ps. 111:10). The fear of the Lord, Christian, is where a lot of our spiritual growth will begin to flourish. It is a gift of God. God provides for us some fear and wisdom in the gift of faith that sets us on a path for more knowledge and wisdom that results in greater fear of the Lord. The fear of the Lord is an affectionate reverence by which a child of God humbly and carefully turns to the Father in respect and honor to His authority. Holy fear is God-given (Ps. 34:11). The natural man does not fear God, because he does not accept the things of the Spirit of God (1 Cor. 2:14). God puts the fear in our hearts of Himself so that we will not turn against Him (Jer. 32:40). "I will give them one heart and one way, that they may fear Me always, for their own good" (Jer. 32:39). What God requires of us, Christian, He promises to work into us. It is God's prerogative to fashion our hearts. A man with a new heart to fear God is a man blessed with wisdom. With our new heart, we become a new creature; old things pass away, new things have come (Ezek. 11:19, 2 Cor. 5:17). It is a heart that is in awe of His majesty and authority. It will dread His wrath and gladly give Him all the glory. He will be our God, and we shall be His people (Jer. 32:38). By the grace of God, we shall develop gracious principles that influence every aspect of our lives. "It is God who is at work in you, both to will and to work for His good pleasure" (Phil. 2:13). The grace of God works in us with fear and trembling by His good pleasure. God gives the whole ability. The grace of God inclines our will to value, desire, hope and trust in God's wisdom and power to please Him for our present and future lives. We begin and learn to reflect God's wisdom in our lives.

May the God of peace, "equip you in every good thing to do His will, working in us that which is pleasing in His sight, through Jesus Christ, to whom be the glory. Amen" (Heb.13:21). The good things fashioned into us is how God prepares us for His presence. God works a clear mind and a clean heart. God works a strength and resolve, and vivid affections with gratitude in us for Jesus. We are not idle robots, but get hungry and thirsty, by the Spirit, for more of Jesus and God's good will to us. There is a scripture passage in Philippians that is very important as to how we grow in grace. In sanctification, we cooperate with God the Holy Spirit. God creates the will to work in you and our responsibility is to take hold of God with fear and trembling (Phil. 2:12-13). The will to do good and the power in you is provided by the Spirit of God, and our responsibility is to discover the Lord's ability in us. Jesus said, "I'm the vine, you are the branches; he who abides in Me, and I in him, he bears much fruit; for apart from Me you can do nothing" (John 15:5). Abide means to live upon Jesus by faith, in love, and being led by His Spirit, with a heart of wisdom and fear and obedience. Amen.

"Thou wilt establish peace for us, since Thou hast also performed for us all our works" (Isa. 26:12). All that has been done in us, to us and for us was done by the Lord. All the goodness, grace, mercies, power and providence we owe to Him, and all the glory is due Him. The work of grace upon my heart was God's work, and not mine. My effort to respect and please God from my wisdom sounded right, but was mostly selfish, and based more on what I thought and hoped for, and not what was in the Bible. I lacked understanding of the Lord, and my obedience was inconsistent. My efforts failed and I lived with guilt. I needed something more to live a true Christian life. I struggled and stumbled for a while, until, by the grace of God, the Lord sent me deeper into His word. I learned that faith comes by hearing the word of the Lord (Rom. 10:17). I learned that the Bible was alive, and in reading it, my spark of spiritual life began to grow more into a fire. "Come, you children, listen to Me; I will teach you the fear of the Lord" (Ps. 34:11). I needed to get away from sports and other distractions in my life. I needed to spend more time with the Lord. I needed to learn more about God to fear Him, and to walk more obediently with Him. "A good understanding, have all those who do His commandments" (Ps. 111:10). We are not just to talk about the commandments, but we are to live by them. It will be hard for you to know peace, and believe you really understand the Bible and the Lord, if you are not living for Him. There is a disconnect when we know the right thing to do and do not do it. There is a weakness in our understanding of the gospel when we do not adhere to the teaching it sets before us. God is not mocked (Gal. 6:7). Ignorance is a serious spiritual disease that is healed by God when He sends us into His living word for knowledge and wisdom. When the fear of the Lord rules in our heart, Christian, we will know a conscientious attention to desire to keep His commandments. God knows that when we know more about Him, we will more earnestly seek His help. Amen.

"If you love Me, you will keep My commandments" (John 14:15). Loving Jesus is not just a feeling; it is an abiding part of a serious relationship. True love will mean a growth unto obedience. The Bible says that "we know that we have come to know Him if we keep His commandments" (1 John 2:3). "If any man is willing to do His will, he shall know of the teaching, whether it is of God, or whether I speak from Myself" (John 7:17). "He who has My commandments and keeps them, he it is who loves Me; and he who loves Me shall be loved by My Father, and I will love him, and will disclose Myself to him" (John 14:21). I was gripped by the promise of Christ being disclosed or manifested to me. The disclosing of Christ to your heart is a spiritual manifestation of His love to you (Eph. 3:16-19). The mind becomes enlightened to know His love and your graces from God become alive and active. You behold your salvation in your heart with comfort and gratitude. You experience the fear of the Lord and recognize a wisdom from above. You know tokens of His love in the study of His word. You have been given understanding and desires to do the will of God. Spiritual intelligence comes to the heart in the exercise of faith and seeks God's glory. "By faith we understand" (Heb. 11:3). God's Spirit of wisdom is at work in our lives, to save us for the purpose He made us for. In the wisdom of God, we first hear the call to receive Jesus into our hearts, and then we hear a call to keep His commandments. In the wisdom of God, He sends us into His word to grow in grace and knowledge and obedience. In the wisdom of God, we fear Him for His greatness and goodness, and go to work with Him, according to His will and pleasure. Amen.

God knows everything (1 John 3:20). For God to be sovereign over all His creation, He has the perfection of knowing everything. God knows everything in the past, present and future, and is aware of every detail in every human being. Though some people think that this is impossible, even for God, they will learn they were wrong. In the future, our conscience will bring forth the truth. God does not wonder about things, Christian, He is a wonder. Wisdom is knowledge guided by understanding, and when it is perfect, is called omniscience. Wisdom is practical and means applied knowledge. Not only does the Lord, our God, know everything, Christian, but He has a perfect goodness. He knows the best way to use this wisdom on our behalf. God has infinite awareness, understanding and insight. God is all powerful or omnipotent (Isa 55:11, Gen. 18:14). Our salvation is possible and reasonable given the abilities of God to perform any kind of work. He appointed us to eternal life (Acts 13:48), and opened our hearts to believe (Acts 16:14, Rom. 8:28-30). God is present everywhere or omnipresent (Ps. 139). God is in every place at the same time. "The Lord Himself goes before you and will be with you" (Deut. 31:8). "I will never desert you, nor will I ever forsake you (Heb. 13:5). Taken together, Christian, these "omni" terms define God's sovereignty and include His providence and Lordship. The nature, wisdom and power of God help us understand the world's creation (Ps. 104:24, Dan. 2:20-21), our person (Job 38:36), the church (Eph. 3:10) and our salvation (Luke 19:10). Amen. God has all these perfect and complete attributes, and at the same time, a lovingkindness to carry out His acts of providence to bring us to Jesus and then home into His heaven.

Whatever it would take, His grace will always be sufficient. Whatever it takes to accomplish His will, you can be confident that God's will, will be done. God's wisdom will be inscrutable (Isa. 40:28), infinite (Ps. 147:5), mighty (Job 36:5), and perfect (Job 37:16). "So shall My word be which goes forth from My mouth; It shall not return to Me empty, without accomplishing what I desire, and without succeeding in the matter for which I sent it" (Isa. 55:11). God has already done great things for you, Christian, with much more to come. You will be holy, and learn to deeply love and trust Him. The promises of mercy and grace upon your soul now will develop into more sanctification and greater comforts the more you walk with Jesus. "You will go out with joy, and be led forth with peace" (Isa. 55:12). You will begin living in the mansion He has prepared for you (John 14:2). The purposes of the gospel in your life will not be returning to the Lord empty. God will finish the work He started (Phil. 1:6). "The grass withers, the flower fades, but the word of our God stands forever" (Isa. 40:8). The world (1 John 2:17), your body with good looks, and your mind with all its hopes and goals, Christian, will fade; but the purpose and promises of God will stand forever. Out of your belly will flow rivers of living water (John 7:38). "You have been born again, not of corruptible seed, but incorruptible, that is, through the living and abiding word of God" (1 Pet. 1:23). Jesus in you will never pass away. You were drawn by God (John 6:44) and quickened by God (John 5:21) for everlasting life with God. Amen.

The Lord knows you intimately, Christian, because He is everywhere and knows everything. What the Lord knows about you, He uses for your good and not against you (Rom. 8:27). We need help to be born again and become a spiritual man. We need help to grow in grace and knowledge in order to remain a spiritual man. God knows that we cannot understand Him as a natural man, and must be cleansed from the defiling nature of our hearts. God knows that sometimes we will choose foolishness and ignorance and reject suggestions about being holy. God knows we will think that He might be no fun; God goes to work in this kind of man, to will and to work for His good pleasure (Phil.2:13). We become more serious about sin and judgment, Jesus and the church, and what our lives might be like when we see God after we die. We may find that trying to get right with God, by quitting habits we know to be wrong, is not working. Failure in the Christian life, after a while, by the grace of God, is humbling and is intended to lead us to the understanding that we need a Savior, or that we need to be closer to the One we thought we already knew. God's wisdom is at work, bringing the spiritual success to you that is born out of surrender to Jesus. Our efforts to please God was a work of our wisdom that proved to be a failure. Unless the Lord steps in, we are lost. We do not know what we need, but God does. We need His presence. We need His wisdom. He sends us into the word for faith in Jesus (Rom. 10:17). We learn that Jesus is God's wisdom for our hearts (1 Cor. 1:30). We learn "that we are His workmanship, created in Christ Jesus for good works, which God prepared beforehand, that we should walk in them (Eph. 2:10). It was never about our wisdom and works, Christian; it was about understanding the Lord, and for this, we had to grow into God's wisdom by the grace of God. Amen.

God's wisdom is to make a covenant with us in Jesus. "I will put My laws into their minds, and I will write them upon their hearts and I will be their God and they will be My people" (Heb. 8:10). "I will be merciful to their iniquities and I will remember their sins no more" (Heb. 8:12). This is the wisdom of God working in us for our eternity, that is, He promises to remember our sins no more, and establish our peace by His Word. In God's wisdom, He chose us to be free from the practice and penalty of sin forever. In God's wisdom, He chose for us to be happy in His presence, and not bear the guilt of sin. In God's wisdom, He chose to build in us a gratitude for His mercy and grace. Somehow, we will remember our sin, I think, but in God's way. We will not remember our sin from regret and weakness or sorrow about missing the mark, but in forgiveness and the gift of His great love. God first loves us into a relationship with Himself, and then provides sufficient grace and wisdom for us to love Him and do our duty (1 John 4:19). The pardon by God opens the door to spiritual blessings. He chose us in the way of His wisdom and power to bring us into the gospel covenant, and then builds us up in it. This is God's wisdom; choosing to work out our salvation, redemption and righteousness for an eternal destiny with Himself in a heavenly residence. Amen.

God knows us and still chose us (Rom. 5:8). Sometimes I feel like Lot when he hesitated to leave Sodom. The angels seized his hand and brought him outside the city of Sodom before brimstone and fire rained down from the Lord out of heaven (Gen. 19:16). Lot and Abraham had separated from each other earlier, because of strife between their herdsman. Abraham gave Lot the first choice of land to move to, and he chose a valley that was well watered near the city of Sodom, which was full of wicked sinners (Gen.

13). Lot walked by sight and was worldly while Abraham walked by faith looking for the city whose builder and maker was God (Heb. 11:10). The world can lure us into hesitating about God and making poor choices. If the Lord had not brought me out of my sinful state, Christian, I would have been ruined by it. It is by God's grace and mercy that we are saved (Eph. 2:8). I gratefully acknowledge God's power and wisdom to save me. I acknowledge that I had many convictions and some misery early on in my spiritual state. I acknowledge that I was weak. I gratefully appreciate the Lord's patient wisdom. I loitered too much of my life in sin and distractions when I should have been in the word of God. The wisdom of God tells us to "seek first His kingdom and His righteousness" (Matt. 6:33). The Bible tells us that if we search for wisdom and cry for discernment, "we will discern the fear of the Lord, and discover the knowledge of God" (Prov. 2:4). Amen.

Our heart is the center of knowledge, understanding, thinking and wisdom. The heart is the center of your personality and character and controls your mind, emotions and will. The heart is essentially the whole man, Christian, and includes all his intellectual and psychological attributes. It is the heart that makes a man and governs his actions (Prov. 4:23). The heart is the spring of your desires and should be watched diligently (Prov. 4:20-23). It is you. We are to love the Lord our God with all our heart (Mark 12:30). The right attitude of the heart for God begins with it being broken to self (Ps. 51:17). A change of heart is needed (Jer. 24:7, Ezek. 11:19). When we are born again, God gives a new heart of flesh (Ezek. 36:26). The fulfillment of these Old Testament prophecies, for a Christian, is Christ dwelling in your heart through faith, being rooted and grounded in love (Eph. 3:17). The pure in Heart shall see God (Matt. 5:8). God knows your heart. "For He knows the secrets of the heart" (Ps. 44:21). God opens (Acts 16:14), enlightens (2 Cor. 4:6) and recreates the heart (Ezek. 11:19). "The Lord searches all hearts, and understands every intent of your thoughts" (1 Chron. 28:9). "For nothing is hidden, except to be revealed; nor has anything been secret, but that it should come to light" (Mark 4:22). By the grace of God, the kingdom of God is hidden within you, that you may share it and not hide from it. With blessing comes duty and responsibility. You cannot hide from God. God searches you and knows when you sit down and rise up. He understands your thoughts and is intimately acquainted with all your ways. He knows your words before they fly off your tongue. The wisdom of God is too high for you to attain. You cannot flee from God's presence (Ps. 139:1-7).

The Lord in His powers of omnipresence and omniscience has searched you and knows you (Ps. 139:1). The Lord God is compassionate and gracious, slow to anger, and abounding in lovingkindness and truth (Ex. 34:6). Though we deserve judgment, God has chosen to deal with us in grace and mercy. God has chosen forgiveness in place of wrath. The price for our freedom was paid in full by Jesus. God, the Father accepted the price that Jesus paid, so His justice for sin was served. The non-believer in Jesus will bear the penalty and the responsibility of paying the price himself. Where would we be without the mercy and power in God's wisdom to save us? The wisdom of God was displayed in the way of our salvation and growth in grace for our sanctification. The victory secured by Christ becomes ours from the mercy in the wisdom and kindness of God. "He heals the brokenhearted and binds up their wounds" (Ps. 147:3). "How blessed is the man who finds wisdom, and the man who gains understanding" (Prov. 3:13). He is the great physician, and we are the patients. The gospel breaks our heart and provides the cure. The gospel is the truth that sets you free and happy. Wisdom is more precious than jewels; it will be life to your soul (Prov. 3:15, 22). Amen.

The Holy Spirit helps our spiritual weakness and limitations due to sin. The Spirit does not take over our responsibility, but lends an indispensable helping hand, especially in regard to our prayers. The Spirit makes intercession for us during the trials of faith with groanings that cannot be uttered or too deep for words (Rom. 8:26-27). Jesus intercedes for us in heaven (Rom. 8:34, Heb. 7:25) and the Spirit in our hearts (Rom. 8:27). We cry out "Abba, Father" (Rom. 8:15), which is a holy, humble, bold petition for help, excited by the Holy Spirit. The Holy Spirit takes hold of our burden, and constrained by love, relieves the pressure. It is the wisdom and power of God, which we cannot fully conceive, at work. How we pray, and the content is important; that is, we pray according to the will of God (1 John 5:14). I think the Holy Spirit prays for us which excites a groan from our heart and lips. The animals and plants of creation groan (Rom. 8:22). We groan waiting for our adoption and evidence of sonship (Rom. 8:23), and the Holy Spirit intercedes within us (Rom. 8:26). The Holy Spirit strengthens us to bear our trial and directs us to God. The groans, I think, are primarily spiritual and nonverbal. The pressures of sin and sorrow are a heavy burden. The groans are about hope and life, Christian, not despair and death. The groans are a difficult time, no doubt, but they are the birth pangs of God's love going to work to rescue our souls, and put them on higher ground. "He who searches the hearts knows what the mind of the Spirit is, because He intercedes for the saints according to the will of God" (Rom. 8:27). God the Father searches our hearts to know what the groanings and longings of the Holy Spirit are for us, in order that He might supply the need we have. In spite of our ignorance and desire to sin, the Lord works on our hearts according to His good and perfect will and purpose. God knows the thoughts we think and provides the help we need to speak. No one but God can gain this kind of knowledge and turn it into wisdom on our behalf. Amen. The sighing in your heart, Christian, is the work of the Spirit of God. His wisdom for us going forward will be fruitful and encouraging. His word will not be returning to Him void (Isa. 55:11). We have a Comforter (John 14:16).

"For My thoughts are not your thoughts, neither are your ways My ways, declares the Lord" (Isa. 55:8). "Man's steps are ordained by the Lord. How then can man understand His way?" (Prov. 20:24). "To the only wise God, through Jesus Christ, be the glory forever. Amen" (Rom. 16:27). God is infinitely wise and always has the perfect knowledge to achieve the best goal in every situation. We think we know what is best for us, or what we think at least will feel good. However, God has much more knowledge and wisdom about what really constitutes the best for our future. The Lord's plan for us is to be humble and loving in Jesus, and to achieve the greatest good for the glory for God, and even for ourselves (2 Cor. 3:18). Some people want what they think, no matter what. They think without God and have no fear of what that might mean. Thinking they are wise they have become fools (Rom. 1:22). "Since the creation of the world His invisible attributes, His eternal power and divine nature have been clearly seen, so they are without excuse" (Rom. 1:20). God gave them over to the lusts in their hearts to impurity, degrading passions and a depraved mind without understanding and righteousness (Rom. 1: 24-32). The world, through its wisdom, does not come to know God. God was well-pleased through the foolishness of the message preached to save those who believe by the gift of faith. The Jews ask for signs, and the Greeks search for wisdom, but Christ became a stumbling block and foolishness to both groups (1 Cor. 1:21-24). God has chosen the foolish things of the world to shame the wise and the weak things of the world to shame the strong, that no man should boast before God (1 Cor. 1:27-29). We are saved by grace and not works. We are saved by the Lord's lovingkindness and work, to boast only in the Lord. Amen. "For as the heavens are higher than the earth, so are My ways higher than your ways, and My thoughts than your thoughts" (Isa. 55:9). Amen

God is more interested in our character than our comfort. Through trials, troubles and sickness, we learn His mercies, faithfulness, perseverance and comfort (1 Cor. 1:3-4, 1 Pet. 1:6-7). We are to focus on what is going on inside of us, rather than what is happening to us. We learn that, "Blessed are those who mourn, for they shall be comforted" (Matt. 5:4). We mourn over our sin, but we rejoice in God as our comforter (John 16:20, Isa. 61:2). We learn to count it all as joy, knowing that the testing of our faith produces endurance (James 1:2-3). We learn "The Lord is near to the broken-hearted, and saves those who are crushed in spirit" (Ps. 34:18). "God is our refuge and strength" (Ps. 46:1). We think that God is not fair sometimes, and that bad things should not happen to good people. We think that physical pain or trouble is because we did something wrong. The Lord knows that the sense of His presence is a wisdom that is bigger than life. Amen. The Lord hears the prayers of the righteous in Jesus. God's eyes are upon them, His ears are open to their cry, and He delivers them out of their trouble (Ps. 34:15-17, Prov. 15:29). Though we have been prodigal children, His thoughts for us are about reconciliation. The Lord's thoughts for us in affliction are about drawing us closer to Himself with spiritual comforts. God's thoughts for us are about mercy. God's plans for you, Christian, are for "your welfare and not calamity to give you a future and a hope" (Jer. 29:11). You will not see the expectations of your fears or fancies, but you will see a spirit of prayer, mercy and faith in Jesus.

The wisdom comes to us in the promise to seek the Lord with all your heart and you will find Him (Jer. 29:13). Seek the Lord by prayer and diligent Bible study, with hope and sincerity, "believing that He is, and that He is a rewarder of those who seek Him" (Heb. 11:6). The rewards you will find from the Lord are priceless. You will know peace in your conscience. The hope you will find will be the witness of the Holy Spirit, that you have been born again, and are in the family of God by adoption. The reward from God is a more perfect wisdom about God, that is, the truth of Christ living in your heart. The reward from God is to keep you from sin and give you knowledge with power for the obedience of faith. Amen. The reward from God is to be moved with fear, like Noah (Heb. 11:7), to build an Ark of faith in Jesus. The reward from God is to see the glory of God and His righteousness. The reward of God is to see Jesus standing at the right hand of the Father, like Stephen (Acts 7:55-57), in the midst of being stoned by the world. The reward from God is a faith that travels deeper into your soul with convictions about the realities of Jesus. You know you have been called to serve the living God in the purpose born from His wisdom. "By His doing you are in Christ Jesus, who became to us wisdom from God" (1 Cor. 1:30). "The mouth of the righteous flows with wisdom" (Prov. 10:31). Once we were foolish and ignorant of the things of the Lord, Christian, but now, by the grace of God, Jesus Christ has been made the true wisdom of our life. Amen. A wise person's mouth flows with praise to God for saving his soul and is grateful for His many blessings. A wise person comforts the afflicted, encourages the weak, gives good advice and points the way to God by Jesus Christ. We will be judged by our words (Matt 12:36-37).

"Little children, let us not love with word or with tongue, but in deed and truth. We shall know by this that we are of the truth, and shall assure our heart before Him, in whatever our heart condemns us; for God is greater than our heart, and knows all things" (1 John 3:18-20). I take this passage as encouraging, Christian, that God is greater than my heart and knows all things. I know my weakness, and I sense the failings in my conscience of not being a perfect Christian for Jesus. I do not doubt that the Lord is fully aware of my sin, my thoughts and my infirmities, and the defiling nature of all this in my soul. "The wishing of doing good is in me, but the doing of good is not. The good that I wish, I do not do; but I practice the very evil that I do not wish. I joyfully concur with the law of God in my inner man but I also find the principle of evil is present with me". (Rom. 7:14-24). I know the conflict of the two natures. If our heart condemns us, we are to confess our sin for cleansing (1 John 1:9). We are to continue in acts of self-giving love, Bible study and prayer. We are to be responsible and allow the Lord to speak to our hearts about our acceptance and forgiveness. In this way, God removes the condemnation (Rom. 8:1). God does not bar us from approaching Him. God is greater than our heart in knowledge, understanding, love and compassion. He is tender with us as children and more patient with us than we deserve. We eventually learn to follow Him in love. God is greater than my conscience. The Lord does not minimize our disobedience, but gives us time to discover His work in us, and handle our responsibility to honor His presence with us. It hurts to miss the Lord. He is omniscient and knows me better than I know myself. He remembers the gospel covenant and that I'm clothed in the righteousness of His Son. This is the only firm ground for my assurance.

God keeps His word and can be trusted (Heb. 6:17-18). The word of God tells me that I should base my hope on the character of

God. Hope in the Lord Jesus is sure and steadfast, and a refuge and an anchor for our soul to hang on to for salvation and eternal life (Heb. 6:18-19). We keep on trusting Jesus, Christian, realizing with gratitude, that we are not earning our salvation. We will always need the grace of God, working from His love, even throughout our eternity. In this life, we learn about God's love and faithfulness for us, in the midst of putting on the armor of God in the struggle against spiritual forces of wickedness (Eph. 6:11-12). It is our responsibility to learn to fight "in the strength of His might" (Eph. 6:10). We will not be perfect, but we will not be losers. I'm reminded of the story of Peter (John 19:25-27). Peter's denial of Jesus grieved him greatly, especially when Jesus asked him three times if he loved Him. Peter's response was "Lord, you know all things; you know that I love you" (John 21:17). He appeals to the omniscience of God rather than his own conscience. Jesus knew what was in a man (John 2:24-25). The Lord searches the heart and tests the mind (Jer. 17:10). All things are laid bare and open for Him to see (Heb. 4:13). He knows how to comfort us and assure us that we belong to Jesus. We are to pray like David. He wanted God to search his heart, and see if there was any offensive way, and then to lead him in paths of righteousness for His name's sake (Ps. 139:23, 23:3). We must listen to our conscience for God's wisdom to teach us truth and give us guidance. The conscience is our organ of faith by which we have our best chance to hear from God. God will be the final judge. Amen.

God's wisdom is called manifold wisdom (Eph. 3:10). The manifold wisdom of God's work in the church is being viewed by principalities and powers in heavenly places. The Spirit of Christ, the church and our redemption, are things that the angels long to look into (1 Pet. 1:12). Our struggle is against spiritual forces in heavenly places, where the angelic hosts witness God's wisdom in salvation through the church. They are learning about God and His wisdom in the redemption of man. It is a wonder of wisdom that they have never seen before. We shall actually even judge the angels (1 Cor. 6:3). Angels were created as servants of God and redeemed humanity (Heb. 1:14). Humans were created in the image and likeness of God (Gen. 1:26-27). Jesus gave His life for human redemption and not angels (Heb. 2:14-16). Some folks have thought that Satan's rebellion was somehow related to God's command that angels were to serve Adam's race. Some folks think that we shall have authority only over the holy angels, since the fallen angels have already been condemned (Jude 6). The angels are ministering spirits, sent forth to minister for those who shall be the heirs of salvation. In the wisdom of God, they are the ministers of divine providence for us. Angels were created by God (Ps. 148:5) as intelligent spirits (2 Sam. 14:20) and excel in wisdom and strength (Ps. 103:20). I believe they help us in our battles against sin and execute the divine will. I believe that they help protect (Ps. 34:7) and comfort us (Acts 27:23-24) as we pass through this world. The Bible says, "He will give His angels charge concerning you, to guard you in all your ways. They will bear you up in their hands" (Ps. 91:11-12). Exactly when and how angels protect us may be unknown, but I think they protect our body, soul and spirit without limit, according to the tender mercies of our God. I think that they faithfully and effectively carry out the commandments of God for us when we grow in grace and knowledge. I think they will be judged a great success for God's glory.

The manifold wisdom of God was evident in the grace revealed for our salvation. When God designed our redemption, He chose His only-begotten Son to perform the work (John 3:16). He is called God's chosen (Isa. 42:1). His name was Jesus. He would save His people from their sins (Matt. 1:21). The wisdom of God in choosing His eternal Son, a divine person, to be our redeemer and mediator gave an infinite value to Him, and eternal favor and value to us as His adopted children. He has infinite power, wisdom, love, mercy and holiness. He was not a created being, could act of His own will and was infinitely dear to His Father. He is called the Beloved (Eph. 1:6) and made us acceptable in the Beloved. "The Father predestined us to adoption as sons through Jesus Christ to Himself, according to the kind intention of His will, to the praise of the glory of His grace which He freely bestowed on us in the Beloved" (Eph. 1:5-6). It shows a divine wisdom by God to choose

Jesus, whom against we had sinned and were enemies (Rom. 5:10), to be our redeemer. Because Christ was accepted, those who are in Him, are accepted. We have a righteousness imputed to us, Christian, by grace through faith. We stand in the Son of the Father's love, accepted and holy with the demands of justice fully satisfied. Jesus prayed that the Father would love believers, just like He loved Jesus (John 17:23,26).

It shows a divine wisdom that He would take our guilt upon Himself and be able to take the penalty. It shows a divine wisdom that God would perform the humbling work of becoming a man through the incarnation, and live in perfect obedience to the law. The "Word became flesh" and lived on the earth (John 1:14). "This is My beloved Son, in whom I'm well-pleased" (Matt. 3:17). He appeared in low outward circumstances in the world (Isa. 53:2). The wisdom of God allowed Him to become a prophet and a teacher. The wisdom of God allowed Him to become a healer. It was in the wisdom of God that He suffered, was condemned and put to death on a wooden cross. It was in the wisdom of God that the One who died and gave His life would be put to death by His own creatures. It was in the wisdom of God that grace through faith in Jesus would be the way that sinners would be saved. It was in the wisdom of God that many would see the criminal who died, while many others would see the Savior. Because He humbled Himself, "God highly exalted Him, and bestowed on Him the name which is above every name, that at the name of Jesus every knee should bow, of those who are in heaven, and on earth, and under the earth, and that every tongue should confess that Jesus Christ is Lord, to the glory of God the Father" (John 5:23).

The Old Testament tells us that the Messiah or Christ should arise out of the house of David (Ps. 132:11, Isa. 11:1). "The Spirit of the Lord will rest on Him, the spirit of wisdom and understanding, the spirit of counsel and strength, the spirit of knowledge and fear of the Lord" (Isa. 11:2). The spirit of wisdom was predicted. "Jesus kept increasing in wisdom and stature, and in favor with God and man" (Luke 2:52). Christ was the power of God and the wisdom of God (1 Cor. 1:24), and recognized even in the city of

Nazareth (Matt. 13:54). In Christ are hidden all the treasures of wisdom and knowledge (Col. 2:3), and by God's doing, we are in Christ Jesus, and He becomes to us wisdom from God (1 Cor. 1:30). The spirit of wisdom is given to us by God (Eph. 1:17), by Christ (Luke 21:15) and is a gift through the spirit (1 Cor. 12:8). Paul prayed and taught that we might know the unsearchable riches of wisdom in Christ (Col. 1:9, 28). If we lack wisdom, Christian, we are encouraged to ask God, in faith without doubt, and He gives to all men generously (James 1:5-6). "The wisdom from above is first pure, then peaceable, gentle, reasonable, full of mercy and good fruits, unwavering without hypocrisy (James 3:17). Wisdom from God is a gift; it is imputed or attributed to us by His presence with us. We grow in grace and knowledge and reflect His wisdom. Amen. The wisdom of this world is foolishness (1 Cor. 3:19) and earthly (James 3:15), can be corrupted (Ezek. 28:17) and cause boasting (Jer. 9:23) and delusions (Isa. 47:10). God was well-pleased through the foolishness of preaching of the message preached to save those who believe (1 Cor. 1:18-21). There is great value in the wisdom of God. "Trust in the Lord with all your heart and do not lean on your own understanding. In all your ways acknowledge Him, and He will make your paths straight (Prov. 3:5-6). The Lord protects us and keeps us from evil when we give attention to His wisdom. "Wisdom is better than jewels (Prov. 8:11). Wisdom produces meekness (James 3:13). It is better to get wisdom than gold. Gold is another's, wisdom is our own; gold is for the body and time, wisdom for the soul and eternity (Matthew Henry).

The gospel in the heart of any person, according to the wisdom of God, is a preserving grace. It is the power of God that stays at the work to complete the Lord's will for our salvation (1 Pet. 2:2). The result of the gospel is our union with Christ, and along the way, to experience a life blessed with the obedience of faith. "And without faith it is impossible to please Him, for he who comes to God must believe that He is and that He is a rewarder of those who seek Him" (Heb. 11:6). Just like Justification and Sanctification are distinct acts of God, Christian, yet inseparable, so are faith and obedience. Our acceptance with God precedes our separation unto God. Faith in Jesus made us sons of God (Gal. 3:26), and bearing fruit or obedience proves us to be His disciples (John 15:8). Faith purifies the heart. Faith is a gift and works by love, we are saved by grace through faith (Eph. 2:8). "We love, because He first loved us" (1 John 4:19). God's wisdom has put in place an obedience, springing from faith in Christ. Our salvation is not a work of ourselves, it is a gift of God (Eph. 2:8). "We are His workmanship, created in Christ Jesus for good works, which God prepared beforehand that we should walk in them" (Eph. 2:10). "To the only wise God through Jesus Christ, be the glory forever. Amen "(Rom. 16:27).

From the standpoint of God, Christian, His choice was to love us. In His wisdom, He chose to give gifts to us, to bring about a glory for us that magnifies His mercy and grace. In His wisdom, God designed and controls His own faithfulness to His own promises. God's sovereign election, gifts and calling are irrevocable (Rom. 11:29), because they are rooted in His perfect and immutable nature. "Oh, the depth of the riches both of the wisdom and knowledge of God! (Rom. 11:32). In His wisdom, God chose the mechanism of faith, not works, to reveal and display His mercy, love and grace on poor sinners. It is by grace then, that God gives a new heart with faith in Jesus, and a new spirit and His own Spirit that we might be careful to walk in His ordinances (Ezek. 36:26-27). The wisdom displayed is unsearchable by the logic in our minds, but knowable by the work of the Lord in our hearts. The trust and assurance of Jesus Christ as Savior is the Spirit's work, nursing us into the comforts of knowing, loving and serving a great God. Our spiritual growth takes place in God's time and way. In His wisdom, He brings forth the circumstances of our coming to Jesus, and the victories over sin we come to realize in our lives. The wisdom of God is worked into the providences of God, that bring our souls nearer to His presence. "With Him are wisdom and might, to Him belong counsel and understanding (Job 12:13). No human being can know the mind of the Lord. "For from Him and through Him and to Him are all things. To Him be the glory forever. Amen" (Rom. 11:36). "He has made everything appropriate in its time. He also set eternity in their heart, yet so that man will not find out the work which God has done from the beginning to the end" (Eccl. 3:11).

God's wisdom can be seen in bringing glory to Himself out of sin. The wisdom of God makes good out of evil and honor to Himself. God may have permitted Adam's fall to allow a greater discovery of His mercy and grace and goodness. "Sin reigned in death, even so grace might reign through righteousness to eternal life through Jesus Christ our Lord" (Rom. 5:21). In His sovereignty God permitted sin; in His justice He punishes sin, and in His wisdom, He brings about good. The unbounded goodness of God's mercy and grace on miserable guilty sinners in Jesus, makes His wisdom illustrious. God draws good out of evil. The fall of the devil had to be allowed by infinite wisdom. The fall of man had to be allowed by infinite wisdom in order to show the virtue of God's cure of the disease of sin. While man ruined his nature, God glorified Himself in the obedience of His Son. God's wisdom appears in the death and resurrection of Jesus for the glory of Christ. To the world, the resurrection is foolishness. "Let no man deceive himself. If any man among you thinks that he is wise in this age, let him become foolish that he may become wise. For the wisdom of the world is foolishness with God" (1 Cor. 3:18-19). "The Lord knows that the reasonings among men are useless. So then let no one boast in men. For all things belong to you, and you belong to Christ; and Christ belongs to God" (1 Cor. 3:20-21,23). Jesus Christ will be the first fruits, and after that those who are Christ's at His coming, then comes the end, when He delivers up the kingdom to the Father" (1 Cor. 15:23-24). In His wisdom, God has set into our hearts that "our citizenship is in heaven, from which we wait for a Savior, the Lord Jesus Christ; who will transform the body of our humble state into conformity with the body of His glory" (Phil. 3:20-21). Amen. God may have permitted sin, not as an end, but to bring forth His good mercy and grace in the mystery of the incarnation of the Savior. In His wisdom, God brought forth the honor of a new creation and our Redeemer. Jesus was "delivered up by the predetermined plan and foreknowledge of God and godless men put Him to death, and God raised Him up again" (Acts 2:23-24). Infinite wisdom made the cross of Jesus, which was a great evil by man, the place of our righteousness and salvation, which was a great good by God.

The good of a nation sometimes comes from the sin of man; even from our sin, God can bring forth good. For example; good came to the family of Jacob from the selling of Joseph to the Midianites (Gen. 37:28). Good came to the Gentiles from the unbelief of the Jewish people (Matt. 22:9) and Jonah's disobedience led to the repentance of the city of Nineveh (Jonah 2:5). The events of sin in our lives are not allowed by God to remain in our hearts. My own personal experiences are a testimony to the damage of sin and the mercy of God. Our conversion to Jesus Christ can be intense and profitable. We are saved from ourselves, by the wisdom of God, for adoption and an inheritance imperishable and undefiled, reserved in heaven (1 Pet. 1:4). "He makes known to us the mystery of His will according to His kind intention" (Eph. 1:9). Without God's love, we would not have holiness, humility and patience, or even know the meaning of love. The remaining sins and corruptions in our hearts keep us running after God for grace to know peace and freedom. The sins of man can lead to his conversion and/or sanctification. My lapses, Christian, have often reminded me how much I always need Jesus. We might sink sometimes in order to recognize we need Him. Paul had a thorn in the flesh to remind him that God's grace was sufficient (2 Cor. 12:7). It is in the wisdom of God to allow a weakness now and then to keep up the honor to Himself in the Redeemer. We are reminded that our righteousness was imputed by grace and not earned. By the grace of God, I find confession when I sin (1 John 1:9). We need God's grace after we are saved. Being reminded daily of the forgiveness of my sin, keeps the fires of gratitude burning. After we are saved, sin humbles us and makes our conscience more tender and able to discover the triggers to sin and the devices of Satan. It sounds counterintuitive, Christian, but the Lord, in His wisdom, can weaken the sin by allowing it to stir and defile us. The soul gets awakened and clings more strongly to Christ for the grace to promote a more holy life. Because of one sin, we become more vigorous against it with stronger desires for repentance (2 Cor. 7:11). Purging of sin, or pruning, is with a hope that God's grace will be fruitful (John 15:2). This is the wisdom of God patiently accomplishing His purpose of forming Christ within us. Amen.

The works of creation are the footsteps of His wisdom; the work of redemption is the face of His wisdom (Stephen Charnock). "But we all, with unveiled face beholding as in a mirror the glory of the Lord, are being transformed into the same image from glory to glory, just as from the Lord the Spirit" (2 Cor. 3:18). An unveiled face is a description of a born-again Christian. By grace through faith, the veil has been removed from the face or heart of the Christian, and he can see Jesus. "He delivered us from the domain of darkness, and transferred us to the kingdom of His beloved Son" (Col. 1:13). The eyes of our heart have been opened to see Jesus as our Lord and Savior. The glory of the wisdom of God is now open and no longer veiled by the Law and our sinful passions. The veil of unbelief has been removed and we experience close face-to-face encounters with the Lord every day. When we look full into God's face, Christian, by reading and studying the Bible, we are apprehended by faith. From this faith, we see the riches of God's glory, the mystery "which is Christ in you, the hope of glory" (Col. 1:27). God's face reveals Jesus as the glory of His wisdom for our redemption. Looking unto Jesus must affect your heart. Beholding Jesus as the Son of God is the secret to holiness. "Whoever confesses that Jesus is the Son of God, God abides in him, and he in God (1 John 4:15). This is eternal life (John 17:3). Amen. We overcome the world, Christian, because our affections have been set upon Christ and our will is yielded to Him. Turn your eyes upon Jesus; look full in His wonderful face; and the things of earth will grow strangely dim in the light of His glory and grace (Helen H. Lemmel, 1922).

The gospel opened up to us God's wisdom. It is called hidden wisdom (1 Tim. 1:17), wisdom in a mystery (1 Cor. 2:7), and manifold wisdom (Eph. 3:10). The wisdom of men and angels cannot understand it. Without revelation and God's help, we could not begin to imagine it. The glory of God, our redemption, the Trinity and the nature of Christ and His death and resurrection, and much more were hidden. He "lavished upon us, in all wisdom and insight: He made known to us the mystery of His will, according to His kind intention which He purposed in Him" (Eph. 1:8). Justice was satisfied in His punishment, and mercy satisfied in our being pardoned. God's wisdom reconciled His honor with our salvation in Himself. God reconciled His hatred of sin with His love for the sinner. The first death, Satan brought upon us in Adam, ruined us; the death Satan brought upon the second Adam, restored us. "Through death He might render powerless him who had the power of death, that is, the devil" (Heb. 2:14). The devil, in his wisdom, ruined his own kingdom. In the wisdom of God, the sinner is pardoned, sanctified and reconciled by the same blood that God is glorified and the rebellion condemned. God did this all for us and His glory, and the price He paid was the death of His only begotten Son.

The love of Christ to die for us, and the love of the Father expressed in it, constrains us to no longer live for ourselves, but for them. This is valuable grounds with incentives for obedience and gratitude to fear God. The gifts from the Lord of faith, love, grace, and comfort provide incentive to follow Him in love. The love of Christ constrains, compels, controls, and empowers us to live not for ourselves, "but for Him who died and rose again on our behalf" (2 Cor. 5:15). "The grace of God has appeared, bringing salvation to all men, instructing us to deny ungodliness" (Titus 2:11-12). Jesus is our example and incentive for obedience. He was obedient unto death for our freedom (Phil. 2:8). We acknowledge the mercy and justice of God and that faith is the important condition of our recovery. God is sovereign, and we are made glad in humility. We fell by unbelief in the consequences of disobeying God, and are saved by believing in a promise which exalts the glory of God's free grace. We sinned by pride, and the wisdom of God recovers us by humbling our souls. I would rather be humbled and have Jesus and be found, than keep my pride without Jesus and be lost. "As many as received Him, to them He gave the right to become the children of God, even to those who believe in His name, who were born not of blood, nor of the will of the flesh, nor of the will of man, but of God" (John 1:12-13). Faith can be described as receiving and/or believing on His name. We were born again by a free act of sovereign grace. In the wisdom of God, we were born of God. This Divine work was accomplished by the Holy Spirit applying the Word in living power with wisdom to our heart. Amen.

God's infinite wisdom appears for our good in everything that happens in our lives. This includes our afflictions, judgments, deliverances, faith, repentance, and growth in grace and knowledge. God's wisdom appears in the choice of our family members, the schools we went to, and the major fields of study, friends and the type of work we had to make a living. The details are not a problem for the Lord to cover for us. God's wisdom appears in the manner He encourages our obedience. His work is suited to our persons and the nature of our sins. "Our adequacy is from God" (2 Cor.3:5). When a man turns to God, Christian, he comes with a corrupted nature unable to be obedient. He can only return to God with God's help. A man is restored to the Lord in His way and His time. God persuades man by faith which embraces promises (Heb. 11:13). Faith is not making good resolutions. Faith is implanted by God, and is the assurance of things hoped for (Heb. 11:1) and can never be lost. Faith is like love; faith "bears all things, believes all things, hopes all things, endures all things" (1 Cor. 13:7). The soul is satisfied in the promises of God. Though the believer may be dying without the promise fulfilled, he has seen enough. The eyes of his understanding have been Divinely enlightened. He knows the wisdom, love, power and goodness of God; seeing the promise from a distance is assurance enough of the reality. God has a wisdom that pierces our hearts with a hope that enables our perseverance. To God be the glory.

In the wisdom of God, we do not become holy overnight but grow in grace and knowledge. Faith and repentance and sanctification are usually discovered to our souls gradually. God's treasures and the gospel were put into weak earthen vessels, that the greatness of the wisdom and power would be known to come from God and not themselves (2 Cor. 4:7). The Christian religion grew stronger by suffering. The blood of martyrs was the seed of progress, defeating the methods of human policy that tried to stamp it out. Paul tells us that he himself was not sufficient in himself to fulfill his calling as an Apostle of Jesus (2 Tim. 1:1) and a teacher (2 Tim. 1:11). Anything of eternal value, Christian, is from and through the Lord. He always has and will provide the sufficient supply of wisdom, grace and power for any appointment He has made for us. A day is coming when we will give an account of the stewardship of our soul (Luke 16:2). The glory from obedient faith is from the Lord's pleasure, and returns to Him in praise and gratitude. God is all-sufficient (Gen. 17:1), our success is derived from His adequacy. "By the grace of God, I'm what I'm, and His grace toward me did not prove in vain; but I labored even more than all of them, yet not I, but the grace of God with me" (1Cor. 15:10). As a natural man, Christian, we live for ourselves without the saving grace of the Lord. By Divine grace, we become a new man. "Therefore, if any man is in Christ, he is a new creature; the old things passed away; behold, new things have come" (2 Cor. 5:17). The new man has eternal life, because he knows Jesus (John 17:3). Whatever good we have is due to the grace of God. Grace is an unmerited favor for our being just as if we never sinned before God. Grace is an unmerited favor that makes us holy before God. Grace is an unmerited favor that gives us the ability to carry out our calling and fulfilling our purpose in life. God is adequate and all-sufficient. We become sons and servants and brothers and sisters in the Christian experience by virtue of the grace of God. Amazing grace, how sweet the song (John Newton, 1779). The wisdom of the Lord thinks about us and does things for us (Ps. 57:2). Amen.

The natural wisdom we are born with is a great gift; but compared to God's wisdom, it is like a weed. Our wisdom starts with self-love and self-interest and is always imperfect. We can learn and improve in our thoughts, but we never rise close to the place the Lord inhabits. A multitude of years should add to our wisdom, but time is no guarantee we will be right. Great men are not always wise; just because someone is older; it does not mean they are going to be righteous in judgment. Being smart is one thing, but showing wisdom is another thing; having the Lord's wisdom is entirely another thing. "The Spirit of God has made me, and the breath of the Almighty has given me life" (Job 33:4). Wisdom "is a spirit in man, and the breath of the Almighty gives them understanding" (Job 32:8). God has given every man a spirit (Gen. 2:7, Eccl. 12:7, Zech. 12:1). I think the soul is an understanding spirit that is able in some measure to discern between good and evil. It is a light which enlightens every man (John 1:9). People "show the work of the law written in their hearts, their conscience bearing witness, and their thoughts alternatively accusing or else defending them, on the day when, according to my gospel, God will judge the secrets of men through Christ Jesus" (Rom. 2:15-16). God shall judge the world in righteousness. "God is declaring to men that all everywhere should repent, because He has fixed a day in which He will judge the world in righteousness through a Man whom He has appointed, having furnished proof to all men by raising Him from the dead" (Acts 17:30-31). This is wisdom from God. "He who has ears to hear, let him hear" (Matt. 11:15). This is a wake-up call.

The gospel reveals the wisdom of God (1 John 5:20). Jesus Christ, by the grace of God, is made wisdom to us (1 Cor. 1:30). We must seek Jesus for God's wisdom. "If any man lacks wisdom, let him ask of God, who gives to all men generously and without reproach, and it will be given to him. But let him ask in faith without any doubting" (James 1:5-6). When I was about twelve years old, I wanted to memorize a piece of scripture, but I did not know which one to select. I ended up memorizing the first part of the book of James; chapter one verses 1-11. I believe that God picked out this passage for me to memorize, Christian, because He knew it would mean something to me further down the road in my life. It had aspects of considering trials as a joy, asking God for wisdom, and about being a double-minded man. As a kid, I knew very little about spiritual life and faith, wisdom, joy and perseverance and the Lord, but God knew they would become important to me in my life. God fashions our hearts (Ps. 33:14-15) and orders our steps (Ps. 37:23, Prov. 16:9, 20:24). I have learned that God is sovereign, and that He works providentially in our lives according to His good will and pleasure. I have learned that the Christian life is a warfare and that "the word of God is living and active" (Heb. 4:12), and "profitable for teaching, for reproof, for correction, for training in righteousness; that the man of God may be adequate, equipped for every good work" (2 Tim. 3:16-17). The wisdom of God, Christian, is received from God. Amen.

God made me willing to do His will, and sent me into His word for faith (Rom. 10:17) to learn the mind of God. "The kingdom of God is not eating and drinking, but righteousness and peace and joy in the Holy Spirit (Rom. 14:17). The faith that I now have, by the grace of God, is a "conviction of things I cannot see" (Heb. 11:1). The gifts of forgiveness of sin and peace with God has made me glad. "If you abide in my word, then you are truly disciples of mine; and you shall know the truth, and the truth shall make you free" (John 8:31-32). "May the God of hope fill you with all joy and peace in believing, that you may abound in hope by the power of the Holy Spirit" (Rom. 15:13). The wisdom of God may be revealed by the experience of endurance in your life. The love of God is poured out into your heart during trials, and the endurance that He gives you will be crowned with God's glory. "Blessed is the man who perseveres under trial; for once he has been approved, he will receive the crown of life, which the Lord has promised to those who love Him" (James 1:12). It is in God's wisdom that we may experience trials and suffer and persevere in Jesus' name. It is difficult but all good, because it takes you on the way to discovering the love of God. The believer finds strength to overcome sin and temptation and endure trials and live for Christ. The believer has been in a war, and has become a learned veteran. It is the wisdom of God, "That whoever wishes to save his life shall lose it; but whoever loses his life for My sake and the gospel shall save it" (Mark 8:35). You save your own life by declining to come to Christ. By denying Christ, you lose the comforts of your natural life, and the joys of spiritual life and eternal life. Whosoever loses his life for Christ, saves it for a relationship with Jesus and eternal life. Amen. The conclusion of God's wisdom for us, Christian, is laid up in joy and freedom for this life, and the eternal joys and peace that come in the saving of our soul when we see Jesus.

"If any of you lack wisdom, let him ask of God," "but let him ask in faith" (James 1:5-6). We usually lack wisdom when we first try to understand our affliction. We just want to get out of it. Then we ask the Lord about it, because we know that He knows something about it and can do something about it. We humble ourselves and seek the Lord, because we know that His wisdom explains the truth about the situation. We pray for understanding and that God's will be done. We want to believe that "all things are working together for good to those who love God, to those who are called according to His purpose" (Rom. 8:28). In our outward troubles, trials, tests, and temptations, and even successes, the devil wants us to sin while God's purpose is to improve our graces. In trials, we can get exposed by our weakness and folly and double-mindedness and then waver in our obedience to God. Sometimes we are not steady or faithful in our minds, and we sin. Sin is a difficult taskmaster and brings about a kind of death experience in the soul and in the body. We know better, but struggle to do better. God sends us into His word to discover the power of truth. We find Jesus and His wisdom convicting us about what to do. It is the wisdom of God at work leading us into paths of righteousness. "In the exercise of His will He brought us forth by the word of truth" (James 1:18), to be first fruits among His creatures. The word of truth is a light of faith for a path selected by the Lord for our good. "Every good thing bestowed and every perfect gift is from above, coming down from the Father of lights, with whom there is no variation" (James 1:17). God gives the light of learning and reason. Only God's work produces the lasting and noble effects of holiness, which is a fruit of God's children. In the wisdom of our God, Christian, He builds our house with renewing grace. He builds up our hearts, establishing His good will. From this work of the Lord, He becomes our treasure. Amen. The light of our faith and holiness and all the consolations we have in this life are from

Him. What we have is from God's will, Christian, and being born again is right at the top of His good gifts to us. God's wisdom is in the spiritual power that enables us to walk obediently with Him, especially in the midst of trials and temptations. The spiritual knowledge and wisdom that God gives us is in all the very armor that we put on to protect our souls (Eph. 6:11).

We must be broken to know the Lord. Broken of our old ways and pride and receive Jesus into our hearts. We must ask in faith for help to believe that Jesus is the only way to be saved. Hope in God. "Turn to Me, and be saved, all the ends of the earth; for I'm God and there is no other" (Isa. 45:22). "I have sworn by Myself, the word has gone forth from My mouth in righteousness and will not turn back, that to Me every knee will bow, every tongue will swear allegiance" (Isa. 45:23). Look by faith to the Savior. In these last days, Jesus is how God has spoken to us; Jesus is the One appointed heir of all things. He is the One who is the exact representation of the Father and upholds all things by the word of His power and wisdom. He is the One who made purification of sins, and sat down at the right hand of the majesty on high (Heb. 1:2-3). Amen

"It is appointed unto man to die once and after this comes judgment" (Heb. 9:27). The idea of death is difficult to grasp. A Christian is prepared in this world by the Lord to enter into another world. We must die, but our comfort is that our time is in His hands. Death is a work that the Lord does for us in His time, power and wisdom. He knows the ones that are His (2 Tim. 2:19). I think that death will usher us into a big change for sure that we know very little about. We do know, "to be absent from the body is to be present with the Lord" (2 Cor. 5:8, John 12:26). Who and what will we remember? What will we learn about our past world, ourselves and others? Will all our sins be seen by others on this day? A day of judgment is coming and the perfections of God's wisdom and glory will be on display. Will we see the Lord's management of our world, and His providence in the lives of the saved and the lost? I look forward to seeing the Lord and His glory from the children He saved as His own. At the same time, I do not want others to see my sin and feel the shame of my thoughts and some of my deeds. They prove I was a sinner. Let God's will and wisdom be done.

We will be judged according to the deeds for what we have done (Rev. 20:12, 22:12). The Bible says that the righteous judgment of God "will render to every man according to his deeds" (Rom. 2:6). This scripture is not describing the basis for salvation, Christian, but the basis for judgment. "All have sinned and fall short of the glory of God" (Rom. 3:23). We are all guilty. Jesus paid the penalty for those who believe and receive Him into their heart. The life that is saved by faith will give evidence of salvation in their character and deeds. Those who do not believe, must pay the penalty for their own sin; they have no substitute. They have no inner life of faith, trust and love for Jesus. They chose to not believe His claims and were not born again. They live outside the salvation of God. They cannot yield the obedience of faith and have no evidence of living and working for the Lord. We do not go back and forth or in and out of the death experience; we are appointed once to die (Heb. 9:27).

The Bible also tells us that "We all must appear before the judgment seat of Christ, that each one may be recompensed for his deeds in the body, according to what he has done, whether good or bad" (2 Cor. 5:10). The Father has given all judgment to the Son to honor Him (John 5:22). The judgment seat of Christ, called the Bema Seat, will be for believers; we will stand before Jesus as our works are judged and rewarded. Each one of us will give an account (Rom. 14:10-12). Most folks think that this judgment will take place after the Rapture, when God's people are taken from the earth. If you are a sincere believer in Jesus, you have peace and have been set free from the law of sin and death (Rom. 8:1). We have been made righteous in the sight of God (2 Cor. 5:21). We will be judged, not according to our sins, but according to the wisdom and righteousness of Jesus. We fight sin from the position of freedom in Jesus, wearing the armor of God (Eph. 6:10-18). You do not fight sin because of your shame and weakness; you fight with spiritual weapons from the victory of Jesus who never sinned and died for your forgiveness of sin. We are already safe in the judgment about our sin by the power received from the victory of Jesus. The Godhead is always interceding for your life. Your sins will not be seen again (Ps. 103:12); they are completely and forever forgiven. In the power and wisdom of God, we will stand before God faultless with great joy (Jude 24). Mercy triumphs over judgment (James 2:13).

We will know the joy of gratefulness and that the grace of God was indeed greater than our sin. It may be that some details of God's wisdom and providence about the judgment will remain obscure or beyond our understanding. I do not know. The vindication of God's faithfulness, goodness, righteousness and providence seems appropriate. The reasonableness of justice strikes me as an act of wisdom. Without a public view of our lives as well as others, it would be difficult to understand the evil hearts of men being changed by the secret wisdom and grace of God. It would be difficult to see the power, love and glory of God drawing us to Jesus. Without some details, it would difficult to fathom the glory of God in our being chosen, adopted, and reconciled through obedience and holiness bringing about our reconciliation. The knowledge of the testimony of Jesus in a man's soul, by the mercy and wisdom of God, would bring clarity and justice for the worship, gratitude and the glory of God. The Lord will be perfect in all His ways. Whatever the reality turns to be, we will be complete and perfect when we see Jesus (1 John 3:2). Amen. The understanding between God's sovereignty and man's responsibility, in part, may remain a mystery. I do not know. "The secret things belong to the Lord" (Deut. 29:29). To God be the glory, and to God will be the glory. Amen.

Our deeds are not the basis for our salvation, Christian; they are the evidence of our salvation. In the wisdom of God, we would be saved by grace through faith, that we might not boast in anyone or about anything, but the Lord (Eph. 2:8-10). There are deeds in the soul and body that come out, and provide some evidence of a true transformation of life, in Christ. It is in God's wisdom to reward varying degrees of faithfulness in the lives of Christians. (Luke

19:12-27, 1 Cor. 3:8, Eph. 6:8). The Bible describes Christians as "God's fellow workers; you are God's field, God's building" (1 Cor. 3:9). The foundation for our house, that is, our soul, is Jesus. We build upon the foundation with gold, silver and precious stones, or we build with wood, hay and straw. Fire will test the quality of each man's work. If a man's work is burned up, he shall suffer loss; but if the work remains, he shall receive a reward (1 Cor. 3:13). Be careful how you build. God is not willing that you build poorly. We were created for good works (Eph. 2:10, Col. 1:10). Our purpose should be to always serve the Lord with our best, with full dependence on Him and leaving the results with Him. From the grace He has given us, and His wisdom to evaluate the work; He knows the true value of the work. The fire, symbolic of God's holiness, will determine what is consumed and what will last into eternity. The wisdom of God and the seeing eye of Christ will see through the phony. The test of fire will determine the quality, not the quantity. Much work with right motives will not make you ashamed at His second coming (1 John 2:28).

You are a building or temple of God, Christian, and the Holy Spirit dwells in you. You are being constructed to be a spiritual house where God dwells. Amen. "To those who by perseverance in doing good seek for glory and honor and immortality, eternal life; but to those who are selfishly ambitious and do not obey the truth, but obey unrighteousness, wrath and indignation, there will be tribulation and distress of every soul of man who does evil" (Rom. 2:7-9). "Faith works with works and as a result of the works, faith is perfected" (James 2:22). "Faith without works is dead" (James 2:26). Works, and not lip service, are the evidence of the reality of our faith in Christ. Saving faith is seen in acts of obedience and charity; not to be saved, but because we are saved (Rom. 1:5,16:26). Saving faith is alive and merciful, and released in your life as works of compassion. Through work, particularly in the church, God builds in your soul a maturity of grace through faith. In God's wisdom, our work in Jesus' name can encourage the faith of other people, and build assurances and convictions that God is alive and that Jesus is the Messiah. Faith is founded on God's promises and is witnessed to by the Spirit in our heart (Rom. 8:16). There can be a comfort, a conviction and peace with God that a particular work by us is approved by God. God has released His wisdom to us through the gift of faith in the Savior. In the wisdom of God, faith starts out in our hearts as a gift. The gift of faith then grows, by the grace of God, to learn about God through Bible study. The gift of faith is then tried and tested and, by the grace of God, grows experiential with a deeper trust of God. Your responsibility is to be "diligent to approve yourself to God as a workman who does not need to be ashamed, handling the word of truth" (2 Tim.2:15). Amen.

I close this letter with some advice and thoughts from Solomon, David's son, who has been considered the wisest man who ever lived. He set his mind to know wisdom, and found out that wisdom can be a striving after the wind. "In much wisdom there is much grief, and increasing knowledge results in increasing pain" (Eccl. 1:18). "He who pursues righteousness and loyalty, finds life, righteousness and honor" (Prov. 21:21). In the New Testament, Jesus said, "Blessed are those that hunger and thirst after righteousness, for they shall be satisfied" (Matt. 5:6). Righteousness is synonymous with salvation and in wisdom; God created both. "Drip down, O heavens from above, and let the clouds pour down righteousness; let the earth open up and salvation bear fruit, and righteousness spring up with it. I, the Lord, have created it" (Isa. 45:8). From God in heaven, Christian, drops down every good and perfect gift. The graces of the Lord and the Holy Spirit for our salvation were determined and freely given and carried out on our behalf by the wisdom from heaven. Our righteousness is imputed to us from the righteousness of Christ, who lived as a man, and died for our forgiveness and reconciliation with the Father. We would have no redemption if God had not commanded the work be carried out for our deliverance from sin and death. In the wisdom of God, we are called to repent, return to God, and receive the righteousness of Christ for salvation. This is a great work that was first born as a thought in the heart of God in heaven; then in the power of His wisdom, He brought forth Jesus Christ for us to be holy.

"You shall be holy, for I'm holy" (1 Pet. 1:16). "He has clothed me with garments of salvation, He has wrapped me in robes of righteousness" (Isa. 61:10). In God's wisdom, Christian, He would have us rejoice and draw water from a spring of salvation (Isa. 12:3). We may know times of struggle in our Christian experience and a sense of joyless withering, but the root for Jesus will always remain fixed by the wisdom of God. Amen.

This is the wisdom of God in you; to hunger and thirst after righteousness, and to yearn for God's image and favor. Though we will know weakness, we desire a greater faith and obedience. The Spirit awakens our conscience, convicts us of guilt and creates our hunger for Jesus Christ, "The Lord our righteousness" (Jer. 23:6). In our desire to be forgiven and restored to the peace of fellowship, the Spirit works into us the importance of confession of sin and humbling ourselves before Him. These are the graceful actions from a renewed heart, by the grace of God, displaying sincere aspirations of godly wisdom. The new man is blessed by God, to know and desire a life that exerts a godly wisdom. The love of Christ surpasses knowledge and is intended to fill your heart up with the Lord's presence, by the grace of God. The Lord intends to fill the heart up with trust, joy, peace and holiness in an experiential knowledge of acceptance by God. A young and/or a weak Christian may at times know the weakness and failure of faith, trust, assurance and obedience to Christ. When a believer is sincere and desires to be right with God, he still has some learning and training to go through. God is patient; although the man may not fully know it, he is being blessed. The hunger and thirst for righteousness is a gift from God (Matt. 5:6). We are His workmanship (Eph. 2:10), and the Lord desires we know His approval. Only God has the wisdom to know how to fill every man's soul with His grace. Paul prayed that we might "know the love of Christ which surpasses knowledge, that you may be filled up to all the fulness of God" (Eph. 3:19). It is the wisdom of God, Christian, to fill you up with Himself. Being full of Jesus is the ultimate and consummate experience of the Christian life. Being made in God's image and rich by His Spirit, we should reflect

His wisdom in our lives. Amen. "O taste and see that the Lord is good" (Ps. 34:8). Faith is the soul's taste that can only be claimed as good when it is experienced. "Faith comes from hearing, and hearing by the word of Christ" (Rom. 10:17). "They who seek the Lord shall not be in want of any good thing" (Ps. 34:10). Taste the Lord, Christian, by reading the Bible. This is God's wisdom for your heart. Amen. "The conclusion, when all has been heard, is: fear God and keep His commandments, because this applies to every person. For God will bring every act to judgment, everything which is hidden, whether it is good or evil (Eccl.12:13-14). Amen.

Providence

"For from Him and through Him and to Him are all things. To Him be the glory forever. Amen"
(Rom. 11:36).

Dear Christian,

"It was grace that taught my heart to fear, and grace my fears relieved; How precious did that grace appear the hour I first believed" (Amazing Grace, John Newton, 1779). The song lyric quoted here is from the second verse of the very popular hymn entitled "Amazing Grace". The song's message of forgiveness and mercy, by the grace of God, has comforted many souls through the years. It speaks to me about grace in the providence of God that can bring a person along a road to Jesus for salvation. God's grace can fearfully get our attention about our sin, and then God's grace can gently relieve the fear in leading us to receive forgiveness of sin in Jesus. Amen. Some people think after they are born into the world, that God takes a step back, and lets them loose to be on their own. Some people think that God has very little to do with the affairs of man, if anything, while they are alive on the earth. Some folks think that they will only see God after they die, in a judgment about the kind of life they lived on the earth. I'm not of these persuasions. The Bible clearly does not describe God as an absentee God. The Christian knows that God has called him, saved him, and is continuing to do a lot of work with him, to prepare him for His presence in His kingdom. The Christian knows that he is what he is by the grace of God (1 Cor. 15:10). The Christian knows that God woke him up about sin, righteousness and judgment (John 16:8-10). The Christian knows that he was born again by the grace of God (John 1:12-13, 3:5). The Christian knows that God works every day in his heart about following Jesus. The Christian knows that it is God who is at work in him, both to will and to work for His good pleasure (Phil. 2:13). The Christian knows that, but by the grace of God, he would be lost after he dies off the earth. It was grace that taught us to come to our senses and hear God, and it was grace that blessed us to hear Jesus and walk with Him. It was grace that taught us to fear God, and it was the same God with grace who relieved our fears. Amen. God rules over all things and has a holy presence in our world. God is always at work to carry out His will, and secure the promises He has made to His Son and believers in the gospel covenant of grace. Amen.

The absolute and universal supremacy of God is plainly affirmed in many scriptures. Though the word "providence" is not specifically used in the scriptures, the truth of Divine providence permeates the whole Bible. The doctrine should make us grateful for salvation and prosperous times, as well as patient in trials and tribulation. The doctrine should make us confident that God will be faithful to complete His work in us, and bring us all the way home where the promises of Jesus will be fulfilled. The definition of providence is the act of seeing and providing for the future. God is an active participant in the world He created, by sustaining it. In the Bible, this refers to God's foresight and power to watch, protect and provide for His creatures. "Thine, O Lord, is the greatness and the power and the glory and the victory and the majesty, indeed everything that is in the heavens and the earth; Thine is the dominion, O Lord, and Thou dost exalt Thyself as head over all. Both riches and honor come from Thee, and Thou dost rule over all, and in Thy hand is power and might; and it lies in Thy hand to make great, and to strengthen everyone" (1 Chron. 29:11-12). In the New Testament, in the Lord's prayer, "For Thine is the kingdom, and the power, and the glory, forever. Amen" (Matt. 6:13). God has the government of the world and the protection of His saints in His hands, to the praise of the glory of His grace.

The New Testament tells us that "We have obtained an inheritance, having been predestined according to His purpose who works all things after the counsel of His will" (Eph. 1:11). "For from Him and through Him and to Him are all things. To Him be the glory forever. Amen" (Rom. 11:36). God can work perfectly with divine energy and power in our lives, whether we acknowledge it or not. He can bring about spiritual blessings in us for His glory. God's purpose for our lives will stand because of His infinite love. Our inheritance is God's plan and will and His heart's desire. We lack the desire, power and will to do the will of God, but God works in us "both to will and to work for His good pleasure" (Phil. 2:13). "He works in us that which is pleasing in His sight, through Jesus Christ, to whom be the glory forever" (Heb. 13:21). In telling us about spiritual gifts, Christian, Paul writes "there are varieties of effects, but the same God who works all things in all persons" (1 Cor. 12:6). Our responsibility is to "not be foolish but understand what the will of the Lord is" (Eph. 5:17). Our responsibility is to do "the will of God from the heart" (Eph. 6:6). God shows great love for our souls. Our response, by the grace of God, is understanding Him from our hearts. Amen. Ignorance and neglect are evidence of folly, while compliance with God is wisdom. An earnest regard for Jesus, by the grace of God, will reveal a sincere faithfulness from you, and wisdom and blessing from God. God will provide (Luke 12:22-24, 2 Cor. 9:8, Phil. 4:19).

God works faithfully in our heart a strong desire and hope to know more about Jesus. We are being blessed when we "press on to know the Lord" (Hosea 6:3). The knowledge we get from God, Christian, is the best. It is by the providence or the work of God in your heart that you are pursuing His wisdom by Bible study. Faith comes by hearing the word of God (Rom. 10:17). "If you cry for discernment, lift your voice for understanding; and search for her as for hidden treasures; then you will discern the fear of the Lord and discover the knowledge of God, for the Lord gives wisdom" (Prov. 2:3-6). If your knowledge improves, and your duty to it follows, then you may expect the mercy of knowing more about God. Amen. "He who has My commandments and keeps them, he it is who loves Me; and he who loves Me shall be loved by My Father, and I will love him, and will disclose Myself to him (John 14:21). The evidence for the providence of God in your life, appears when Christ is more spiritually disclosed to your heart and mind. More grace is evidence of His love and work in securing your heart for Himself. More grace to realize how deep the love of God is, and more faith that leads to a greater sense of His presence and comfort. More grace to understand the scripture. Christ may be present in your heart to share the gospel, and serve others at your local church for God's glory. The heart has found a more believing place of rest in the knowledge and confidence of the power of God to save. There is a trust in the idea that the Lord was always with you, all throughout your life, working on your behalf to reveal a Savior for salvation from the penalty of sin. You were always in His hands. All things have been working together for good (Rom. 8:28). You "delight yourself in the Lord; knowing that He will give you the desires of your heart" (Ps. 37:3), that is, a new man in Jesus and holiness. "This was in accordance with the eternal purpose which He carried out in Christ Jesus our Lord" (Eph. 3:11). There are unsearchable riches in Christ, Christian, and God knows how to plant these treasures in your soul. "God is opposed to the proud, but gives grace to the humble" and "draw near to God and He will draw near to you" (James 4:6,8). Amen.

"The Lord has made all things for Himself" (Prov. 16:4). We are the people to be blessed by Him. From eternity God designed our world to be a stage on which He would display and work His manifold grace, love and wisdom for the redemption of sinners. The sovereign operations by God for people and the nations on the earth is His providence. What He ordained is being accomplished. In the providence of God, He provides. God's purposes are executed through God's actions "after the counsel of His own will" (Eph. 1:11). God has an eternal purpose that reveals His grace and love.

"There is an appointed time for everything. And there is a time for every event under heaven". For example, "A time to give birth and a time to die" (Eccl. 3:1-2). The providence of God works at night and during the day and in all the seasons of our lives. God's providence is in our emotions, love, hate, relationships, war and peace (Eccl. 3:2-8). "He has made everything appropriate in its time. He has also set eternity in their heart, yet so that man will not find out the work which God has done from the beginning even to the end" (Eccl. 3:11). The word "beautiful" for this verse is used in the KJV for "appropriate" in the New American Standard Bible. Everything will have been done in the perfect way and time. There is a wonderful harmony and a complete beauty in the Divine providence, and it will be the wonder of eternity, manifesting the grace of God. The word "world" is used in this same verse by the KJV for "eternity" in the New American Standard Bible. The word "world" used here is not meant to mean a sinful love of the world, but rather that there is so much already known, and so much more to be known, in the world, we cannot grasp it all. Our capacity is small and our lives so short, we cannot understand the work of God. We find out that His ways are unsearchable and past our ways of finding out. We cannot therefore, see the beauty and understand our world (Rom. 11:33). We get a glimpse in time of what is going on. We cannot see the big picture, that is, the beginning and the end. We live in the middle of the Divine counsel. We notice little of the Divine providence in our own lives because we are so possessed of ourselves and our world. Every human being has a gift from God though, that makes them aware or hope for something more than the vanities of this world. God has set a longing for purpose and meaning in life that only finds an answer in Himself. Life is but a vapor (James 4:14) but the soul lives forever (John 3:16). The mystery of God and the beauty of Providence, some future day will be more clearly seen. We will be going home, Christian, into the wonders of God. Amen.

God has an unchanging eternal purpose for us as we live on this earth. He can accomplish all His own purpose for us because He is all-powerful. The Holy Spirit seeks to work in our lives to fulfill what God has already planned. Before the world was made, God had plans that centered in Christ, that involved saving our souls and the church, to display His wisdom, power, love and surpassing grace (Eph. 2:7). We were on His mind and in His heart to be in the gathering, as His bride, that would honor the Son throughout eternity. We had to be born, and then born again by receiving Jesus and the gifts of forgiveness and faith. We were adopted into the family of God and inherit the eternal life He died for us to receive. It was necessary for us to be conformed to His Son to walk with Jesus. "For we are His workmanship, created in Christ Jesus for good works, which God prepared beforehand, that we should walk in them" (Eph. 2:10). "The Lord will accomplish what concerns me; Thy lovingkindness Lord is everlasting: Do not forsake the work of your hands" (Ps. 138:8). We become a masterpiece of God. The magnificent, great and comforting point is, God acted, in us and for us to keep our side of the covenant of gospel grace. He had no problem keeping His part of the covenant of gospel grace, it was our part or side that needed power that He was willing to give, in order for us to be saved. The agreement will be our greatest blessing ever. The grace of God for us is found in the unsearchable riches of Christ. Thank you, Jesus. God provided for the glory and honor of Christ. It was by a special "operation" or the providence of God that we become an acceptable bride for Jesus. By His spirit of grace, Christian, we are worked into being a new creation that is holy and sincere. To God be the glory. My redemption was planned and worked out by God. Amen. My confidence is in Him and the work of His hands, not in mine. My hope of perseverance is in the Lord's promise to finish the work (Phil.1:6), and not in my diligent efforts. I'm responsible to work out my salvation with fear and trembling (Phil. 2:12). It is a gift from God that I'm in Jesus. The truth is, He deserves all the glory, and I'm blessed to understand and believe this with all my heart and soul. I willingly and gladly commend myself into His hands.

The doctrine of God's providence tells us that God knows and sees and ordains everything in our lives. He plans and therefore knows, when and where we will be born and how, when and where we will die. He chooses our parents, siblings, friends and spouse we have in our life. He decides where we go to school and the colleges we attend, and our major field of study. He picks out the cities and homes we live in, and the church we will attend. The definition of providence is the divine guidance of people and things. God determines the circumstances of our lives and the points in time when we will receive Jesus, and are shaped into the image of Christ. "We know that God causes all things to work together for good to those who love God, to those who are called according to His purpose" (Rom. 8:28). For whom He foreknew; He predestined, called, justified and glorified (Rom. 8:29-30). Nothing happens by chance; God's will shall be done. These ideas are hard for some folks to grasp and understand and therefore difficult to accept. They are spiritually discerned, and can be difficult even for some believers to also recognize. The providence of God is something I have learned by the grace of God. I received it a lot better in my life after Bible study, and considering my own life's experiences. I totally believe in God's power and ability to act in my life. At certain times in my life, I clearly could not see what the Lord was doing. Looking back, I think I can see or understand some events much more clearly today. The doctrine of God's providence implies that God knows what He is doing, and has the wisdom and power to control events according to His good pleasure. We see God's providence through the eye of faith. Amen.

The doctrine of God's providence implies the Lord is in control of all events, both important and those seemingly unimportant. The Lord cannot make mistakes and has the ability to finish the work according to His original design and purpose. What is implied is true. The Bible teaches that God is sovereign, has perfect wisdom and goodness in the plans of every circumstance. It all works for our salvation and His glory (1 Chron. 29:11-12). God's truth teaches us that "in Him we live and move and exist" (Acts 17:28). He "upholds all things by the word of His power" (Heb.1:3) and determines our steps (Prov. 16:9). "Our God is in the heavens; He does whatever He pleases" (Ps. 115:3). "The eyes of the Lord are in every place, watching the evil and the good"

(Prov.13:3). This denotes omniscience and an ability to distinguish between people and their actions. The eyes of God see secret sins, services of love and our sorrows. God gave man a conscience, I think, so he could have a set of eyes to distinguish the sin in his own behavior the way the Lord does. We were made in the image of God. Being born again with a new spirit gives us the potential to see the Lord's providential work in our own lives. This blessing fuels our faith and assurance that His eye is upon us to secure our continued growth in grace and knowledge. Amen.

"The Lord has established His throne in the heavens; and His sovereignty rules over all" (Ps. 103:19). The Lord reigns universally in the universe over all time and places, and always will. All kinds of men; big and little, smart or ignorant, strong or weak, mean or gentle and the willing and unwilling are all under His influence and power. A clear view of God's supreme providence in understanding our world is one of the most delightful of spiritual gifts. He was with me all the time in my life, Christian, and I know that He is with you also. "The Lord is righteous in all His ways, and kind in all His deeds. The Lord is near to all who call upon Him" (Ps. 145:17-18). We cannot discover the depths of God in our own way; we must be humbled first and come to Jesus which is God's way. This is drawing near to God, by the grace of God; He opens the door to salvation and reconciliation. "Behold, I stand at the door and knock; if anyone hears my voice and opens the door, I will come to him, and will dine with him, and he with Me" (Rev. 3:20). God steps into our lives at appropriate times, determined by His wisdom, and accomplishes a task in His power for His designed future purpose. We understand by faith (Heb. 11:3).

The most important example of providence for us to know about was the life of Jesus. The Bible tells us that numerous prophecies or predictions about His life were fulfilled. This is shown by the Old Testament prophecies (Isa. 7:14, 9:6, 53:1-12) that were fulfilled in His life as described in the New Testament (Matt. 1:18-25, John 20:1-9, Acts 2:32, 3:15). The story of Joseph in Genesis is also a good example of the providence of God (Gen, 37-45). In this story, his brothers were going to kill him, but instead sold him into slavery. He spent some time in jail but he ended up becoming a ruler in Egypt. A famine arose in Israel, and his brothers ended up going to Egypt to get grain to survive the famine. They met up with Joseph, who told them, "Now do not be angry or grieved with themselves, because you sold me here; for God sent me before you to preserve life" (Gen 45:5). Joseph's perspective was all about what God was doing in his life. God providentially took care of them all; He fulfilled His purpose. Another story in the book of Daniel records the words of King Nebuchadnezzar after he was humbled because of pride (Dan 4). "God does according to His will in the host of heaven and among the inhabitants of the earth" (Dan. 4:35). We learn the power of God from the providence of God, by the grace of God. He works in our lives in times and ways that serve His purpose and pleasure. God is good (John 3:16, Luke 18:19). "For the Lord is good; His lovingkindness is everlasting, and His faithfulness to all generations" (Ps. 100:5). The character of God is gracious, kind, good, and loving. He is merciful and forgiving. He is a God of all grace (1 Pet. 5:10). He is the author and finisher of our faith (Heb. 12:2). God is the origin of the grace and work of faith with power in our souls. He is in control and directs everything to its appointed end for His own glory. The providence of God is the grace of God working in love for our best interest. Praise the Lord. Amen.

The providence of God is manifested in the world. "He upholds all things by the word of His power" (Heb. 1:3). The Lord Jesus holds all things together in their proper relationship by His own power alone. He maintains the universe and guides its growth and development. The Lord impacts all the changes, even erosion, nothing is excluded. "The very hairs of your head are all numbered" (Matt. 10:30). "While the earth remains, seedtime and harvest, and cold and heat, and summer and winter, and day and night shall not cease" (Gen. 8:22). God made it all, Christian, and He is preserving the world, the earth and all that is on it (Neh. 9:6). "He made every nation of mankind that lives on all the face of the earth, having determined their appointed times, and the boundaries of their habitation, that they should seek God, for in Him we live and move and exist" (Acts 17:26-28). We live in constant dependence upon the providence of God; because of His power and fatherly care, our frail lives are prolonged. In Him we move; that is, our souls and bodies carry out their thoughts and actions. In Him we have our being, capable of knowing God.

Men may forget that there is a God, and a providence that all things are ordained in heaven. They see the forces and passions of some men, but not always the work of God. "But God is the judge; He puts down one, and exalts another" (Ps. 75:7). Countries rise and fall at His bidding. People are serving His purpose in order to confirm His own counsel and pleasure. God is infinitely wise and good and His grace is His own to give. "I will have mercy on whom I will have mercy" (Rom. 9:15) and "Thou art our Father, we are the clay, and Thou our potter; and all of us are the work of Thy hand" (Isa. 64:8). "O Lord, how many are Thy works! In wisdom Thou hast made them all; the earth is full of Thy possessions" (Ps. 104:24). The whole of these verses, Christian, speak of the sovereignty of God. He made us into the shape that we are for the purpose He designed we should fulfill. We were made in His image, and our construction is unique. Though we were made in His likeness, we became a fallen race because of sin. God knew that He would be remolding us, so He made a perfect plan for our salvation and reconciliation in His Son, Jesus. He draws us to Jesus, and by His grace and love, molds us into the shape He wants us to be. We reflect His image. All along this path, with Bible study and the help of the Holy Spirit, we learn to let God be God.

"Trust in the Lord with all your heart, and do not lean to your own understanding. In all your ways acknowledge Him, and He will make your paths straight" (Prov. 3:5-6). We reach out and are encouraged by faith and our prayers to depend upon God's providence. The confidence about our life must be in His wisdom, power and goodness for our earthly affairs. We must trust and follow God, that by His providence we will discover what is best for our hearts. We must seek His hand in our prayers to lead us into paths of righteousness for our peace and His glory. We must humbly seek His help and be grateful for His providence. He has promised to direct us. His is the greatness, power, the glory, victory and the majesty. Whatever strength we have, Christian, God gave it to us (1 Chron. 19:11-12). Never forget, "The Lord gave, and the Lord hath taken away; blessed be the name of the Lord" (Job 1:21). We must own the divine providence, and not always be taking our own life into our own hands for our work, play and leisure. When we discover God, by His grace, we can find our divine purpose for being alive. God gave us everything, and He may take from us whatever He pleases, whenever He pleases. Amen.

"Thy hands have made me and fashioned me; give me understanding, that I may learn Thy commandments. I know O Lord, that Thy judgments are right, and that Thou in faithfulness hast afflicted me" (Ps. 119: 73, 75). It is always good to remember, Christian, you did not make yourself short or tall, white or black or brown, male or female. You did not decide when you would appear in history and into what country you would be born. God made you! He made you with His own hands in love and wisdom. The body He gave is wondrously made (Ps. 139:14). Parts of it you may not like at times, but do not complain to God. He never makes a mistake. I can only imagine how complex our soul will be in heaven bearing His image. Please Lord, let me have spiritual judgment that I may keep your commandments and always be at peace with you. Help me think and treat people with grace. Help me to study the Bible to grow in faith and understanding, and to stay close to you with obedience. God's plan is to be close to you. He knows that we are prone to wander. Sometimes we fall into sin and/or get overly distracted by worldly affairs. The Lord may allow an affliction to get our attention, and put us back on track. He always acts providentially with a sincere intention of doing you good. You will only be really safe when you are close to the Lord. God knows that fame, money and good health can expose us to temptation, to sin, and/or neglect walking with Him. Affliction may help us get our priorities more in line with our hopes in His favor, and more earnestly desire the delights of a clear conscience. Divine providence, though the experience may be difficult at times, deserves our gratitude. When we reorganize our priorities and avoid vanities, our life is more clearly blessed. In adversity, the Lord does not leave us, but stays close to complete the work of growing us more and more by His grace to be like Jesus.

God has the attributes of omniscience and omnipresence that would be necessary to support the ability of God to work providentially in our live's. He watches over us. "O Lord; Thou hast searched me and known me. Thou dost know when I sit down and when I rise up; Thou dost understand my thought from afar. Thou hast enclosed me behind and before, and laid Thy hand upon me. Such knowledge is too wonderful for me" (Ps. 139:1-2, 5-6). God knows your nature and character and completely understands you. We will never be beyond His observation of us. God takes notice of the motions of your body and mind. He is acquainted with all your ways, and He still loves you. The knowledge of God should fill us with awe that we do not sin, and confidence because He is our God with us (Immanuel). The knowledge God has about us and the way He has chosen to deal with us should give us a measure of delight. We are in the hands of a God that is merciful, kind, generous, loving and graceful. Amen. That we cannot escape His power is a good thing. He has His hand upon us in a way that He folded His arms around us. "The steps of a man are established by the Lord; and He delights in his way. When he falls, he shall not be hurled headlong; because it is the Lord who holds his hand" (Ps. 37:23-24). He leads us and sustains us, and when necessary, recovers us to Himself. "Delight yourself in the Lord; and He will give you the desires of your heart. Commit your way to the Lord, trust also in Him, and He will do it" (Ps. 37:3-4). The future is certain, and our joy, because of Him, will be forevermore. Amen. My mind reaches out sometimes to understand God's power, Christian, but I cannot reach it. It is too high. My heart reaches out to understand God's love, Christian, but I cannot reach into it. It is too high also. What I have is a plea to let me live up to the knowledge I have in Jesus. Let me worship and adore you in spirit and in truth. Let me honor you with my life and service, and always give you all the glory. By your providence and grace and Thy Spirit, lead me in the way everlasting. Amen.

Some human beings live their life most of the time without considering or thinking at all about the providence of God. They live their life with little spiritual truth and power from God. They might think about dying, and then, in fear, wonder about what happens next. Thoughts about Evolution tell them that nothing happens. The word of God tells them that they will give an account of their lives (Rom. 14:12). The world, the flesh and the devil make them feel that giving an account is not what they want to do. Giving up or surrendering their life to Someone else does not sound like fun or a victory. We can be haunted by a life that knows something about God but lives far away from Him. They do not realize that God already knows all about them. We can trap ourselves in places and relationships that prevent us from getting closer to God and personally knowing Him. We need God's grace and mercy, but we may be weak about finding out how to go about getting it. We need God, but we are deaf, blind, and ignorant. We are born as a natural man (1 Cor. 2:14) and cannot wake up on our own. We need a miracle. We need to be born again. Bearing the burden of sin alone is too much for us; we need a Savior. We need Jesus. God is patient with us. He allows our situations and circumstance in life to be such that they give way to a lost state that shows great need but no easy answer. God may be drawing them providentially to Himself, but they do not know it. Jesus came to seek and to save those who are lost (Luke 19:10), that they might know an abundant life. In our world, the thief comes to only steal, kill, and destroy (John 10:10). Some people know the thief and the natural life first, and by the grace of God, wake up to spiritual life. God may work at this time through His Spirit providentially to touch their spirit and they begin to know life. God sends us into His word to get the grace of faith and the truth of religion (Rom. 10:17). The word of God is alive (Heb. 10:12). There is a huge difference between knowing about God and believing on Him. It is important that you sense a welcome from the Lord and a love for Him. This difference comes into your heart, because God is working with His power, mercy, and grace and providing the gift of faith for your soul. The devil will challenge this new stance with doubt and leave you unwilling to respond to God's overtures. The truth can set you free (John 8:32).

We are born naturally in this world which means without a spiritual strength. We first think we must work to get God's approval. We think we must be holy and serve Him before we can be saved from the penalty of sin. To be a spiritual man, we must be born again, and we do not know what this means or how it is accomplished for us. A natural man is ignorant of God and does not know Jesus. He must learn to receive what Jesus has already done, and grow in grace and knowledge of His love (1 John 4:19). We must hear from the Lord. We must become like a letter of Christ, written not with ink, but with the Spirit of the living God, not on tablets of stone, but on tablets of human hearts (2 Cor. 3:3). The changed heart and life will be the evidence of being renewed by the grace and providence of God. We must die before we can be resurrected with Jesus. That is, we must die to self (Gal. 5:20), die to our desires and passions (Gal. 5:17, 5:24) and die to the world (Gal. 3:14). The more you die, the more you will know freedom. You must be diligent to pray, worship, serve and study the Bible a little bit every day. This is not a work for salvation, but rather the pathway that God has chosen for us to discover what He has put into us when we come to Jesus. The church can be a big helper. We needed a miracle and God came to us in His providential power and love to give us a gift of faith. Amen. To God be all the glory. "Faith is the assurance of things hoped for, the conviction of things not seen" (Heb. 11:1). It is God at work, releasing understanding, assurance, and conviction that Jesus is the Christ, the Son of the living God. It is God at work in you releasing confidence into your heart that the Bible is the word of God about Jesus (Heb. 1:1-2). God speaks to our hearts about His Son. It is a providential act of God's goodness for your soul. Amen.

God's loving work in us, leads us to believe that Jesus will save our soul. Believing becomes great joy and peace, and importantly, leads to obedience. Believing may start as an influence and thought, then becomes a persuasion and finally a deep conviction that "God is able to guard what I have entrusted to Him until that day" (2Tim. 1:12). It is in the gift of faith that the Lord begins to let you see His providence at work. Faith comes from reading, studying, and letting your heart be engaged in Bible study. Reading the Bible is the place where the Lord teaches you about His sovereignty and providence. In faith, we become committed to Christ for the salvation of our soul. Salvation is the forgiveness of our sin and a reconciliation with God. We are not preserved for eternity by faith, because we will see Him, and He will see us. We are preserved by the promises made in the grace of God. A day is coming, when we will give an account of the stewardship of our soul (Luke 16:2). The possession of the Gospel is not just a notion to entertain your mind, but to engage you in the practice of holiness. The Holy Spirit dwells in you and by the power of God's grace, enables you to keep your purity. You still use your best endeavors with the assistance of the Holy Spirit to keep living by what you have learned. Faith and obedience go together. Christians are called to holiness (1 Pet. 1:15-16) and acts of charity (Acts 20:35). Faith as a result of works becomes more complete, mature, and fully grown (i.e., perfect) (James 2:22).

We learn that the truth of faith makes it act. Acts of self-denial and responding to calls from the Lord for service result in a more complete faith. The works do not save you, but they do provide a witness in you and before the world for the practice of God's way of life. By this I mean, God speaks to our hearts through a believing faith in action. "We are His workmanship, created in Christ Jesus for good works which God prepared beforehand that we should walk in them" (Eph. 2:10). His voice demonstrates intimacy and confirms that you are His child. It is a voice that delivers encouragement in a providential way that you never forget. When you act, it shows more than opinions about Jesus and glorifies God. You will be known by your fruit (Matt. 7:17). "Everyone who hears these words of Mine, and acts upon them, may be compared to a wise man, who built his house upon the rock" (Matt. 7:24). God allows faith in Jesus to be tried and tested to reveal to you the reality of it in your life and to others. We learn from His providence that we are being prepared on earth for His presence in Heaven. We learn from His providence that we are the sheep of His pasture. We learn from His providence about the lovingkindness of His hands. We learn from His providence that we are changing into His image by the loving power of God.

How great is it to receive the gift of faith from God (Eph. 2:8)? How great is it to have a life of faith that follows from it? How great is it to know you can depend upon and trust God for the future? "God causes all things to work together for good to those who love God and are called according to His purpose" (Rom. 8:28). We may not be much in the world, but we already have in Him all we will ever need or want for eternity. I think about Jesus a lot every day. I think about Him loving me from His perfections and not from my failures and sin. I think about Jesus in my mind with understanding and in my heart with love. Why would I do this? It is God's grace convicting me that we all will be alive in the future, and that we will give an account of our life at the judgment seat of Christ (2 Cor. 5:10). I believe our future habitation will be spiritual, and with the Lord. The goodness of God will pass our understanding. On earth, by faith, we get the taste. There are things, "which the eye has not seen, the ear has not heard which have not entered the heart of man that God has prepared for those who love Him "(1 Cor. 2:9). The key is in knowing, in spite of your sin, that you are falling in love with Jesus. The key is in knowing that you are not the person you used to be. The key is in knowing that the Lord has healed you and is taking care of your life. You do not work hard in your mind to get these things, but rather, you will know you have them by the amazing providence of God. Amen.

The man who loves God has received not the spirit of the world, but the Spirit who is from God (1 Cor. 2:12). The wisdom in the Gospel is out of the sphere of human discovery and therefore not sensed by the natural man. He does not know the love of God. In the Old Testament, the same passage for 1 Cor. 2:9 shown above also appears in Isaiah 64:4. At the end of this Old Testament passage, it says, "for the one who waits for Him" (Isa. 64:4), while at the end of the New Testament passage it says, "for those who love Him" (1 Cor. 2:9). Waiting and watching upon the Lord is the evidence of your love for Him. The devil will cast doubts into your mind, but you will know your heart is waiting for Jesus. We have great joys awaiting us in Heaven, but now the blessing is known by faith as a spiritual foretaste of His power and glory to come in eternity. "Though I walk through the valley of the shadow of death, I fear no evil; for Thou art with me; Thy rod and Thy staff, they comfort me" (Ps. 23:4). Amen. We are not blind but patient. Believers are happy with what the Lord has prepared for them. "Because Thy lovingkindness is better than life, my lips will praise Thee" (Ps. 63:3). God's love is the dearest and His mercy is everlasting. No matter how it goes in this world, in Him we live. I hope to see you living with Jesus. I hope to see your spirit knit to the Spirit of God. I hope to see you worshiping God. I hope to see you waiting on God. I hope that you behold in your mind the Lord loving you magnificently. If you live in these hopes, Christian, then you are being blessed in the providence of God. Amen.

"How blessed is the one whom Thou dost choose, and bring near to Thee, to dwell in Thy courts. We will be satisfied with the goodness of Thy house, Thy holy temple" (Ps. 65:4). You are chosen of God. This is a secret truth you will keep in your most private thoughts and not argue about with other people. Though some folks strongly detest this truth, the Bible speaks clearly for this truth. Man does not fully understand what God means. You will hold this truth to be dear, because you will know that He loved you before you loved Him (1 John 4:19). God draws you by His grace and providence into an intimate fellowship. He becomes the husband of your heart. In spite of your sins, ignorance, and complacent thoughts; He brings you near to His heart and loves on you. The call of God is firm, steady, persistent, patient, and effectual. God's call brings you into His courts revealing His mercy, forgiveness, and acceptance. The Christian experience satisfies the heart beyond conception. "Behold, what manner of love the Father hath bestowed upon us that we should be called the sons of God" (1 John 3:1). His love subdues our unwillingness and leads us to new depths of abiding with the Lord that are indeed pleasurable.

We strongly desire to follow Jesus in obedience, and welcome with more assurance the promise of Heaven. You were born the first time from natural parents which will lead to physical death, but the new birth in Jesus will be permanent. The inner presence of the Lord from being born again will never dwindle, disappear, and die; it is life everlasting. "The gifts and the calling of God are irrevocable" (Rom. 11:29). God does not repent of the fact that He chose you, called you, and made for you a presence with Himself in eternity. We go from being heirs of sin and guilt to a place of dignity as the sons of God. We go from rags of sin to riches in the love of God. A holy God is not ashamed to be called our Father and to call us sons. Amen.

We are to "work out our salvation with fear and trembling; for it is God who is at work in you, both to will and to work for His good pleasure" (Phil. 2:12-13). This is the grace of God and His providence in action. God is love (1 John 4:8), and He enables us to love Himself, your own self and others, especially the children of God (1 John 5:2). From His love, He puts us on the road leading to the obedience of faith (Rom. 1:5, 16:26). Love is practical. "If you love Me, you will keep my commandments" (John 14:15). Follow the Spirit, Christian, and you will have the comforts of the Spirit. Amen. The performance of our duty to the laws of Christ will not be perfect (1 John 1:8-10), but we must have a conscientious care to perform His commands. We are not to grieve the Spirit (Eph. 4:30) and quench the Spirit (1 Thess. 5:19). I remember when I was younger and struggling with the verse John 14:15. I thought that if I did not keep His commandments, I did not love Him. The devil got a grip on me and just made me feel guilt. It is by grace that we love Jesus. It is by grace that we show a truthful obedience. The principle of love to Christ matures in the true Christian. Since you love Him, you will keep His commandments. We grow by grace and knowledge closer to Jesus. In fear and trembling we discover His presence, and learn to love Him. When we love Him, we keep His commandments; cheerfully, impartially, and with perseverance. We never cease to love Him, and in trust, never regret to follow Him. Our salvation is not based on works but on Jesus (Eph. 2:8-10,

Titus 3:5). Our responsibilities are not works. Amen. First, we have the commandments; then we keep them by the working love of the Helper, the Holy Spirit, whom the Father sent in Jesus' name (John 14:21-26). We grow in faith, being comforted that He who began a good work in you will perfect it until the day of Christ Jesus (Phil. 1:6). He guides us in paths of righteousness for His name's sake (Ps. 23:3). He providentially guides our thoughts and steps with holy guidance and divine motives. God is faithful. In surrender, we are victorious for the glory of His name, not our name. His name is magnified. Now, live as though you have a holy, loving, and merciful Father above you, a precious and beloved soul within you, and a glory yet to be revealed for an eternity before you. Amen.

Writing three books to you, Christian, has been filled with both joy and work. You know the saying, "there is no gain without pain". My gain has been immeasurably beneficial. I believe that God used you in this way to help motivate me to write. I'm no writer, and it is impossible for me to understand how I did all this writing, except that the Lord was with me. It was God's will that I spend more time in His word. God knew that if I spent more time in His word, I would be drawing nearer to Jesus. God knew that He would be drawing nearer to me (James 4:8). God knows exactly how great the gift of faith is for a human being to have, and I'm sure He remembered how He has ordained men to receive it (Rom. 10:17). In the providence of God, Christian, he sent you for me. He used writing as the way for me to discover more of His love, mercy, and goodness. He used writing as the way for me to grow in grace and knowledge. He used writing as the way in my old age to remember that He has been with me all the time (Isa. 46:4). "The Lord will accomplish what concerns me" (Ps. 138:8). This has been great gain without pain. Amen. It was work, but the Lord was with me and the blessings from His presence completely overshadow the sweat in work. I sensed His presence a lot and could not wait sometimes to get back to my desk. In writing, He erased any potential pain and allowed in me the privilege of praise and worship. There is absolutely a great God in Heaven, and He has providentially planned on coming for you. Amen.

God's purposes can take our lifetime to unravel. Our purpose(s) with the Lord will vary according to His wisdom. Grace was on the way for me in the Lord's time and way. Amen. "They that wait upon the Lord shall gain new strength; they will mount up with wings like eagles, they will run and not get tired, they will walk and not become weary" (Isa. 40:31). The main theme that I think ended up defining me, my life, my heart, and purpose was worked out in the providence of God. I freely admit, Christian, that I did not see and understand all this before it happened. In fact, it is probably the safest to say, that I never saw anything until it happened. Even then, it has taken a while to appreciate the Lord's handiwork. I was not completely oblivious to the Lord in the close calls I had to make, but I was immature and most of the time did not know His voice well enough to proceed with full confidence. I feel that sometimes the Lord stepped in and moved; not without me, but in a way of sovereignty that my mind believes and yet cannot fully grasp.

Spiritual life is in the Lord's domain, we get glimpses of His presence. We must be born again (John 3:5). I wrote about some of this in the book Letters to Christian, pages 56-88. We are to walk by faith, not by sight (2 Cor. 5:7). Sin will make you feel naked, like Adam and Eve in the garden of Eden, before God covered them up with a garment of skin. Likewise, sin will make us feel naked, but God's grace puts a robe of righteousness and garments of praise on us. It is God that is preparing you for His purpose, Christian, and it is the Lord that has given you His Spirit, as a witness and testimony of Jesus (2 Cor. 5:5). The future is with Christ and His glory. Amen. What goes on in this life is the preparation for the future, the very presence of God. It takes God's love and power and grace to transform your heart to a place where it will be safe to come into His presence, and receive the inheritance reserved for you. God providentially builds faith for us in this life that will be turned into sight in the life to come. Amen.

How has God the Father prepared you to "fit into" His presence? He called you to purity and honesty in this world, and sincerity with Jesus. It is by His grace that we are born again and receive the gift of faith in Jesus. Being born again, we are forgiven of sin and accounted as justified before God (i.e., justification). We are declared righteous before God. Amen. We are delivered from the penalty of sin. Further, we are set apart or sanctified or delivered from the pollution and potency of sin, by the grace of God (i.e., sanctification). This action is attributed to both the Holy Spirit and the believer in the paradox of grace. It is a mystery exactly how truth and love mature within us. It involves both God's sovereignty and man's responsibility. It is a transformation resulting in purity, goodness, and godliness. Amen. "He who calls you is faithful, and He will do it" (1 Thess. 5:24). "Pursue peace with all men and the sanctification without which no one shall see the Lord "(Heb. 12:14). From the work of the Holy Spirit in our hearts, we realize the gift of eternal life. Knowing Jesus is eternal life (John 17:3). From the providence of God, we learn to walk by faith. We put off the old man and put on the new man (Eph.4:22-24). We focus on the new world coming and not the old one that is dying. Faith is taking God at His word and trusting Christ. Walking by sight is living in this world. Walking by faith is living in another world. The building of your spiritual life is a gift of the grace of God, which means it is the work of God, which is by the providence of God. We are responsible to apply ourselves to the means that God has provided, that is, prayer, worship, and Bible study. The experience of this grace, Christian, is your assurance of the Lord's interest and purpose. The blessing will be best realized from your eye of understanding the spiritual nature of the events in your life. This comfort from the Lord is grace from Providence, confirming the truth that Jesus was alive and died for you. We did not actually see Jesus, but the Holy Spirit confirms the truth of His life. Faith is the victory (1 John 5:4). When the Holy Spirit speaks, a child of God hears Him because he has been born again with a believing heart. Amen.

What has happened in my life that I can look back on and remember and believe the Lord was acting in my life? The voice and the actions of God are the work of God. The work of the Lord is by grace, and is what we call the providence of God. In the struggles against sin and the situations of my life, God was planning and executing my salvation, peace, and eternal joy. The Lord has provided for my needs, and I'm grateful. The Lord God has oversight, Christian, over all the important things in your life as well as every detail. God has perfect wisdom and unlimited power to control and carry out His purpose of shaping you into the image of Jesus Christ (Rom. 8:29). "For in Him we live and move and exist (Acts 17:28). He is able. The keys of providence swing at the girdle of Christ (Charles Spurgeon). By the grace of God, we are enabled to discern His hand in our life. The result for our hearts is an encouraging strength and comfort that everything in our lives is in the Divine purpose. God has ordained for you, Christian, when and where you would be born and who your parents would be. God has ordained what your infancy, youth, and adulthood would be like. God has ordained that you will not die before your time and that you will not live beyond it. God has ordained the freedom of your will and the regret you have from your mistakes. God has ordained the best and worst moments of your life. To God be the glory. God has ordained that faith in Jesus will be your choice. There is no decision or work that you will do that will save you; Jesus saves. There is no such thing as blind fate or chance, Christian; there is only a kind and loving Father moved by love, mercy, and grace. "Humble yourself under the mighty hand of God, casting all your anxiety upon Him, because He cares for you" (1 Pet. 5:6). God may let you be poor to learn to trust Him. God will give you everything you need. Amen. The longer I live, the more deeply I'm convinced that the future glory of God will be revealed by His mysterious providence over our earthly lives. Amen.

Let me briefly review from my life, what I believe, constitute the providences of God in my life. These are things, both big and little, that I clearly and dearly remember. They are things I have thought about, believe, and recognize by the gift of faith from my loving Father in Heaven. Faith comes by hearing the word of Christ (Rom. 10:17). Amen. Two places that I think qualify for recognition of the development of faith in my life are the church and the Bible. By the providence of God, Christian, I kept finding a church. It started when I was young at the Salvation Army, and continued through High School at the West Seattle Christian Church. Though my attendance was once a month for a while, and only in the summers during my undergraduate years in college, I still lived with the idea of the importance of going to church. In graduate school, I got married and returned going to Church all year round. We found a church when we lived in Austin, Minnesota, and in Galveston, Texas at the University Baptist Church. In Birmingham, I was faithful through the years at Bluff Park Baptist Church and more recently at the Church of the Highlands. By the grace of God, I kept finding and going to church. By the grace of God, I worked in these churches and developed friendships. By the grace of God, I tithed and regularly heard the word of God. I grew in the knowledge of the Bible and loved the brethren. I died more to self and grew in holiness. By the grace of God, in Texas, I began to read more, study and better understand the scripture. I found a few good commentaries that made me think. The Lord used my time in the church to draw me closer to Himself, deeper into His word, closer to other believers and to take part in more work around the church. This was the providence of God gently growing me spiritually in the truth. Getting closer to the Lord in church and Bible study does not leave you the same, it blesses you. Amen.

I have had many experiences that I believe were providential. They gave me confidence that the Lord knows me, and that He has touched my heart. I described some of this in my first book to you in the letter on hearing the voice of the Lord (Letters to Christian, pg. 29). I remember receiving a wooden plaque for kindness from the Salvation Army, which I still have to this day. I especially remember the Lord's power and presence when I was walking the aisle to receive Jesus, and being baptized at West Seattle Christian Church. At this early point in my life, He gave me the gift of faith and a Helper, the Holy Spirit. He stepped in to help me make a decision about coming to Jesus. He has stepped in to help me make decisions about schools to attend, like Genesee Elementary, Western Washington State College and graduate school instead of medical school. After I interviewed, He gave me a peace about going to graduate school at the University of Washington. He showed me the lady I would be married to for over 48 years when I was in ninth grade. It was in the providence of God that He would show me my future wife and keep us together. He provided for our future in decisions about where to go for post-graduate and faculty work in Minnesota, Texas and finally Birmingham, Alabama. He showed me the home we were to live in before it went up for sale. He called me to be a Deacon and to serve in a jail ministry. He called me to be holy. I give the Lord, my God, the glory for the grace to become obedient. He gives me the peace of cleansing from unrighteousness (1 John 1:9). He has provided for all my needs. He blessed us with a believing daughter. He has protected us and given us strength and good health to serve Him in gladness. Amen.

The Lord shows us tokens of His love every day. He has us, and nothing can separate us from His love. Amen. The vehicles we drive are gifts from His hand. The places we have lived in and the grandson that we help and serve are from the wisdom and kindness of the grace of God. Any struggle we have can bring a blessing in the providence of God; it can teach patience and humility and eventually peace and gratitude. Amen. He was faithful to warn and help me in the temptations to sin. He was faithful to warn me about certain people and going to certain places that might nourish sin in my life. He put a hedge around me that helped my conscience fear the consequences of not listening to His voice. Amen. He made me sensitive about being careful about sin. He kept me in church and especially in His word. He let the word into my heart and showed me His love. He nourished me to grow more in His grace. Thank you, Lord Jesus. He became my assurance. He showed me my forgiveness, adoption, and inheritance. He became my Prince of peace (Isa. 9:6). He gave me a new heart. I have been changed by the word of God, Christian; a little faith, by the grace of God, can grow into great facts. A little fact is very pleasing but not completely satisfied and begs for more faith. The new man waxes stronger, and the old man fades away. Amen. We become God's masterpiece. There is no disappointment in the gift from the Lord called the obedience of Faith. "I'd rather have Jesus than silver or gold. I'd rather have Jesus than riches untold. I'd rather have Jesus than anything this world affords today" (I'd rather have Jesus, George Shea).

Your life is a gift from God, and the purpose you have in life is also a gift chosen by God. He gives the grace and opportunity for the expression(s) of your gift(s) according to His providence. In my life, I have struggled to identify my gift from God. The devil will be gleeful about your ignorance; because if you do not know what it is, you are going to have trouble honoring the Lord in exercising it. I have learned a lot of the Bible and gained some wisdom, but my gift is not wisdom or knowledge. I have taught a lot of Sunday school classes, but my gift is not teaching. However, on occasion I have recognized these gifts in other believers. Many times, I know what they know but that does not make it my gift. I sense my spirit respectfully yielding to these folks when their gift from the Lord is being used. It is not only what you know but how you share it. I do some preaching in the jail, but my gift is not preaching. The fact that no one follows me reveals I'm no leader. The whole idea of administration, though important, is foreign to my nature. I do not prophecy, except when I give a testimony of Jesus (Rev. 19:10). I've done a lot of different kinds of service over the years, so service was probably my gift at one time. Currently though, we are not serving significantly in our local church. We do tithe, and show some mercy at times as a Christian kindness, but not to the frequency, depth, or extent that I would sense constituted the gift of mercy. "To each one is given the manifestation of the Spirit for the common good" (1 Cor. 12:7). To my knowledge, I have never healed anyone, though I have prayed for their healing. I have never spoken in tongues or heard tongues being used and therefore not shared an interpretation of tongues. For most of my life, I think my gift was service. The gift of service was present in Seattle and Minnesota, but especially became predominate in Texas and Alabama. I taught Sunday School classes, served on numerous committees, and routinely gave my body to the Building and Properties Committee for inside and outside jobs. I was not trying to save myself; I just thought it was the right thing to do. I felt the presence of the Lord many times in this service. Amen. I became a deacon, by the grace of God.

Today though, I think I have the gift of encouragement (Rom. 12:8). The gift of encouragement from the Lord was developed in me over time, and especially realized by me, during my visits to the jails. The extra study for lessons and especially the writing of three books has contributed significantly to the building up of the truth of God in my heart. The jail has been the place for the expression of this gift over the past thirty years. To God be the glory. My favorite and most important topic of encouragement in the Bible is the sovereignty and providence of God. "All things work together for good to those who love God, to those who are called according to His purpose" (Rom. 8:28). "Nothing is impossible with God" (Luke 1:37), and it is never too late to repent (1 John 1:9). I like to share 1 Peter 1:3-8 and 1 Peter 5:6-10, because they mention about being distressed and suffering a little while, if necessary, through various trials. Though tested by fire, the Lord can confirm and establish people, and their faith can be found to result in praise and glory for God. Amen. We must all learn that we are God's workmanship (Eph. 2:8, Phil. 2:12-13)). We live in His grace and for His purposes and not our own selfish interest but for His glory. Amen. I have peace and a sense of fulfillment that the faith that the Lord has given me is prevailing, to His honor and glory. Amen. We have great value because of Jesus and so do other human beings. We are our brother's keeper. I pray that the expression of your gifts from God, Christian, will be known as your greatest blessings. "Only one life to live, 'twill soon be past, only what is done for Jesus will last" (C.T. Studd, missionary to China, 1860-1931). Blessed assurance, Jesus is mine! O what a foretaste of glory divine! Heir of salvation, purchase of God. Born of His Spirit, washed in His blood. This is my story, this is my song, praising my Savior all the day long (Blessed Assurance, Fanny Crosby, 1873). God Bless you.

"As many as received Him, to them He gave the right to become children of God, even to those who believe in His name who were born not of blood (i.e., earthly parents), nor of the will of the flesh (i.e., your hopes), nor of the will of man (i.e., your friends or me), but of God" (John 1:12-13). Amen. Thus, you see that grace does not run in the blood or received as a matter of heredity, or of the will of others for you. The natural man is opposed to God, and the well-meaning efforts of friends and even the Pastor have no power to regenerate your soul. The new birth is of God (Eph. 2:8). The new birth you have in your heart, Christian, is from the word of God as the means (1 Pet.1:23) and the Holy Spirit of God as the author (1 John 3:9). The new birth is a Divine work. The inner spiritual life that God gives cannot go away. It is in you to stay. It is established by the Holy Spirit applying the Word in living power to your heart. The love of God in the power of your regeneration means your adoption into the family of God. You have an eternal spiritual ancestry from Jesus Christ, the lamb of God. You believe because you have been ordained to eternal life (Acts 13:48). You can expect the love of God, not as something you earned, but rather because you have been born of God. "You are His workmanship, created in Christ Jesus for good works, which God prepared beforehand, that you should walk in them" (Eph. 2:10). Being God's workmanship has God's graceful providence built up into it. Amen.

"We love Him because He first loved us" (1 John 4:19). God's love is the motive for our love. We are saved by grace through faith (Eph. 2:8) and faith works by His love. Amen. To those who love God, all things work together for good. They are called, predestined, justified, conformed to His image, and will be glorified. If God is on their side, who can be against them (Rom 8:28-31). We become the children of His pasture and learn to love. You can know your election and adoption, Christian, by your conformity to the image of Christ (2 Thess. 2:13). Our salvation was ordained by God (Eph. 1:4-5, 1 Cor. 1:27-30) and at the same time, it is to be "worked out "by us with fear and trembling (Phil. 2:12). The role that God performs is clearly indispensable, necessary and gracious (John 3:5, 6:44, Eph. 2:8-9, Phil. 2:13). We are His workmanship and the beneficiaries of His providential grace (Eph. 2:10). What must you do? The Bible exhorts you to "keep your heart with all diligence; for out of it are the issues of life" (Prov. 4:23). The responsibility to keep your heart for God is yours, Christian, and you will feel this. At the same time, the power to do this, is from God, and you will feel this also (Phil.2:12-13). Jesus said, "I am the vine, you are the branches; he who abides in Me, and I in him, he bears much fruit; for apart from me you can do nothing" (John 15:5). Our union with Christ and being led by His Spirit is productive of all good. The experience of salvation is by the sovereignty of God and the responsibility of man working together. Faith in Jesus becomes the victory. You discover God's presence by its patient work in your heart. Amen.

The grace of God, in providence, many times may be a mystery to us, but never to God. Though things can get tough and afflictions heavy, remember that God has reserved the right of what He allows and does, to Himself. At the same time, He promised to never take away His lovingkindness from us. God has secured you. You are God's heritage; He is our great Ancestor (Eph 4:1-5). When I consider the nature of God as perfect in love, mercy and wisdom, Christian, my spirit casts my soul up into the wind for Himself. Amen. God has this promise to people who have nothing and think they are nothing. God has this promise for the confused and depressed. God has this promise of heaven with Jesus to people who also have something and think they are something. They also have yet to learn the power of God. We are never orphans with God the Father, God in His Son opened the door, He made the way. He leads us to surrender our hearts to Himself as the way to know His victory. We are adopted by God. Amen. Our whole life becomes His masterpiece. We grow from the natural life to the spiritual life. We grow in grace and knowledge and this glorifies God. You will know the Love of God, your sonship, and a spiritual livelihood because He lives. At first when some folks hear about Jesus, they hope it is true, but do not feel the assurances from faith. The longer they wait or delay, the more power the world, the flesh and the devil can work over them, and they do not choose Jesus. If they would read their Bible, go to church, pray, tithe, and serve, they may begin to experience the power of faith for obedience. The obedience in a new man is when the assurances of faith will come deeper into the heart that Jesus is alive. The grace of assurance from God, Christian, is the flower of true religion. "Seek first His Kingdom and His righteousness; and all these things shall be added unto you" (Matt.6:33).

Someday, your life may be all in a flame, but it will never be consumed. What I mean here, is that fear may grip you deeply, but "God has not given us a spirit of timidity, but of power and love and discipline" (1 Tim. 1:7). God gives a spirit of courage to encounter dangers and difficulties and a spirit of love to God and our fellow man. God gives us the spirit of a sound mind, with words of truth and encouragement. God has changed our heart, Christian, to rise above the fear of man, this world and even ourselves. We are weaned from the world and urged forward to the peace of heaven. The wheels of God's providence are full of eyes (John Flavel). When we fear and worry, we make our burdens heavier. Jesus said, "Come unto me all you are weary and heavy-laden, and I will give you rest" (Matt. 11:28). God gives a rest now by grace which will be perfected in glory. Another yoke to bear sounds like more work, but a yoke from Jesus fits and helps us carry the burden. The yoke of Jesus is made of love and delivers spiritual assistance in the way of encouragements and consolation. It is in yielding and surrender to the Lord that we prove ourselves to be His servants. In love, He works to keep our hearts for Himself. "Do not fear, for I have redeemed you; I have called you by name: you are mine! When you pass through the waters, I will be with you. When you walk through the fire, you will not be scorched" (Isa. 43:1-2).

When you let into your heart the fear of man, you must let out the fear of God. When you let into your heart the fear of God, the fear of man must leave. Although our hearts can start out with some corruption in the beginning, after coming to Jesus, our heart becomes our best part. The way we think and the way we act gets set on the Lord, by the grace of God. The Spirit of God dwelling in you, Christian, is the mark of your adoption.

The Spirit of God's presence can be discerned and reflected by the Lord's graceful operations. It is a spiritual surgery. The word of God is living and sharp, piercing between the soul and spirit allowing you to hear and judge your own thoughts (Heb. 4:12). This dissection allows you to be converted and comforted, and to understand and value your adoption into God's family. You are a new creature, not like the flesh of a natural man, but of the spirit. God created you and formed you into a human being beforehand, that you should walk with Him (Eph.2:10). Amen. You have love and mercy in your heart because of Jesus. This proves the grace of God for you and your sonship. God lets you see this work of grace in your own soul. God is love, and He is your eternal Father. The best is yet to come. You have been redeemed by the blood of God's Son. Blessed assurance Jesus is mine, oh what a foretaste of glory divine (Fanny Crosby,1873). God knows your name and will provide you with a new name (Rev. 2:17). God shows you His care and blesses you with His kindness and grace. Those children that are in the family of God were called and created by His grace and for His glory in eternity. When you die, Christian, I believe that you will not go alone; Jesus will be with you. He promised as a Father, He would never leave you or desert you (Heb. 13:5). No one is more important, bigger, or more powerful than God. I believe Him. Amen.

"Blessed be the God and Father of our Lord Jesus Christ, who according to His great mercy has caused us to be born again to a living hope through the resurrection of Jesus Christ from the dead, to obtain an inheritance which is imperishable and undefiled and will not fade away, reserved in heaven for you" (1Pet. 1:3-4). A very important part to understand about your life, and the best, is in the meaning of being born again. Having a new heart, a new spirit, and the Holy Spirit (Ezek. 36:26-27) is a gift from our Father in heaven. The hope, by faith about Jesus, is alive and providentially matures in this life. We grow to deeply realize the salvation of our soul and look forward to the gift of a spiritual inheritance for the children of God that awaits our presence. The inheritance is distant in time and place and is preserved and reserved for us who believe in Jesus by the grace of God. God's plan all along was for us to be called the children of God (1 John 3:1). We receive a spirit of adoption as sons by which we cry out "Abba, Father" and become fellow heirs with Christ (Rom. 8:15,17). Praise the Lord, Christian, that we can know this cry for His help and holiness. He predestined us to adoption as sons through Jesus Christ to Himself (Eph. 1:5). In this life, we are being kept by His goodness; in heaven, we will be preserved by His providence for His eternal glory. Amen.

The Christian life is a journey, a race, and a battle. As athletes, we are called to forget what lies behind, and with our eyes fixed on Jesus, to cast aside every hindrance to complete the race of faith (Heb. 12:2). The eye on Jesus is important when your heart is engaged. Having your heart engaged is important when you read the Bible. Your heart will burn for Him. Amen. Worshipping two masters (i.e., Jesus and myself), I know today, was worshiping the Lord, my Father with a careless heart. The Lord had to feel this infirmity from me, and I regret this. Instead of casting me aside, Christian, He gave me grace. While I was yet a sinner, Christ died for me (Rom. 5:8). For a while, my conscience was not quiet, my life was a struggle, and my church life was fruitless. I had a faith with works, but without full obedience and little assurance. "God is not mocked, whatsoever a man sows, this he will also reap" (Gal.6:7). I was on a diet from the word of God. Almost 45 years ago or so, I went off this diet and started feasting more and more on the word of God. God changed my heart. I was not initially surprised by joy like C.S. Lewis, but I was surprised by peace. The peace passed my understanding and convicted me of the Father's love for me in Jesus. The joy for me followed after the peace was established. I believe I'm a Christian today by the grace of God. I was chosen in Him before my time on earth began (Eph. 1:4). It is the grace of God, working providentially, that convinces us we are saved and insures we will not fail to get to heaven (Phil. 1:6). Our faith will always be real, but the sense of God's presence or assurance and power, may slip a little if we are disobedient or ignore the Bible. It is important to remember what He did, and when, and how the Lord has already worked in your life. Do not dwell on your weakness so much. Recall His help in the past, and feel confident that He will help you in the present time. God helps those who help themselves, and God helps those who cannot help themselves. God's purpose is to save you by His power, so that you may know freedom in Jesus and the joy of walking with Him. God freely chose you for this outcome. He did not choose you because you somehow earned it. He saw your need and chose to fill it with His love. He loved you first (1 John 4:19). All the graces in your life; faith, hope, love and work, are the effect of His providential grace. A believer in Jesus discovers God's workmanship and knows where to give all the glory. The Lord is our destiny; we are His children.

"Delight yourself in the Lord; and He will give you the desires of your heart" (Ps. 37:4). The desires of the natural man will perish, but the desires of the new man shall live with the Spirit of God. The world, the flesh and the devil will cast doubts into your soul to try to kill you and steal the Truth from you. Jesus came that you might have life and might have it abundantly (John 10:10). God is bigger than a lie. Jesus is the bread of life, the light of the world, the good Shepherd, the resurrection and the way, the truth, and the life; no one comes to the Father, but through Him (John 6:35, 8:12, 10:11, 11:25, 14:6). Amen. When you answered the call to surrender to Jesus and gave Him your heart, you received the greatest blessing in your life. The Lord will accomplish what concerns you (Ps. 138:8). Thank you, Jesus. "Now the God of peace, who brought up from the dead the great Shepherd of the sheep through the blood of the eternal

Covenant, even Jesus our Lord, equip you in every good thing to do His will, working in us that which is pleasing in His sight, through Jesus Christ, to whom be the glory forever and ever. Amen." (Heb. 13:20-21).

Patience

"The Lord is not slow about His promise, as some count slowness, but is patient toward you, not wishing for any to perish but for all to come to repentance" (2 Pet. 3:9).

Dear Christian,

Patience is part of God's perfect character, a divine attribute. God's patience controls the timing in the sovereign plan of God, makes forgiveness possible, and reveals the love of God for us. God is patient in His dealings with sinful man, and we are to learn to be patient in the face of trials and afflictions. We are the recipients of His patience, and by the grace of God, grow spiritually to reflect this fruit of the Spirit (Gal. 5:22).

I know for a fact that God is patient, because He was patient with me. At one time in my life, I pushed off into some of the troubling waters of life; by the grace of God, I came back home. I was a weak Christian for a while, and it took me some time to order my life right. We need the work of the Lord for us in the area of His patience. I feel like I know some of the experiences of the prodigal son coming home (Luke 15:11-24), and the man that once was blind but now he can see (John 9:13-25). I know the misery of sin and learned the patience and enduring love of God. I know what it means to be a weak Christian, and I know how great the mercy and patience of God can be. The definition of patience is the ability to bear trials without grumbling. The trials that God bears from us, Christian, He patiently bears. He always knew we would need His mercy and compassion to be saved. What I know about God today makes it difficult for me to believe He grumbled at me, no matter how much I may have disappointed Him. I'm His child. He sent His Son for me. In dying for us, Jesus answered all the questions that may have tried His patience. He took the work of our salvation up into His own hands. Amen.

The Gospel originated in the mind of God. Our redemption and every circumstance relating to our salvation was settled in His purpose and choice. He showed compassion and gave patience to a ruined people whose names He wrote in the Lamb's book of life (Rev. 21:27). God's hand of patience protects us (John 10:29) and exalts us (1 Pet. 5:6). "Do not fear, for I am with you; do not anxiously look about you, for I am your God. I will strengthen you, surely I will help you, surely I will uphold you with My righteous right hand" (Isa.41:10). God's patience is not evidence or an expression that He does not care for you. The work of enlightening the world, and awakening our conscience about sin, subduing our corruptions and respecting our will is what God patiently does, and He deserves the glory. The plan for our salvation, that God brought forth, would be accomplished in perseverance, or through endurance and with patience. God's superior strength to carry on the work of sanctification and overcome the sinner establishes a deeper conviction that God is at work. The heart of stone being changed into a heart of flesh, is a patient work of God. It is not me saving myself, but rather, by the grace of God, a building up of gratitude and glory for the Lord. It brings a solid hope, that though I struggle, He maintains the covenant in my heart by the work of the Holy Spirit. God is at work, patiently fulfilling the promise that Jesus saves. "It is God who is at work in you, both to will and to work for His good pleasure" (Phil. 2:13). Amen.

What is God really like? Some folks think that there is no God, and we just live under a power called "chance" which somehow has an ability to drive a process called evolution. Some folks believe that there is a God, but that He is not involved in human affairs. Some folks believe everyone will be saved, and by their deeds, their place after death might be a little better if they are good. Some folks believe we cannot know if God is real. Some folks think that God is a difficult taskmaster and always ready to punish them for how they live their lives. They think He is angry and demanding something from them all the time. Some folks like their sin, and the idea of holiness is not attractive to them, so they avoid decisions about God. Some folks do not trust the Bible as the word of God. All this, I believe is a mistake. The Bible is alive and active and sharper than any two-edged sword (Heb. 4:12). The natural man does not want to be cut by it. The Bible tells us the truth about God. It is a spiritual book that nurses faith into the person reading it, which is why it becomes important to read it to begin to know God. The choice to remain ignorant is not the correct decision. This decision is not the path the Lord has chosen for working out your salvation with fear and trembling. Faith comes by hearing and/or reading the word of God (Rom. 10:17). Faith opens the heart to understand spiritually the word of God, and change it from being a heart of stone to a heart of flesh. We are saved by grace through faith, and it is a gift from God (Eph. 2:8). God has the power in Himself to be patient, merciful and understanding. We have victory in Jesus for salvation in His time. We have the victory over sin and self, the world and others, and even understanding God by His enduring and patient love. All this comes to our hearts after we receive Him. He remains in our hearts over our lifetime to work patiently by faith to accomplish His purpose. We become the righteous who learn to live by faith (Hab. 2:4).

Patience is manifested in God's nature. In the Old Testament passage describing the replacement of the tablets for the Ten Commandments, God proclaimed the name of the Lord by which He would make Himself known. "The Lord, the Lord God, compassionate and gracious, slow to anger, and abounding in lovingkindness and truth; Who keeps lovingkindness for thousands, who forgives iniquity, transgression and sin; yet He will by no means leave the guilty unpunished" (Ex. 34:6-7). God is good.

He is merciful and gracious and abundant in goodness and truth. He forgives sin of all sorts, but will not clear the impenitent guilty without some satisfaction to His justice and honor. He is slow to anger or long-suffering, and waits to be gracious and merciful. The goodness of God, Christian, helps us not to be afraid of the power in His greatness. Peter tells us that "The Lord is not slow about His promise, as some count slowness, but is patient toward you, not wishing for any to perish but for all to come to repentance" (2 Pet. 3:9). God is always on time. There are a group of blessed folks chosen before the foundation of the world (Eph. 1:4), that are to grow in grace and knowledge. They are, by the grace of God, to live by faith and advance in holiness. They are to discover and do their calling, and be ready and prepared to meet God. They are to know repentance. "I tell you, no, but unless you repent, you will all likewise perish" (Luke 13:3). We all deserve to perish, Christian, but God has decided that repentance will be the way to escape it. Repentance is absolutely necessary for salvation. A merciful God does not take pleasure in the death and punishment of sinners. God longs that all would be saved, but He knows that many will reject Him. God's good desire for mankind does not refer to the ultimate determining will of God. The Bible clearly teaches both the sovereignty of God and the free will of man for salvation. God is willing and patient to save a man, but that man may not be willing to be saved. He may prefer self in his mind and push aside the thoughts of eternal life. He does not choose the Lord and lives in His absence without the forgiveness of sin. He will not receive Jesus into his heart. The design of God's patience is for those chosen to salvation. It is for those to be given time to grow in the belief of the truth and sanctification through the Spirit, to fulfill their calling (Heb.12:14). Amen.

"Be diligent to be found by Him in peace, spotless and blameless, and regard the patience of the Lord to be salvation (2 Pet. 3:15). The word "regard" written above, is like to "consider it all joy when you encounter various trials, knowing that the testing of your faith produces endurance" (James 1:2-3). The words "consider" and "regard", Christian, should be based on the true knowledge of God and what God is doing in our lives through trials. These may be difficult, challenging and stressful times in your life. At the same time, we know most importantly that the Lord is with us, and is at work in us by grace with the Spirit. Our character is developing a strength to stand under the difficult circumstances of trials. God intends patience and perseverance to develop as a virtue with hope for God's glory. Self-control has more to do with handling the pleasures of your life, while patience and perseverance relate more to the difficulties and problems of life. There is a bravery in this fight, like one sees in a good soldier. "You will be distressed by various trials, that the proof of your faith, being more precious than gold which is perishable, even though tested by fire, may be found to result in praise and glory and honor at the revelation of Jesus Christ" (1 Pet. 1:6-7). In the history of your life, Christian, will be the evidence that in your trouble, you trusted Christ by faith. To God be the glory. The outcome of your faith is the salvation of your soul (1 Pet. 1:9). "Blessed is the man that perseveres under trial; for once he has been approved, he will receive the crown of life, which the Lord has promised to all those who love Him" (James 1:12). When you stand before the judgment seat of Christ (2 Cor. 5:10), Christian, the trial of your faith will be revealed as the glory of Christ. You belong to Him, and He was faithful to protect you. "After you have suffered a little while, the God of all grace, who called you to His eternal glory in Christ, will Himself perfect, confirm, strengthen, and establish you" (1 Pet. 5:10). The goal of the Lord is your perfection, that is, to be more like Jesus and have your heart alive for Him. Amen.

"Do not think lightly of the riches of His kindness and forbearance and patience, not knowing that the kindness of God leads us to repentance" (Rom. 2:4). The kindness of God leading us to repentance is a great work for us, in which God shows great patience with us. I needed God's patient work in my life to save my soul, because sometimes I did not listen to Him right away. God calls men to repentance. I used to think that repentance was to reform myself. Repentance is a change of mind, heart and will. The sorrow that is according to the will of God produces a repentance without regret (2 Cor. 6:10). Repentance is a gift of God (Acts 11:18, 2 Tim. 2:25, Rom. 2:4). Repentance is hearing an alarm bell or getting a wake-up call that sin is not a joke. You can develop an anger about yourself and sin. You no longer want sin in your life and you are turning to Christ for help. You dream of freedom from sin and develop a desire to clear your name by Jesus (2 Cor. 7:11). Repentance is a difficult work that requires the power of God to change or to be converted from sin to God. True repentance includes a broken heart with groans for offending such a good and loving God. True repentance includes a deep loathing of ourselves and feeling the shame of sin.

A true repentance goes from faith to faith in Jesus and strength to strength against all sins. Amen. God is patient while we grow in the grace of repentance, which we will need for the remainder of our days. Repentance is a battle that takes time. We learn our weakness, the power of God, and the value and necessity to confess our sins for cleansing (1 John 1:9). In repentance we learn to avoid occasions to sin, destroy the triggers and press the darts to sin from the devil out of our minds. We gain experience, Christian, of the Lord supporting us in the battle. We value the discovery of the work of the Lord in our souls. We take great delight in obedience and develop a true enjoyment and a passion to be holy. "Let the word of Christ richly dwell within you" (Col. 3:16). Godliness with contentment is great gain (1 Tim. 6:6). The work of God in the gift of repentance will raise you up with Christ, Christian, above the world and your old self. The gift of repentance growing in you means you have been chosen of God to be holy in preparation for His presence. Therefore, "Put on a heart of compassion, kindness, humility, gentleness and patience; bearing with one another and forgiving each other" (Col. 3:12-14). Let the peace, love, joy, strength and patience of God rule in your heart. Amen.

One of the reasons God is patient is to show His power. "What if God, although willing to demonstrate His wrath and to make His power known, endured with much patience vessels of wrath prepared for destruction? And He did so in order that He might make known the riches of His glory upon vessels of mercy, which He prepared beforehand for glory" (Rom. 9:22-23). "All have sinned and fallen short of the glory of God" (Rom. 3:23) and deserve death and eternal punishment (Rom. 6:23). God did not prepare vessels of wrath for destruction. God gives ample opportunity for the sinner to repent and escape His wrath. Vessels of wrath are prepared for destruction by their own sin and rebellion. We store up God's wrath against ourselves (Rom. 2:5). The Lord was patient with vessels, but they rejected His truth. God created Hades for the devil and His angels, and did not give them the gift of repentance (Matt. 25:41). Hades was not made to destroy man. The responsibility is on man to work out his salvation with fear and trembling (Phil. 2:12), and in this way, discover what God has placed in him. God does have objects of mercy that He prepares beforehand for glory (Eph. 2:10, Rom. 9:23). The vessel of mercy sees the wrath and power and love of God in Jesus. The vessel of mercy sees the riches and experiences the patience of God in a growth of His grace and knowledge. God's purpose is to show the riches of His grace and glory on vessels of mercy. Man has no rights, Christian, God can do as He pleases and is justified no matter what He does. Men are without excuse (Rom. 1:20). It is a mystery how God prepared some men and women for glory before the foundation of the world (Eph. 1:4). He was not obligated to chose anyone. He chose Paul (Gal. 1:15-16). The Holy Spirit calls and leads a person to receive repentance and faith and salvation in Jesus. It seems clear that not every man accepts the call. I do not know enough about the deep things of God; or for that matter about a man, that leads him to ignore or reject the invitation to come to Jesus. I believe that God was patient and righteous. Every man has been born with a measure of faith, that when he hears God's word, has the ability to open the door and let God in (John 3:15-16, Rev. 3:20). Amen.

"The fruit of the Spirit is love, joy, peace, patience, kindness, goodness, faithfulness, gentleness, self-control; against such things there is no law" (Gal. 5:22). Patience is a bearing of pain or enduring trials without complaint. Additional words that describe patience are long-suffering, perseverance, forbearance, tolerance and endurance. The fruit of the Spirit is expressed or reflected in man by the new nature from God, and becomes ours by the grace of God. We are to live and walk by the Spirit (Gal. 5:25). "The flesh sets its desire against the Spirit, and the Spirit works against the flesh; for these are in opposition to one another, so that you may not do the things that you please" (Gal. 5:17). Thus, we have two contrasting powers within us, Christian; one is natural which brings forth the sinful fruit of the flesh, while the other is supernatural and bears the fruit of the Spirit. We are born as natural men (1 Cor. 2:14), and must be born again (John 3:5) to be led by the Spirit. The Spirit produces the character of Jesus in the believer. Paul entreats us to "walk in a manner worthy of the calling with which you have been called, with all humility and gentleness, with patience, showing forbearance to one another in love" (Eph. 4:1-2). Paul wanted the members of the Church "to preserve the unity of the Spirit in the bond of peace" (Eph. 4:3). Be calm. The ongoing work of sanctification in the life of the believer, by the power of the Holy Spirit, is to conform us to the image with the character of Jesus Christ. Amen.

We are to know and live with a courageous endurance over time in difficult circumstances. Patience is a "long holding out" in the mind before it gives into action. Patience is an emotional quietness in the face of unfavorable circumstances. It is described by God's patience against sinful men that leads to repentance (Rom. 2:4). It is described of Jesus when He was reviled and suffering at the hands of evil men, "He uttered no threats, but kept entrusting Himself to Him who judges righteously (1 Pet. 1:23). Patience is a capacity for self-control. Do not be easily offended or make quick judgments. Be patient with foolish, blind, unteachable or ungrateful people. Being right about something will never change a person's mind who has chosen what they believe for whatever valid reason they think they have. It only leads to arguments. Patience bears insults and wrongs without bitterness and complaint. Though we might have the ability to embarrass or take revenge against unpleasant people, we are to know the spirit of being calm and gracious by the grace of God. Be mindful of the patience that the Lord has shown you in the face of all your provocations against Him. If the Lord had been a man without patience, He could have been justified in wiping us off the earth a long time ago for our disobedience in the Garden of Eden or at the time of the flood when God waited during the construction of the ark (1 Pet. 3:20).

God is patient during our repentance (Rom. 2:4), during our growth in grace and knowledge (Rom. 9:22), and during our sanctification and salvation (1 Tim. 1:16). Keep looking for a new heaven and earth in which righteousness will dwell. Keep hearing the promises of God, and keep the aim of your life to sanctify Jesus in your heart. No matter what you're suffering or your trouble may come to, keep a good conscience. "It is better, if God will it so, that you suffer for doing what is right rather than for doing what is wrong" (1 Pet. 3:17). Therefore, Christian, look into the future for God's goodness and righteousness and "be diligent to be found by Him in peace, spotless and blameless" (2 Pet. 3:14). Let your renewed conscience be your guide (John 14:16-17). "Regard the patience of the Lord to be salvation" (2 Pet. 3:15). The great patience of God, Christian, is allowing you time to repent. The patience of the Lord means He has mercy in giving you time to "work out your salvation with fear and trembling" (Phil. 2:12). Heaven is a prepared place for a prepared people. In your patience, seek knowledge and understanding, in hopes that it shall be given you from the Lord. The patience and peace of God that passes your understanding is a gift from the Lord. The gifts of God are evidence of His love for you. Be patient and diligent, Christian; God is merciful and generous in His time. "Press on to know the Lord" (Hosea 6:3). At the right time and in the right way, He pours more knowledge into your heart about His ways. Knowing the Lord, our God, will make you patient. Since they are spiritual gifts you need, and are looking for, they must and should and will, only come from His hand.

God's grace will give you a mind to know and understand His word, and a heart to love Him. Taken together, they build sincerity and conviction, which converts the will and affections into the grace of obedience and service which glorifies God. The lazy, obstinate and hypocritical man remains ignorant of the Lord. "The fear of the Lord is the beginning of wisdom; a good understanding, have all those who do His commandments" (Ps. 111:10). True religion is the most important wisdom, and obedience to God, the just and appropriate response. The important test of this wisdom is how deeply fixed it becomes in your heart. Does this wisdom steer your heart towards heaven with a new hope and a repentance that you do not regret? Does this wisdom allow a discovery of your purpose in life? When the fear of the Lord is ruling in your heart, there will be a strong conscientious work on your part to keep His commandments. You will be at war with yourself and the devil, and your patience will be tried and tested. We will not be perfect, but we will know a great difference in our walk by being with Jesus. To God be the glory. "If any man is willing to do His will, he shall know" more, and more clearly the teachings of Christ (John 7:17). The Lord is patient with us, and you must be patient with yourself. God is in charge of His own gifts of grace, Christian, and will give us knowledge and understanding in His own time. He knows our hearts, and our abilities and disabilities. He knows how to improve our "light" and when to secure us by divine grace. Be patient, we grow in grace and knowledge and mature in the Lord's time as a Christian. We "are being transformed into the same image from glory to glory, just as from the Lord, the Spirit" (2 Cor. 3:18). The work of the Holy Spirit brings us into a conformity to Christ in His time, by the grace of God, for God's glory. Thank you, Jesus.

There are numerous exhortations in the Bible for Christians to be patient. The writer of Hebrews exhorts believers to "be imitators of those who through faith and patience inherit the promises" (Heb. 6:12). He gives the example of Abraham to whom God promised Isaac as a blessing. He gives the examples of some Old Testament folks who trusted the promises of God, but died in faith, without receiving the promises. They desired a better country, that is a heavenly one. They came into their inheritance with patience, and God was not ashamed to be called their God (Heb. 11:13,16). The trial of faith we have in this world, may be easier sometimes, because we already have some experience with the promises of

God. Perfection awaits our presence in heaven. The gift of faith tells us that God is true, and it satisfies our soul. We have a spirit of adoption and know that a place is being prepared for us. We will grow spiritually and then come into our inheritance by faith and patience. God implants the grace of patience to give time to grow our desires, enliven our affections and to better build up our hearts in knowledge and gratitude for such a great salvation. We will move into our perfectly designed homes filled with the love and the glory of God. It is our duty to be faithful and trust the outcome to God, who cannot lie (Heb. 6:18).

Patience can be a trying experience, but we are to run to our Refuge, that is Christ, and the hope that is set before us from His victory over sin and death. On every occasion that I have been patient, I have not regretted holding my breath. Like every one else, Christian, I have felt mistreated and misrepresented at times. Some of the times, I wish that I had spoken up for myself; but today, I'm glad I kept my mouth shut. Some people like confrontations, but I'm not one of them. Peace with all men about most things is a good policy, and arguments solve nothing. In Colossians, Paul exhorts the believers to put on a heart of patience, bearing with one another, and remembering how much the Lord forgave us (Col. 3:12-13). It is usually a good idea to wait most of the time to speak out. Self-control is a virtue of the Holy Spirit. Self-control is a godly virtue that the Holy Spirit produces in our lives. Let the peace of Christ rule in your heart and reflect the patience of God (Col. 3:15).

In Jesus, we show patience toward our Christian experience. We can get disappointed at failure and weakness for the Lord when we know the right thing to do and do not do it (James 4:17). When we sin, we realize and learn how much we need the Lord. We find ourselves struggling against sin, and hoping and waiting on the Lord at the same time. We fear the future, yet we do not give up. God's promises can seem delayed or taking too long to get answers for situations we are facing. We wait. We should wait in prayer and Bible study, recognizing that the Lord knows our situation, and already has the perfect solution on the way. The family, your job, your health, sin and your prayers are despairing sometimes, and you need a bearing patience with yourself. Waiting for the Lord to work needs patience. Where else can we go? Only Jesus has the answers to any and all questions and especially the important ones, called forgiveness of sin and eternal life (John 6:68). Whenever we wait and need to be patient, whenever we are struggling against sin and whenever we feel lost or confused, faith comes to the rescue. Amen.

Faith is a gift of God (Eph. 2:8), and is defined as the assurance of things hoped for and the conviction of things not seen (Heb. 11:1). We are justified by Faith (Rom. 5:1). "This is the work of God, that you believe in Him who He has sent" (John 6:29). Amen. This is what God requires. It is not works but faith in Him. A work by man panders to his pride, which is something that he can boast in and glory about. Salvation is not earned by a religious life, but is a free gift received by faith (Rom. 6:23). The work of faith is the work of God. Without faith you cannot please God (Heb. 11:6). Faith working in us subjects our soul to God working on us, which leads our soul in working for Him. He is a rewarder of those who seek Him (Heb. 11:6). We grow out of the natural man and develop and mature, by the grace of God, into a spiritual man by faith in believing in Christ. Be patient, Christian, "every good thing bestowed and every perfect gift is from above, coming down from the Father of lights" (James 1:17). Be patient, Christian, "In the exercise of His will He brought us forth by the word of truth, so that we might be the first fruits of His creatures" (James 1:18). This is God's plan for you in Jesus; every day you have was ordained for you before there was one of them (Ps. 139:16). "He who began a good work in you will perfect it until the day of Christ Jesus" (Phil. 1:6).

Hope in the Lord, though He may seem to tarry or be late, never disappoints. He is never late. This hope in Jesus we have as an anchor grows deeper in us and will mean more to us than our very lives. Hope in Jesus covers all kinds of circumstances. "This hope, we have as an anchor of the soul, a hope both sure and steadfast, and one which enters within the veil" (Heb. 6:19). "Therefore, we do not lose heart" (2 Cor. 4:16). "For in hope we have been saved, but if we hope for what we do not see, with perseverance we wait eagerly for it" (Rom. 8:24-25). With patience we wait, knowing that the Lord's promises will never be in vain. We are saved by grace (Eph. 2:8), but the condition in which we are saved is hope. We hope in God, that is Jesus, and deal with the Lord upon trust. He is trustworthy. "Blessed is the man that trusts in the Lord, whose trust is the Lord" (Jer. 17:7). Our duty is to trust and hope in the Lord and depend upon Him. We shall be like a fruitful tree planted by the water (Jer. 17:8). What this means is that the trust that honors God will yield an inward peace and satisfaction. Their life will be a harvest of holiness, and their work will be productive for the benefit of others and the glory of God. Jesus is always on His way toward us to take us home. We grow in grace and knowledge to a spiritual maturity, that takes time to appear in our heart. If it seems that He is late in coming, that is on us, because His timing will be perfect and can be no other way. Amen.

The author of our patience is God. "May the God who gives perseverance and encouragement grant you to be of the same mind with one another according to Christ Jesus" (Rom. 15:5). The example of patience for us was Christ. "May the Lord direct your hearts into the love of God and into the steadfastness of Christ" (2 Thess. 3:5). The source of patience is the Spirit (Gal. 5:22). The scriptures were written, Christian, that we might know God, and that you may "believe that Jesus is the Christ, the Son of the living God; and that believing you may have life in His name" (John 20:31, 1 John 5:13). "For whatever was written in earlier times was written for our instruction, that through perseverance and the encouragement of the scriptures we might have hope" (Rom. 15:4). There is nothing unprofitable in the scripture. Faith comes by hearing and reading the word of God (Rom. 1:17). Faith goes beyond reason and believes many times before we have a complete understanding, but always trusts the Lord. Faith accepts all things as part of God's will. "Without faith it is impossible to please Him" (Heb. 11:6), Faith waits, Christian; in waiting patiently, your heart is responding to the love of God. Amen. Faith waits patiently by yielding a mind of trust to God. Faith receives a peace with God and rests about going forward into the glory that God has prepared for His children. The Bible tells us that "tribulation brings about perseverance; and perseverance, proven character; and proven character, hope" (Rom. 5:3-4). This is a hope that waits patiently, because it is not disappointed. The Holy Spirit is at work now in our hearts pouring forth the love of God (Rom. 5:5). Tribulation works a Christian patience into our souls. Patience is the building block for character and hope. We learn character in times of difficulty. Man is tested by adversity and learns that God's grace for it will always be sufficient. (2 Cor. 12:9). Never give up, be patient and strengthen your heart with Bible study for the coming of the Lord is at hand (James 5:8).

A day of judgment is coming when God "will render to every man according to his deeds: to those who by perseverance in doing good seek for glory and honor and immortality, eternal life" (Rom. 2:7). Those that fix their hearts on God and do well will win the crown. Seeking the kingdom of God in our hopes and desires, with a strong and patient spirit, will enable a good fortitude for deeds bringing forth fruit. The deeds are not to be saved, but rather the way a saved man will conduct himself. Being born again changes what you pay attention to by setting up new priorities in your heart for God's glory. Paul prays that we all may be filled with spiritual wisdom and walk in a manner that pleases the Lord. He prays that we may bear fruit and increase in the knowledge of God. He prays that we may be strengthened with all power for the attaining of all the steadfastness and patience; joyously giving thanks to the Father (Col. 1:9-12). Never forget, that God in His grace, mercy and patience first seeks and finds us. "We love, because He first loved us" (1 John 4:19). We seek Jesus and a Christlikeness, and the honor that comes from God, because He is good. We seek eternal life in Christ Jesus, our Lord, because God is good. We seek God, by the grace of God. God's patience for us lies inside His goodness. Amen.

The world's expectation for tribulation and patience in bearing a trial is gloom and despair, and then a gladness to be separated from it. Patience in our troubles of life, by the grace of God, is to have joy. We are to count trials as joy (James 1:2). Being strengthened by God is joy, but we have to know what trouble is like before we value His lovingkindness and rescue from it. Everything that happens in our life is with God's will and purpose and presence. With the Lord in our hearts, we are to look to the future and wait on Him. As His child, we have His mercy and love, and are being made fit for His eternal presence and our inheritance. Our duty is to be confident in His grace and grateful for His kindness. "He is our God and we are His people and the sheep of His hand" (Ps. 95:7). Amen.

The Bible has a parable that tells us something about the Lord's patience that also turns out to be my favorite parable. The parable is the story of the Prodigal Son (Luke 15:11-32). It is an encouraging story that speaks perfectly to the human condition. It speaks about our sinful actions in the behavior of the younger son, and our self-righteous pharisee-like actions in the older son. It speaks magnificently of the father which is a picture of the Lord. The conversion of sinners is very pleasing to God. In the story, the younger son wanted his inheritance early in his life, so he could go out and spend it on his pleasure. He essentially dishonored the father and wanted him dead. We have free will, Christian, to choose sin, but the consequences we do not choose. "Sin will take you further than you ever wanted to stray, cost you more than you ever thought you would have to pay, and keep you longer than you ever thought you would stay" (author unknown). The young son squandered his inheritance with righteous living. You think you can run secretly away, but you cannot hide from God (Ps. 139). He understands your thoughts from afar and always knows where you are; nothing is hidden from God. We make poor choices when we think sin is fun. The young son became poor and in need. A famine hit the land and his finances and friends dried up. Sin promised him freedom, success and a happy life, but instead gave him slavery, failure and almost the wages of sin, death (Rom. 6:23). The young man got really desperate and took a job feeding swine. "The one who sows to his own flesh shall from the flesh reap corruption, but the one who sows to the Spirit shall from the Spirit reap eternal life" (Gal. 6:8). He was alone and hungry, and by the grace of God, he began to think, that is, "he came to his senses" (Luke 15:17). He began to realize the cost of sin and the serious mistake he had made being apart from his father. Sin eventually makes us hurt and hungry, and feeling lost and helpless. The Lord is waking us up when we hear this alarm bell. In this affliction, the young son starts looking into another direction. The sense this makes in him, is to look back to his father. The young son decides to go back home. In our lives, we may think we want or need to try sin but at some time, by the grace of God, we also may reach the end of our rope or the bottom of the pit. The fact that we need to go home can be a humbling and tough lesson, but a good one. The Lord was always waiting for us to come home.

God is at work both to will and work for His good pleasure (Phil. 2:13). The grace of God works in the considerations that take place in our senses about what to do. In His grace and patience, we are given time to reflect and compare the wages of sin to the wages of being in His house. We may suffer some consequences from our sin, but what is important, is that we go back home. We pray and maybe pick up the Bible. By the grace of God, the ear is opened to hear, and the mind to understanding that God's plan for our live is the best one. We waded into water that has gotten too deep for us, and the Lord is in the will of our consideration to wade back out and go home to be free. "The hearing ear and the seeing eye, the Lord has made both of them" (Prov. 20:12). The patience of God in His providence has been at work, and the power of His mercy and love is drawing you back to Himself. We see the mistakes in our choices without God and the poor outcomes with all the undesirable consequences. We are exposed as being foolish and prideful and appear now humbled and regretful. The young son confesses that he has sinned and remembers his father's goodness. He decides to go back home to his father in honest humility and repentance. When he was on his way back to his father, Christian, the Bible tells us that "while he was still a long way off, his father saw him, and felt compassion for him and ran and embraced him"

(Luke 15:20). Before the son could show repentance with his father, the father was on the run to greet him and welcome him home. The father understood the son and chose to be kind and gracious, revealing his compassion and mercy. At work in the father, while he waited, was the grace of patience. The father assured him of his welcome and pardon. This is a superb picture, Christian, of the love of God. This is a magnificent picture of the righteousness of Christ imputed to a sinner and his being restored as a child of God. Amen. This is an awe-inspiring picture that shows the healing of our soul in the gift of forgiveness by the Father. We are clothed with a robe of righteousness, and given a "ring" on the hand signifying we have been sealed by the Holy Spirit. We are given shoes for our feet, intimating that we are to go forward with resolve being a Christian. We are to go forward sharing what we have learned about the goodness of God with others in a lost world. He came home to a feast, the fatted calf. Amen.

For all that come home to Jesus, they come home to a feast for their souls. He is the bread of life (John 6:35). The Lord nourishes and sustains our body and the life in our soul. "He makes me lie down in green pastures; He leads me beside still waters. He restores my soul; He guides me in paths of righteousness for His name's sake" (Ps. 23:2-3). We are drawn to Christ or else we perish in our sins. Though we come to Christ sometimes from a bad condition, Christian, He does not think Himself dishonored. He is honored to be called upon by a person in such a troubled and desperate case. God is honored to save and heal lost sinners and weak Christians, if they but call upon His name. There is great joy in heaven over one sinner that repents (Luke 15:7). He knows we need His power to be saved. We can be difficult sinners, which means we will need the perfections in God's patience. The patience of the father in the parable described above, is a rich description of the excellent kindness the Lord has for us as we grow in grace and knowledge. God is patient to save and grow us with grace for the changes we need to make to survive His presence. He gracefully and patiently builds and transforms our lives, so that our joy will be made complete. Amen.

In the parable of the prodigal son, the father was looking for the return of the son. So, it is for us also; the Father has His eye upon us, we belong to Jesus. God's word will not be returning to Him void (Isa. 55:11). As believers, we are God's elect (Rom. 8:29-33, Luke 18:7, 2 Tim. 1:9). Election is God's purpose and cannot fail. He runs to meet us, with feet of mercy. He waits to embrace us and not upbraid us. We come home, but we are really coming back to our heavenly Father. We have been chosen by God before the foundation of the world (Eph. 1:4). Believers are the ones that God the Father gave to the Son (John 17:24). Jesus Christ's reward is the reward for His obedience to the Father (Phil. 2:8-11). "All that the Father gives Me shall come to Me" (John 6:37). "My sheep hear My voice, and I know them, and they follow Me. My Father, who has given them to Me, is greater than all; and no one is able to snatch them out of the Father's hand (John 10:27,29). Amen. Someday, Christian, you may wander out into the far away country of sin, and it may not be so easy to come home. If true, I want you to begin to take steps coming back home. I believe that the Lord will be running out to meet you. God's purpose in waiting for you is to fulfill His promise to the Son and to you that your joy may be complete. Jesus said, "These things I have spoken to you, that My joy may be in you, and that your joy may be made full" (John 15:11). You will find that the joy of the world is empty, but the joy found in communion with Jesus will be rejoicing and full. The apostle John wrote the things he did for us, "so that our joy may be made complete" (1 John 1:4). It is our responsibility, in part, to maintain our joy by reading the Bible with an open heart, and allow the Holy Spirit to speak and fill our hearts and build a rich faith in Jesus. A Christian sees light at the end of life's tunnel with joy unspeakable and full of glory. The light will be Jesus.

"For My thoughts are not your thoughts, neither are your ways My ways. For as the heavens are higher than the earth, so are My ways higher then your ways, and My thoughts than your thoughts, declares the Lord" (Isa. 55:8). We think sometimes that God is a difficult taskmaster; unwilling to forgive and be reconciled to man. Instead, He opens a door and encourages us to depend upon

Christ for the pardon of sin. God has chosen graces in the beauty of forgiveness and patience over judgment. God's holiness and justice are satisfied in the sacrifice of Himself in Jesus. The Bible says, "you shall go out with joy, and be led forth in peace with singing" (Isa. 55:12). This verse was written about the redemption of the Jews out of Babylon from captivity, but relates also to Gospel times. The grace of God will set those at liberty who were in bondage to sin with great joy. The people whose characters were as a thorn and a briar shall become graceful (Isa. 55:13). The people will be encouraged and God will be glorified. The covenant of grace will be filled with God's patience. Amen. The Lord longs to be gracious and compassionate (Isa. 30:18). God's patience shows power over Himself. "He who is slow to anger is better then the mighty, and he who rules his spirit, than he who captures a city" (Prov. 16:32). The conquest of ourselves will take place in God's gracious attribute and gift, of patience.

God is patient (Ex. 34:6). The examples or descriptions of God's patience in the Bible start in Genesis and continue throughout the Bible. Thus, we see God's patience in the lives of Adam and Eve. God might have struck them dead for disobedience in the Garden of Eden but let Adam live to be 930 years old (Gen. 5:5). God showed patience in the corruption of mankind in the days of Noah (Gen. 6) and in the rebellion at the tower of Babel (Gen. 11). God showed patience with the Egyptians in Egypt and with the Israelites in the wilderness (Ex. 16). God showed patience with the obstinate Jewish people when they built the Golden Calf (Ex. 32:9). He repeatedly showed patience for the people of Israel in the time of the Judges and with the kings of Israel and Judah (Judges 3-14, 1 and 2 Kings). He showed patience in allowing the exiles to return from captivity in Babylon (Jer. 29:10, Ezra 1). God was slow to anger against the Gentiles who were practicing all kinds of unrighteousness and trying to turn religion into a fable (Rom. 1:29-32). Even in our own lives, Christian, when we are tempted to sin and inclined to surrender to our fleshly desires, God is patient and remembers we are but dust (Ps. 103:14). When we argue within ourselves about sin, and experience a breach in our loyalty to Christ, He does not treat us in the way we deserve for our ungrateful bearing with Him. He is patient for us to learn the power of sin, and the great need we have of His grace for spiritual warfare. Sometimes we suffer and bleed, but not to death. Thank you, Jesus.

In His patience, Christian, God many times will speak words of warning about judgment and the consequences of sin to our hearts. He warned Adam and Eve not to eat from the tree of the knowledge of good and evil (Gen. 2:17). He had Noah warn the people about their wickedness and the coming flood (Gen. 6,7). He warned Joseph to prepare for a famine in Egypt (Gen. 41). He used the prophets to warn the Jewish people about apostasy (Jer.2) and captivity and the consequences of their sin (Jer. 25). He warned them they should not seek help from Egypt, but rather from Himself (Isa. 31). Jonah warned Nineveh (Jonah 1). God has a right to punish, but He warns us of what we deserve if we continue in sin and encourages us to choose His mercy. We make mistakes in our choices and lose some battles for the majesty of God. But because God is patient, we still are enabled to seek Jesus and trust His word that He would never leave us or forsake us (Heb. 13:5). "At night my soul longs for Thee diligently" (Isa. 26:9). God is patient with the wicked also, but they do not learn righteousness, practice confession with the Lord or perceive His Majesty. Sometimes the Lord will threaten and exercise lesser judgments to get our attention about repentance. Sometimes though, because the sentence is not executed quickly, the hearts of men are given fully to do evil (Eccl. 8:11).

Why is God patient? The Lord is patient toward men, because He does not want them to perish. He wants you to look for a new heaven and a new earth where righteousness dwells. He wants you to be found in peace, spotless and blameless, and regard the patience of the Lord to be salvation (2 Pet. 3:13-15). The delay of the second coming of Jesus is to give more time for folks to repent and grow in grace according to the previous design of God. It is not a delay in the way it is not going to happen. We are to consider the second coming of Jesus paramount to the security of our soul, and look with hope and anticipation for His appearance. We are to be patient toward the Lord about His coming again, recognizing that the time He does come will be the perfect moment according to His good pleasure. God is willing to bear our growing in grace, holiness and knowledge, that you have space to repent as preparation for living in heaven. God waits that He may be more gracious. He will reveal the riches of His grace in kindness towards us in Christ Jesus (Eph. 2:7). This event will be magnificent and fixed in our hearts for eternity. "Things which eye has not seen and ear has not heard, and which have not entered the heart of man, all that God has prepared for those that love Him" (1Cor. 2:9).

The Lord's patience in my life, Christian, is a miracle I know for sure. I needed His patience. The patience in the Gospel is a divine revelation to my heart. It is not hard for me to believe that there will be wonderful things in the home that the Lord has prepared for us in His Father's house (John 14:2-3). It troubles me that I was weak and struggled to be fully obedient for a number of years. It troubles me that I was careless at times and tried God's patience. I suffered and was confused in weakness and ignorance for a while with the conflict between the old man and the new man (Rom. 7:14-24). "For the good that I wish, I did not do; but I practiced the evil that I did not wish" (Rom. 7:19). My conversion through this time was slow, but steady. One sin at a time dropped out of my life by the grace of God. God was patient. I joyfully concurred with the law of God in my inner man, but the law of sin waged war against the law of my mind. I was a wretched man. I stayed in the fight by the grace of God, and I was set free by the grace of God. "Thanks be to God through Jesus Christ our Lord" (Rom. 7:25). "The law of the Spirit of life in Christ Jesus has set you free from the law of sin and death" (Rom. 8:2). Amen.

The time of God's patience and long-suffering for our salvation and sanctification has an end. The time is in the Lord's hands, and this is a good thing. Amen. Our eternity in heaven is only possible because of the work and merits of Jesus Christ. The time of God's patience ends when we die. The days we are invited to accept Jesus or to be reminded about our salvation from the Lord are over. The time is marked by His long-suffering, not by our patience. We still will sin (1 John 1:8) and need confession (1 John 1:9) after conversion. During this time, God still remains patient, as we grow in grace out of the ways of sin in our hearts. It is a great comfort, Christian, that God is the One who gives perseverance and patience, and encouragement and consolation after we come to Jesus. The work the Lord finishes will make us like-minded with Christ (Rom. 15:5, Phil. 1:6). If He was willing to endure, with much patience, vessels of wrath fitted for destruction, He will have sufficient mercy and patience for those vessels prepared for glory by faith and repentance (Rom. 9:22-23). If the Lord gives us a heart to see the love of Jesus, then that is the mercy we need to be saved. To be saved is to be made spiritually alive in Christ. Repentance keeps springing up in me, by the grace of God, which means His patience is still directed for me to trust Christ. God forbid that somehow in my struggle to live for Jesus, and being led by the Spirit, I would take encouragement to sin. Are we to continue in sin that grace may increase? (Rom. 6:1-2). That I want what is best for me is true; it is also true, I want to be holy and please the Lord and live for Jesus. I want to be led by the Spirit of God. I believe, by the grace of God, that what is best for me, is whatever the Lord God has for me. Amen. God's patience is a safe ground to trust in the promises of God. God is faithful, and "The just shall live by faith" (Rom. 1:17).

The patience of God is a comfort in our infirmities. The devil wants me to believe that I must keep getting better on my own to please God. The devil wants me to focus more on what I need to do in order to firmly secure the salvation of my soul. The devil wants me to believe that my acceptance with God is always on a weighing balance. If I do enough or more good things compared to bad, then the balance of my life will be considered good enough to be saved. The devil wants me to focus on my work and life, which will always be insufficient and meager, and accept the idea that God is an unfair and impossible to please taskmaster. The truth and the facts are: Jesus paid it all. Turn your eyes upon Jesus. "A battered reed He will not break off, and a smoldering wick He will not put out, until He leads justice to victory" (Matt. 12:20). A Christian may be weak like a bruised reed and have little life or heat like a smoking flax, but our God is rich in compassion and patience. The design of the Gospel of Jesus Christ for salvation encourages sincerity. Though we have significant infirmities, God accepts an upright and willing mind instead of a sinless obedience. Our fear and trembling (Phil. 2:12) are strongly supported and not discouraged. The Lord is tender toward us, Christian, even when we are weak. He knows that is when we need Him the most. He accepts the willingness of the spirit and passes by the weakness of the flesh. A Christian has true grace and is the child of a King. Amen.

"A book of remembrance has been written" that records conversations of "those who fear the Lord and who esteem His name" (Mal. 3:16). The Lord says that these folks are His, and He "will spare them as a man spares his own son who serves him" (Mal. 3:17). God takes notice of us, and in particular, the gracious words that come out of our mouths as a testimony to Jesus as the Christ. God remembers the love, kindness, prayers and service of His children. "Thou hast taken account of my wanderings; put my tears in Thy bottle; are they not in Thy book? (Ps. 56:8). God remembers our afflictions and keeps an account. The trial of our faith is precious in His sight. God gives the honest heart and to Him be the glory. We are a peculiar treasure of God in this world. We are vessels of mercy to be spared and owned by God, as our Father, throughout eternity. The patience of God will be owned by His children as a rich portion of His glory. Amen.

The study of the patience of God is for our encouragement. God's patience gives us time to repent and grow in grace and knowledge of the Bible and the Lord, our God. Without God's patience, there would be no prospect of heaven in our eternal life. God's patience teaches us about His goodness and love and the tenderness of His nature. The study of God's patience will make you more serious about repentance and grateful that God is merciful. I live in the providence of God. He has healed me and preserves me with a daily supply of grace. How can I sin against Him who holds my life together? From one sin in the garden of Eden, death entered our world. From one sin, Moses was excluded from the promise land. From one sin, Ananias and Sapphira lost their lives. Consider how many times and for how many years we have sinned, yet His patience has remained. A lot of "small" sins and some "big" sins, and neglect of repentance and confession and careless worship have followed me for too many years. Sins of ignorance, lack of diligent Bible study, and resisting, quenching and grieving the Holy Spirit, sadly, have been a part of my life. God was patient and merciful, Christian, and by His grace, blessed me to open my heart to Jesus before I died. Consider where you would be, if the Lord stopped His patient ways with you.

We are carried away and enticed by our own lust, which gives birth to sin. When sin is accomplished, it brings forth death (James 1:14-15). This is the path of all natural men born once in this world. We must receive Christ into our hearts and be born again to receive the gift of the Holy Spirit and faith. This is God's work and way for a life that escapes spiritual death because of sin. To God be the glory. We must be forgiven of sin, and have the penalty for our sin paid for by Christ, or else we will have to pay our own penalty. It is a man's choice. Sadly, since a man does not have the ability to make this payment alone, according to the Bible, he is separated from God for eternity. The sin of resisting the Holy Spirit by rejecting Jesus Christ as Savior and Lord is committed by the unbeliever (Acts 7:51). This is a solemn word that shows a man that is uncircumcised in his heart. It shows a man unwilling or stubborn in his flesh to work through the convictions in his conscience, that the Lord took to claim him for salvation. In the heart of God's elect, this resistance is overpowered and after a struggle, the throne of Christ is set up in his soul. God's patience and love works with us in the struggle. Grace is greater than our sin (Rom. 5:20-21). God leads justice in us to a great victory in Jesus. Amen.

God's grace of perfect patience for our life on earth will not depart His children until they enter heaven. One example of God's patience was shown in the life of Paul. Paul was grateful to God, who considered him faithful and put him into service. Though he was previously a great sinner and acted ignorantly in unbelief, God showed him mercy (1 Tim. 1:12-13). "He found mercy that Jesus might demonstrate His perfect patience, as an example for those who would believe in Him for eternal life" (1 Tim. 1:16). Paul was a pattern for the sake of himself and others, that Jesus shows great patience in the conversion of great sinners. God showed him faith and love in Jesus, that great sinners might not despair of the grace of God. We too can be found in His mercy and patience and believe in Christ for eternal life.

The consideration of Divine patience, Christian, should leave us with strong desires to be grateful to God. They should also leave us with desires to be patient with others, in the way He has been patient with us. To be patient, is to be like the Lord. "Therefore, you are to be perfect, as your heavenly Father is perfect" (Matt. 5:48). It is our duty as Christians, to press on to lay hold of that for which we were apprehended by Christ. We aim at perfection in grace and holiness, and desire to know Him and the power of His resurrection (Phil. 3:10-12). We have a goal in the Christian life; it is a maturity to be in the likeness of Jesus. We grow in grace and knowledge. We read the Bible and discover the goodness and patience of God to bring us to holiness and to love Him in return (1 John 4:19). We learn the truth about God. "If you abide in My word, then you are truly disciples of Mine; and you shall know the truth, and the truth shall make you free" (John 8:31-32). If we abide in His word, then we are disciples indeed. It is not how a man begins, Christian, but how he continues and ends that distinguishes a true disciple. Being made in God's image and rich in His Spirit, you should reflect His patience in your life. God gives the gift of patience to us and empowers its use in our lives (2 Tim. 2:1, James 1:3). In time, we learn to seek and walk, by the grace of God, in the gift of an obedience of faith in Jesus. The promise for an obedient believer, is that he will be loved by God and that Jesus will manifest or disclose Himself to us (John 14:21). Jesus becomes a glorious reality to us and the written Word luminous.

We gain a greater sense of being chosen and transformed by the Spirit of God. We learn the joy of the Lord (John 15:11). We learn the terrific truth that God was patient. "Now to the King eternal, immortal, invisible, the only God, be honor and glory forever and ever. Amen" (1 Tim. 1:17).

Goodness

"O taste and see that the Lord is good; how blessed is the man that takes refuge in Him" (Ps. 34:8).

Dear Christian,

In this life, we start out as "a natural man, which does not accept the things of the Spirit of God, for they seem to be foolishness to him" (1 Cor. 2:14). The deep truth about the goodness of God is unknown to us. The truth about sin, because it sounds more interesting and might feel good, is more welcome into our hearts. We do not really know about God's goodness yet, but we get the feeling that the church and maybe God too are not the place we are going to have a good time. Eventually, we end up having some trouble in life, struggle with certain situations, experience jealousies and strife and adverse circumstances. Taken together, all this does not seem to be consistent with the ideas of a good God. We have had a lot of wars between nations which have littered our world history with dead people. We have diseases, accidents, sickness and addictions and some good people die young. The world is awash with ideas of the evolution of man, which dares to suggest there is no God. The universe does not appear to be a very friendly place if we live by the survival of the fittest. Some folks think that if there is a God, He is indifferent and does not care about people. Some folks think that God is not involved with the ongoing universe He created or the people in it. Besides, He might have trouble keeping track of so many folks. Some people dismiss God because they do not like the idea of being accountable to God. The opinion of God they harbor is wrong because it is uninformed.

It is imperative that we seek and discover the good truth about God by reading the word of God. The Bible tells us that faith comes by hearing the word of God (Rom. 10:17). For some folks, this might start with the only verse they have heard or know. "For God so loved the world that He gave His only begotten Son, that whoever believes in Him should not perish, but have eternal life" (John 3:16). By the grace of God, this verse can get a hold in their heart and does not let go. When you read the Bible, you find that it tells us, "The Lord is good; His lovingkindness is everlasting and His faithfulness to all generations" (Ps. 100:5). The Bible also tells us that "the whole world lies in the power of the evil one" (1John 5:19). This is not good. "The god of this world has blinded the minds of the unbelieving, that they might not see the light of the gospel of the glory of Christ, who is the image of God" (2 Cor. 4:4). The prince of the power of the air is the spirit that works in the sons of disobedience (Eph. 2:2). This is not good. The ruler of this world will be cast out (John 12:31). The great dragon and his angels have been thrown down (Rev. 12:9). The Bible tells us that the Son of God appeared for this purpose, that He might destroy the works of the devil" (1 John 3:8). This is good news. Amen.

There is absolute perfection in God's nature and nothing can be added to it to make it better. "The goodness of God endures continually" (Ps. 52:1). Some versions of the Bible, like the New American Standard, replaces the word "goodness" with "lovingkindness". God is really the only good God (Mark 10:18). "God is love" (1 John 4:8). God is originally good; it is His essence. God is infinitely, immutably and eternally good. In creation, God was good. "God saw everything He had made, and behold, it was very good" (Gen. 1:31). "The earth is full of the lovingkindness of the Lord" (Ps. 33:5). God's goodness is His glory. Amen. Moses had heard the voice of the Lord from the fire (Ex. 2:3-4), and out of a pillar of cloud (Ex. 33:9), but he wanted to see more. Moses wanted to see the ways of God (Ex. 33:13) and to see His glory (Ex. 33:18). God gave a gracious reply to the request of Moses. He said "I Myself will make all My goodness pass before you, and will proclaim the name of the Lord before you, and I will be gracious to whom I will be gracious, and will show compassion on whom I will show compassion" (Ex. 33:19). The Lord answered the request of Moses by letting him see His glory, when He was passing by, he could not see His face but only His back (Ex. 33:22-23). At the time the Lord passed by him, He proclaimed, "The Lord, the Lord God, merciful and gracious, long-suffering and abundant in goodness and truth" (Ex. 34:6). We know God more by His mercy, Christian, than His majesty. We know God more by faith than by sight. We know God more by the wisdom in His word, than by whatever our hopes and personal opinions may be. We will come to know God by His abundant goodness. Amen.

"For Thou hast magnified Thy word according to all Thy name" (Ps. 138:2). Beyond all question, Christian, the word of God discloses to us the most we can know about God, and our pardon of sin and salvation. These things are learned from God and not our schools of philosophy. There is a great tenderness in God, and a great goodness of God that will be in His glory. The devil just wants you to see God as a kill-joy and tough taskmaster. The goodness of God is revealed to us by the grace of God. Amen. The word of God is clear about how to be saved, though many have chosen to remain blind and/or ignorant about what God requires of us. The word of God is clear that God is good. He is merciful, gracious and long-suffering. There is joy in the discovery that God is love and good, and is pleased to be gracious. Let this God be your God. God's prerogative is to save; God's grace is His own to give (Rev. 4:11), and God's sovereignty appears in God's goodness (Ex. 33:19, Rom. 9:15). "So, then it does not depend on the man who wills or the man who runs, but on God who has mercy" (Rom. 9:16). He is the potter, and we are the clay (Isa. 29:16). God "did this so He might make known the riches of His glory upon vessels of mercy, which He prepared beforehand for glory" (Rom.

9:23). "We must come trembling to the Lord and His goodness" (Hosea 3:5). We are to work out "our salvation with fear and trembling" (Phil. 2:12). We are not only to fear the Lord because of His power and greatness, but also because of His goodness and mercy. To fear God's goodness, Christian, means to be amazed He chose you to admire, adore and worship Him in spirit and truth. It is our responsibility to be careful to honor the Lord and not offend His goodness.

"There is forgiveness with Thee, that Thou mayest be feared" (Ps. 130:4). We rejoice with trembling in the goodness of God. We did not earn God's goodness, and we do not deserve it, nevertheless, our hearts receive this great wonder. Our understanding of forgiveness leaves us with a fear and awe of God. God expresses such a great goodness for our sinful souls, that fear is our response. We humbly receive His word, and know a sense of peace and honor by the gracious work of the Holy Spirit. The grace for me, while others may be passed by is a deep mystery, that I must leave with the Lord. I know that God's word is true and good. I know that God is sovereign, and perfect in judgment. God owns us, we have been bought with a price (1 Cor. 6:20). In His secret eternal will and counsel, He decided on the persons He would give effectual grace to. God is a debtor to no man, and His grace is His own to give. The work of your salvation, Christian, is well ordered and certain. The preservation and supply for His children with the riches of Christ is the goodness of God. The preparation of our soul for heaven by sanctification is God's work of mercy, preparing a weak vessel for His glory. We are called and prepared beforehand for His presence so that no man can boast, and because God is good.

"How great is Thy goodness, which Thou hast stored up for those who fear Thee, which Thou hast wrought for those who take refuge in Thee, before the sons of man!" (Ps. 31:19). God alone has all the perfections necessary to define what is good. God is the source of all good and everything He does is all good. God is especially good to His children. God stores up into our hearts a fear of the Lord, that is, respect and reverence for Himself. He builds up in us the hopes He is safe as a refuge. We are adopted children and the Lord knows how to give us good things (Matt. 7:11). It is God's gift of faith that grows us up as His children, and then the adoption by God, seals our place as heirs with His riches. We are disciplined as God's children; this also is His goodness to us. It is laying up for us an obedience, which will lead to greater comforts and service according to His will and the gifts He provides. You cannot really conceive of what it means to your soul to have a friend in Jesus, until you have received Him into your heart. Sadly, it is clear to me that those who hate God and talk poorly of Jesus do not know what they are talking about. God's goodness will set a man's soul aflame. Read the word, meditate on it and let your soul sail up to the Lord in admiration and the fear of His goodness. God's faithfulness is good: He turns mourning into dancing and girds us with gladness. We sing praises and give thanks because His glory will be a good thing for us. God's faithfulness to the covenant of grace supports our believing in Christ and our trusting in His strength. Christ becomes the refuge from which we behold the goodness of God. "Surely goodness and lovingkindness will follow me all the days of my life" (Ps. 23:6). "For the Lord is good; His lovingkindness is everlasting and His faithfulness to all generations" (Ps. 100:5). Amen.

The goodness of God's character promotes the happiness of His children. God is holy (1 Pet. 1:6), and He is not a liar (Num. 23:19). He does not change His mind. I cannot imagine a God who is evil or would lie to the children He created. I cannot imagine a God who would make promises and not keep them or not be able to keep them. I cannot imagine a God who is not telling us the truth about eternal life with Jesus in heaven (John 3:16). God is love (1 John 4:8). I cannot imagine a God who would tell us about the love of God, and it was all a fiction. I cannot imagine a God who is waiting for us to die, so He can punish us. The Bible tells us that God is forgiving and a refuge (Ps. 46), and will remember our sins no more (Heb. 8:12). I cannot believe that God would tell us one thing and do another. God says that "when He appears, we shall be like Him, because we shall see Him just as He is" (1John 3:2).

God's word is true and trustworthy, Christian, and you can have confidence in it. "You have been born again not of seed which is perishable but imperishable, that is, through the living and abiding word of God" (1 Pet. 1:23). I have experienced the word of faith in my heart by hearing the word of Christ (Rom. 10:17). Amen. "The word of the Lord abides forever" (1 Pet. 1:25). His grace has brought me safe this far in my life. I know that "He who began a good work in you will perfect it until the day of Christ Jesus" (Phil. 1:6). I have experienced "the fruit of righteousness which comes through Jesus Christ, to the glory and praise of God" (Phil.1:11). I'm not perfect, but I have a peace, that by the grace of God, passes my understanding about righteousness. I believe the Bible is true and powerful, and reading it gave me a true knowledge that God is holy and good, really good.

God has a good purpose for everything that goes on in your life. In His way and time, He will rescue you from your earthly trouble and trials and temptations to sin. You will learn to boast in the Lord and not yourself. After you die, it will be the goodness and power of God that will be keeping the promise of releasing your soul into His heavenly presence. The wisdom and power of God is able to deliver you from the furnace of burning fire (Dan. 3:17). You are not being used or manipulated or abused by God. He is saving your soul for a happy eternal life. Salvation is only possible through His plan and His way. We are saved by grace when we come to Jesus and receive His righteousness to "wear" as a robe to stand safely in the presence of God. Amen. He will be standing with you in judgment. Your faith and the church itself are built upon a rock, and the gates of Hades shall not prevail against it (Matt. 16:18). Some think the rock designates Peter, some Christ, but most I think take it as the truth and faith from the confession of Christ as the Son of God. The foundation and assurance of salvation, in Christianity, lies in the heart of believers. A Christian's trust is in the sacrifice of Jesus on the cross. A Christian knows that God is true and that God is good. Amen. The good work of God's grace in your soul has just begun; it was God who started it in regeneration, and He will finish it for His glory in your glorification. God's work is always good and perfect. It honors God when we live right and abound in good works. "According to Thy lovingkindness remember Thou me, For Thy goodness' sake, O Lord" (Ps. 25:7). To God be the glory.

The goodness of God has been described as abundant (Ex. 34:6) and great (Ps. 31:19). "The lovingkindness of God endures all day long" (Ps. 52:1). "The Lord is good to all and His mercies are over all His works" (Ps. 145:9). Even those who hate Him, breath air and eat food, and have the sun shine on them. The world was planned for happiness. Though sin marred God's work, Christian, the curse was met by Jesus. He is God's perfect goodness to heal us from bondage and any disease. God has a sympathy for human misery. "Good and upright is the Lord; therefore, He instructs sinners in the way" (Ps. 25:8). In God's sovereignty, He chooses a people for Himself and pardons them in mercy, which is good. We grow in knowledge and strength from His work of providence. We grow by His wisdom and power, which is good. Our obedience and purity, is a beam of His goodness. "How blessed is the one whom Thou dost choose, and bring near to Thee, to dwell in Thy courts, we will be satisfied with the goodness of Thy house, Thy holy temple" (Ps. 65:4). Blessed is the man who God has chosen, and subdued his unwillingness to come to Jesus. Blessed is the man that God works His transforming grace into that leads to his acceptance, obedience, sonship and happiness. Acceptance means we have been brought near to a good God. Acceptance leads us to peaceful abiding, and the sense we are at home with a good God. Amen.

Home is where we know His love and peace, and that our dwelling place is with the Lord. Once we were lost, but now we have been found (Luke 15:24); once we were blind, but now we can see (John 9:25). Nearness to the Lord is the foundation of true happiness. God does not give this goodness to you, Christian, to take it away. "Do you think lightly of the riches of His kindness and forbearance and patience, not knowing that the kindness of God leads you to repentance?" (Rom. 2:4). "The gifts and the calling of God are irrevocable" (Rom. 11:29). This is all good.

Amen. Permanence from the word of God means perseverance, and becomes highly precious to a Christian. The promise of surviving takes away the nature of man to fear the future. This everlasting sensation in the spirit of a saved man shows that our God is a really good God. "Rock of ages, cleft for me, let me hide myself in Thee" (Rock of Ages, Augustus Toplady,1776). At the same time, I remind you that we are always responsible to "work out our salvation with fear and trembling" (Phil. 2:12). God clearly does the miracle of saving our soul, which we clearly cannot do. Our responsibility is to receive this gift of goodness from God, and be responsible with it. It also comes with enabling grace. This may be hard to understand, or appear as a mystery to us, but I'm confident that God is good and righteous in His dealings with us. The call of God to be holy is clearer than the understanding of how and why He has called us. It makes me sick to sin against God, Christian, because I know I have sinned against His goodness to me. It is His love, patience and goodness that leads me to confess and repent of my sin (1 John 1:9). God has great mercy in store for us. It is a great goodness, that we do not deserve, that we are effectually called home by God's grace, and in spite of our weakness, it is without His repentance. God is not sorry that He gave us grace to be saved. Thank you, Jesus.

God depends on no one else for His goodness, He has it in and of Himself; it is His essence to be good. No one else has a goodness they can claim because it initially all came from God. God is infinitely and immutably good. Divine goodness can be known by angels and a vast number of human beings. "The goodness of God endures forever" (Ps. 52:1). Nothing can possibly be better than God. God has a good will and does good to others, especially His children. The goodness of God is His choice and way. The goodness of God is in the predisposition of His perfections, to deal with us well and in His righteousness. "Everything created by God is good" (1 Tim. 4:4). The goodness of God embraces all of His attributes. He is all good. It is grace, patience, truth, pity, righteousness, compassion and holiness. The goodness of God makes His wisdom and power work for us. Our creation and redemption are the proof of His goodness. Amen. Goodness is the motive of His action, and His wisdom and power serve the divine action. The responsibilities we have with the Lord, Christian, are not for His advantages, but for our own good. "What does the Lord require from you, but to fear the Lord your God, to walk in all His ways and love Him, and to serve the Lord your God with all your heart and with all your soul, and to keep the Lord's commandments and His statutes which I'm commanding you today for your good?" (Deut. 10:12-13). In creation, God's goodness would become known, not for Him to acquire anything. God cannot be vain or do anything to puff Himself up, He is already complete. We discover God's goodness, because He chose to reveal it to us. The revelation of this nature of God was not to bless Himself, but to communicate something of His goodness to us. We know that God is love (1 John 4:8), God is light (1 John 1:5), God is holy (1 Pet. 1:16), God is faithful (1 Cor. 10:13), God is spirit (John 4:24) and that God is good (Ps. 34:8). Amen.

"I would have despaired unless I had believed I would see the goodness of the Lord in the land of the living. Wait for the Lord; be strong and let you heart take courage" (Ps. 27:13-14). "The earth is full of Thy lovingkindness O Lord" (Ps. 119:64). God is good to all, but not to the same extent. God is the Lord of what He gives, Christian, His grace is His own. His wisdom rules the distribution of His goodness. Since I believe in God's goodness, I want to honor Him by faith and love Him and share His goodness with others. "Thou art good and do good" (Ps. 119:68). The goodness of God is worthy of praise. The justice of God is a part of the goodness in His nature (Ex. 34:7). The guilty would not be cleared. The design of laws with the punishment of offenders is to promote goodness and restrain evil and protect the innocent. The judgments of God are good (Ps. 119). The afflictions that God allows in our lives is good. They are good for our glory and eternal good. God judges us that we might not be condemned with the world (1 Cor. 11:32).

Affliction is a sign of God's love. "My son, do not regard lightly the discipline of the Lord, nor faint when you are reproved by Him; for those whom the Lord loves He disciplines. It is for discipline that we endure" (Heb. 12:5-7). It is the kindness and goodness of God that we bear some trouble in this world than to be miserable for an eternity. He helps us now, to prevent our ruin. By the grace of God, Christian, you have come to know the Father of spirits; if you are subject to Him, you shall live (Heb. 12:9). In the midst of affliction, God remembers mercy. God deals with the heart. Nothing touches you apart from the will of the Father in heaven. Therefore, do not look upon your trial and affliction as unnecessary. God's afflictions are for your profit. You are not being punished for your sins. God has already dealt with your sins in Jesus. He was our substitute, and we cannot be charged with guilt and condemned. The believer is not punished, but may be disciplined for his good. Your suffering will be tempered by the providence of God. Usually, we take our problems too seriously and focus on the experience, rather than the goodness that is coming into our lives because God is at work in us. We will be growing closer to Jesus. He will provide for you the most rewarding experiences and pleasures in your life. Amen

God's discipline enhances your spiritual life. It is evidence of His presence and Fatherly love, and your adoption. "God disciplines us for our good, that we may share His holiness" (Heb. 12:10). Discipline to our flesh and blood is one thing that our flesh may not understand. Usually, we are not able to use the reasoning from our carnal minds to discover the reality of sanctified tribulation. It is above us and beyond our reach. The discernment of our discipline comes in the understanding of our faith. Our discipline begins when we come to Jesus and are born again of the Spirit. We are being fashioned by God into a new man. We are disciplined to become the man that God wants us to be. Adversity and disappointment from His hand are designed to make us stronger in Jesus, and that is a good thing. We are trained by discipline. It may be rigorous, strenuous and self-sacrificing training of the body and the mind, like an athlete. This is the grace of God, Christian, working into our wills a desire in our hearts to run the race and "exercise self-control in all things" (1 Cor. 9:25). Life can have a lot of struggles in it, both little ones and big ones.

The good things I have received have come out of my trouble and not my successes. "Affliction is the best piece of furniture in my house" (Charles Spurgeon). Afterwards Christian, the purpose for God's work in your life, including the temptations, trials and tests, will have a better understanding. Discipline will yield the peaceful fruit of righteousness to those who have been trained by it (Heb. 12:11). I'm not perfect, Christian, but I know this verse to be true. It may take too much time for your training, by your measure, but God knows your heart. He knows what you need to be spiritually strong, and will accomplish His goal in His perfect time. The affliction or discipline will produce peace and holiness. Without holiness no man will see the Lord (Heb. 12:14). Amen.

The stress for your salvation is laid upon your holiness. You will know the importance and emphasis of being right with God to walk with God. God is being good to you when He faithfully speaks words of wisdom about holiness to your heart. God is being good to us when He builds our interest and desires to understand the Bible and seek salvation. God is being good to us when He sends us into the Bible for faith and gives desires to walk by the Spirit after Jesus. "We know that God causes all things to work together for good to those who love God, to those who are called according to His purpose" (Rom. 8:28). Though afflictions in themselves are trouble to us, the effects are overruled and directed by an all-wise God for our good. They are useful. Afflictions train believers and promote salvation. Afflictions can be disappointing sorrows and dash our hopes, which does not sound that good. We hope that God will only be good to us, because we are His children. The good news is that the providence of God is working on, and by, the believer's side; this is all good. There is a spiritual good that God brings forth from affliction. God builds faith, which is the assurance of things hoped for (Heb. 11:1). Faith is tested and becomes embattled, but the purpose of God cannot be thwarted, and we become stronger. "If God be for us, who is against us?" (Rom. 8:31). The Lord, Christian, becomes the strength of our life, and this is all good. Amen.

The goodness of God is revealed in creation. From nothing, He created an incredible variety of creatures and tremendous diversity in human beings. To be with Jesus is a lot better than not to be. From dust, He brought forth a man, which is a very complicated biological masterpiece. "For Thou didst form my inward parts; Thou didst weave me in my mother's womb. I will give thanks to Thee, for I'm fearfully and wonderfully made; wonderful are Thy works, and my soul knows it very well" (Ps. 139:13-14). The discoveries of the anatomy and physiology of man, show us a number of complicated organ systems that are all integrated to function as a unit. The body is able to run and jump, see, hear, smell, touch and speak. We have intelligence and can express feelings. We have a soul with a conscience that can understand things, and a will to make choices. We were made after God's image in holiness. "Let Us make man in Our image, according to Our likeness" (Gen. 1:26). Though unborn, the Bible tells us that God took care of us and brought us into the light. The goodness of God was with us all the time, even in the beginning when we were being formed. Amen.

The goodness of God remains with you during your lifetime to bring you to Jesus for salvation. God will faithfully keep you and discipline you for holiness and his eternal presence in heaven. Because He is good, His grace will always be sufficient for you. You came from God and will return to Him. In the meantime, on earth you will live and thrive in a world He made to support your life and bring you delight. In the meantime, you will grow in grace and knowledge and live long enough on earth to accomplish His divine purpose for you. God put all things under man's feet, and gave him dominion over the other creatures (Gen. 1:26, Ps. 8:6-8). "How majestic is your name in all the earth" (Ps. 8:9). God gave man water and light, animals and plants for necessity and delight. "The earth is full of Thy possessions" (Ps. 104:24). God gave delight in the beauty of colors to see, odors for our nose to smell. Harmony of sounds to hear and food to please the palate. God gave us laws and governments to regulate and govern us for our own good (Rom. 13:1-7). God created man upright (Eccles. 7:29). Our renewed lives enjoy the righteous ways of God, because they establish peace in our communities (Ps. 119:164-165). God promises man a mighty goodness with an eternal reward after the earthly life. He promises good future blessings with the Lord, in a place we cannot fully conceive of now, but we know it will be good. We will see how large the Lord's goodness really is. We believe it will be an amazing goodness, and such a place that it will surpass any idea of good we may have in our minds from this life.

The gospel is good will to all men. "Glory to God in the highest, and on earth peace, good will toward men" (Luke 2:14). We have good reason to celebrate God's goodness in redemption. To God, this will be glory in the highest. To man, this good will means our peace. This good will means our praise to Him forevermore will arise from His own grace and mercy. When man fell from God's created goodness, we did not fall from His infinite goodness. Divine goodness recovered us, Amen. It was a miraculous goodness for God to send His only begotten Son (John 3:16), while we were yet sinners (Rom. 5:8), for our freedom and salvation. God is love (1John 4:8), and this goodness in Him is love. We will forever worship God as a God of love. The gospel comes from God's infinite goodness and is called the "glorious gospel of the blessed God" (1 Tim. 1:11). We are delivered from the corruption of our nature, and the punishment for our sin. We are delivered from ignorance and free to understand that God is very good. He restores a rebellious creature, defiled by sin, and pays the penalty Himself. In His Son's death, we are forgiven of sin, adopted into the family of God, and reconciled to the Father. We deserved to die under a curse, and God showed us a remarkable goodness. "The grace of God has appeared, bringing salvation to all men" (Titus 2:11). The grace of God for us is His Son. We cannot value the merit of Jesus Christ alone, but must also remember the goodness of the Father and the Holy Spirit. The purpose of redemption, born out of the goodness of God, preceded the merit of Christ. God sent His Son (John 3:16,34). Christ gave Himself and is called the lamb of God (John 1:29) and the wisdom of God (1 Cor. 1:30). The goodness of God for our salvation was the Divine goodness worked out by the Father, the Son and the Holy Spirit. This work was a bountiful goodness and an immense goodness. God gave the highest gift possible for our redemption in His Son, a gift as dear to Him as Himself. He saved us by grace to grow into His own image; to reflect His goodness, and the brightness of His glory (Heb. 1:3). His gifts for hearts and souls are a great testimony of His goodness for us. Amen.

The goodness of God appears in the nature of our bodies. In creation we were similar to animals in our body, and to angels in our spirit. In creation, God made man in the image of God (Gen,1:26). That is, He gave man a soul, which is an intelligent immortal spirit with understanding, will and power. God's image included righteousness and holiness (Eph. 4:24, Col. 3:10, Eccl. 7:29). Man was holy and happy. Man lost a lot by the fall, but God's grace and goodness were greater than man's sin (Rom. 5:20-21). After the fall, God put enmity between the serpent's seed and Eve's seed, and said; "He shall bruise you on the head, and you shall bruise him on the heel (Gen. 3:15). The Savior is the seed of the woman. Satan shall bruise his heel or human nature with suffering and death. The devil put into the heart of Judas to betray Christ, Peter to deny Him, the chief priests to prosecute Him and Pilate to condemn Him. Christ's heel was bruised when His feet were pierced at the crucifixion. In the life of Christ, He triumphed over the devil by casting him out of the bodies of people and rescued them from his power. It was "Through death He rendered powerless him who had the power of death, that is, the devil" (Heb. 2:14). By His death, He gave an incurable blow to the head of the devil's kingdom which cannot be healed. By the grace of God, the Lord treads Satan under our feet (Rom. 16:20) and will soon cast him into the lake of fire (Rev. 20:10). Because of the triumph of Jesus, Christian; when we receive Him into our heart, we get a new nature with the promise of forgiveness and heaven. From the triumph of Jesus, we learn the grace of God's goodness. Amen.

In God's goodness, we can be born again and receive a new heart and a new spirit (Ezek. 36:26). In God's goodness, He chose to put His Spirit in us and cause us to walk in His statutes (Ezek. 36:27). As a new man, we have His godly nature in us, and by the grace of God are called brothers (Heb.2:11). Our nature before Christ was higher than the animals (Gen. 1:26-28), but lower than the angels (Ps. 8:5). In God's goodness to us, He makes us one with Himself. Amen.

"For in Him all the fulness of Deity dwells in bodily form, and in Him we have been made complete (Col. 2:9-10). We wait eagerly for the redemption of our body (Rom. 8:23). "It is sown a perishable body, it is raised an imperishable body; it is sown in dishonor, it is raised in glory; it is sown in weakness; it is raised in power; it is sown a natural body, it is raised a spiritual body (1 Cor. 15: 42-44). We must be changed from mortal to immortality. We wait for the Lord Jesus Christ; who will transfer the body of our humble state into conformity with the body of His glory" (Phil. 3:21). The Son of God assumed our nature in Christ, and went back to heaven to be at the Father's right hand, far above all authority and every name that is named (Eph. 1; 20-21). The Son was to be the "head over all things to the church, which is His body, the fulness of Him who fills all in all" (Eph. 1: 22-23). In the goodness of God, our nature is joined to a heavenly Person, one equal with God (Phil. 2:6). Because of Christ, God has shown us spiritual favor, which will be all glorious. To show such sinners and rebels as us, these gracious acts of goodness, is beyond my human understanding, but I pray never beyond my eternal gratitude.

The goodness of God was clearly manifest in both the Old and New Covenants that He made with man. It was from the goodness of God that He would make any covenant with man at all, and then make a New Covenant which was so much better than the Old Covenant. It was a greater goodness that He would establish a covenant of grace, than keep the covenant of works. The first or old covenant was according to the law; if you are not obedient and sin, you must die. The second or New Covenant was by grace; if you believe in the merits of Jesus Christ, you shall live. "For you are not under law, but under grace" (Rom. 6:14). In the first covenant, He is a Lord, and in the second covenant, He is a Husband. The New Covenant is richer in mercy and love. The first covenant was human and failed, while the second covenant was divine and immutable. The rewards in the first covenant were earned, whereas in the second covenant, the rewards are a gift of grace. The righteousness of the first covenant was the righteousness of a man, while the righteousness of the second covenant was the righteousness of God (2 Cor. 5:21). The first covenant required obedience, while the second covenant required sincerity. The New Covenant had better promises for justification and sanctification than the Old Covenant (Heb. 8:6). The New Covenant has promises of the Lord's acceptance and assistance for progress and perseverance in grace and holiness and glory in heaven. The New Covenant reveals God's mercy, love, wisdom and grace. It is His Son that purchased it and the Holy Spirit that builds it into our souls. Amen. To God be the glory. The goodness of God in the New Covenant is written on our hearts and put into our minds, with a promise that He will be our God, and we shall be His people (Heb. 8:10). It is the goodness of God that He lays the foundation and provides the grace and strength for us to do our part. The Lord gives us a good understanding and stays with us as we learn to believe and trust in Jesus. The Lord gives a heart to love His laws and a conscience to hear His work to guide our soul. He gives the power to practice them and profess them. The Lord gives the strength and truth to be sincere. God is faithful and His grace is always sufficient. God's love for us in Jesus is what fills the New Covenant with all His goodness.

The true goodness of God for our salvation is shown to be remarkable, in providing the necessary gift of faith. We are "saved by grace through faith; and that not of ourselves, it is the gift of God; not as a result of works, that no one should boast. For we are His workmanship, created in Christ Jesus for good works" (Eph. 2:8-10). If we have difficulty receiving the Lord, Christian, it most likely lies in the nature of our pride and the stubbornness of our will. So long as we continue to think we know better about what is righteous, we cannot rise to the humble place of knowing an obedience of faith with the Lord. The condition of the New Covenant is a sincere though many times weak faith. It is a faith nursed along by the work of the Holy Spirit in the providence of

God. In our view, as a natural man it might seem too humbling. Our covenant with the Lord is called an evangelical covenant; meaning it is Bible-based, sincere and renewed by us through confession (1 John 1:9). To enter the covenant, God draws us to first consider and then receive Jesus into our hearts for the forgiveness of our sin (John 3:16). God accepts what His Son did for us in dying on a cross to pay our penalty for sin. When we receive Christ, we are born again (John 3:3), and receive a new heart and spirit and the gift of faith (Ezek. 36:26). Faith grows from grace to grace (John 1:16, 2 Pet. 3:18). "The righteousness of God is revealed from faith to faith; as it is written, but the righteous man shall live by faith" (Rom. 1:17). By the grace of faith, we grow into a willingness in our soul to let God be God, believe Jesus is our mediator and walk by the Spirit. Faith honors God and humbles us. God is gentle and patient, and loving in the work of keeping us constant in our obedience. God is faithful. He came to earth and died for us that we "might have life, and might have it abundantly" (John 10:10). Life can be good, but to have spiritual life in fulness and from the dead, is abundant and really good. Amen.

God's goodness is evident in the lives of all kinds of men. His power for goodness works in bad men's lives and even in the lives of men who hate Him. God is able to turn any man to Christ. He can snatch people that are totally misinformed. He captured Paul on the road to Damascus when he was planning to arrest believers and bring them bound to Jerusalem (Acts 9). He has rescued folks that "were formerly alienated and hostile in mind, engaged in evil deeds" (Col. 1:21), and reconciled them to the gospel. He has looked after folks that have turned their back on Him and closed down their conscience. He can turn folks who seem to enjoy their sin disease with all its misery and distractions, and convict them of the consequences of their behavior. Man, no matter how bad or self-righteous he may be, cannot raise himself out of sin and self to receive God's grace of goodness. Being aware of God and growing in grace and knowledge is not what a natural man is looking for to complete his life. Only God can set the hook in a man's jaw and turn him to salvation. Waking a man up and imputing the righteousness of Jesus to a sinner is a miracle of grace and a good work of God. God's goodness can also appear in His answers to our prayers. We are encouraged to ask, seek and knock and be persistent in prayer for God's help. The heavenly Father knows how to give good things to those who ask Him (Matt. 7:11). Good gifts are called the Holy Spirit in another passage (Luke 11:13). Amen. "The Lord longs to be gracious to you. And, therefore He waits on high to have compassion on you. For the Lord is a God of justice; how blessed are those who long for Him" (Isa. 30:18). It is never too late to call upon God. So long as you have breath, His goodness leads Him to wait in love, keeping the door of life open.

God is patient, Christian, and knows we are but dust and weak. He knows we will have an imperfect obedience. He knows that sometimes we only have a will for Him and not a work; even then, His goodness does not lead Him to reject us. "Thou hast taken account of my wanderings; put my tears in a bottle; are they not in Thy book?" (Ps. 56:8). The trial of our faith in Jesus is precious in the Father's sight. God has an exact knowledge of us, and has even felt our infirmities, and is still good and generous in His estimation of us. The devil wants you to take up hard thoughts about God. The devil would have us believe that God is a tough taskmaster; when the truth is, He is a good, tender and gracious heavenly Father. O Lord, I know I have behaved poorly at times and been weak in the battle against sin. I have tears in a bottle. The tears are because I knew of your goodness, and I know I still missed the mark. The Lord was present to help me, but sometimes I was not willing to be helped. It is a wretched experience for a believer. It is part of being broken to self, and the way to more deeply appreciate the Lord's goodness in His patience. I experienced being sick of myself and sick of sin. We are never perfect and live with reminders to sin. At the same time, we know we have the Lord and the goodness of His law ruling in our hearts. By the grace of God, we keep attaining some victory, but the deepest sense of triumph awaits the presence of Jesus in heaven. I know, He can keep me from stumbling and can make me stand in His presence blameless with great joy (Jude 25). The tears will be remembered to bear testimony of the truth and sincerity of the gift of faith in my heart from the Lord. The tears will be remembered to tell the story of God's goodness versus the devil's malevolent designs and my natural ways of life. The tears will reveal the goodness of God in the triumph of Jesus and the work of the Holy Spirit to save my soul. To God will be the glory. The cry of faith for God and His goodness will prove to be a dreadful thing to my spiritual enemies. "If God is for us, who is against us?" (Rom. 8:31).

The goodness of God is experienced in temptation. The Lord is fully aware of all that goes on when we are tempted and how we respond. God is at the beginning, during, and at the end of every temptation. He knows our corruption, and the weak areas where temptation exerts power over our desires and will. The conflict of the two natures, the law of sin and the law of God in the inner man (Rom. 7:22-23), is clearly described in the Bible (Ro. 7:14-25). We do not practice what we would like to do, but do the very thing we hate (Rom. 7:15). Evil is present in us at the same time we have the love and spirit from God. We win some battles, and we lose some battles. We will never be perfect in this world (1 John 1:8), but we will not bleed to death or be lost. "If we confess our sins, He is faithful and just to forgive us of our sins and to cleanse us of all unrighteousness" (1 John 1:9). Be sincere and honest with the Lord in your cry and prayer of confession to God for His help. God is faithful; He understands our frailties. Be diligent and patient and keep on seeking the Lord. He will respond with grace and power in His time and way. God is faithful to the covenant He made with us in Jesus and righteous to Himself and His Son who provided the sacrifice. Your responsibility is confession of sin, and though already forgiven and saved, your confession is agreeing with God that you still need and want to live for Jesus. The cleansing upon confession is an immense goodness on the part of God. Amen. You will know the peace and your acceptance with God by humbling yourself in this way before the Lord. You will be grateful with the Lord for the nature of this goodness in His essence. Confession is not a license to sin. Forgiveness is a great blessing of God. Forgiveness is from the hand of a great and perfectly good King.

"There is forgiveness with Thee, that Thou mayest be feared" (Ps.130:4). Forgiving love from God reveals His willing goodness to us and produces the awe that describes the fear. Gratitude for pardon produces more awe and reverence for the Lord than punishment. God is good, and we fear Him for His mercy and justice. A true fear of God, Christian, will not make you careless about committing sin. He has promised us that the gates of Hades will not overpower His people (Matt. 16:18). He has promised that "no temptation has overtaken you but such as is common to man; and God is faithful, who will not allow you to be tempted beyond what you are able, but with the temptation will provide the way of escape also, that you may be able to endure it" (1 Cor. 10:13). "But in all these things we overwhelmingly conquer through Him who loved us" (Rom. 8:37). In temptation, we gain more evidence of His real presence with us to help us be good and strong. The goodness of God can shorten a temptation. The goodness of God can weaken the effects of temptation, and strengthen us against it by providing the spiritual armor to put on (Eph. 6: 10-17). We need God's grace with us, because our natural strength alone will never be enough to defeat the passions for sin. Sin has defiled and weakened us so much, Christian, that we cannot overpower the spiritual forces of wickedness alone. They are able to fight by a different set of rules, but God has provided us with the full armor of God that we may resist and stand firm to protect our souls (Eph. 6:13-14). Get into the word of God to learn how to put on this armor. By the grace of God, we grow stronger after battles with sin, and gain victories that nourish our faith and confidence in Jesus. Heaven will be populated by a people chosen by God, who will be veterans of spiritual warfare. God gives the grace for victory in battle, and this is a very good thing. Paul's thorn in the flesh was to prevent the pride in his spirit (2 Cor. 12:7), while the devil's purpose was to discourage and defeat his ministry. Remember that God gives grace to the humble, but He resists the proud (James 4:6). A Christian usually knows almost immediately when he is tempted to sin; by the grace of God, his heart will fly to the Lord for help. This is a good thing. Temptations can make us stronger and fit for service. Remember that Peter stumbled and denied Jesus (John 18:17-27, and later became more courageous in the cause of the gospel (Acts 2). God brings something good out of our temptations. Amen.

When we chose to sin, it stabs at our hearts and robs us of our peace. When we sin, we turn away from God's goodness. When we sin, we reveal a contempt and an evil inside us that chooses ourselves above His providence. When we sin, we neglect His goodness which was designed to lead us to repentance (Rom. 2:4). The abuse of God's goodness has cost a lot, to a lot of folks. Consider: the angels that followed Satan, Adam and his posterity, the pre-flood world, and the Jewish nation. God's grace prevailed, but it cost the life of Jesus. We abuse God's goodness when we forget His mercies and ignore the church. We abuse God's goodness when we complain about our situation and His providence. We abuse God's goodness when we expect Him to serve us or answer our prayers in a certain way. We abuse God's goodness when we trust more in our gifts than the Giver. We abuse God's goodness when we sin more freely from the benefits that He gives to us. We abuse God's goodness when His benefits encourage our pride, ease, security and sensuality. The devil wants you to think that God is unkind and not good and only sees your faults. We abuse the Lord with how we think about Him, and when we fail to be grateful every day for Jesus. Amen

The goodness of God is a great comfort, Christian, that steps into everything in our lives. God knows everything; in fact, He always knew everything. He cannot be surprised by what you think or do or, for that matter, anything that is going on in the world. God is providentially at work preparing His people to be the Bride of Christ. God is bringing forth everything into our lives, by His providential goodness and care, for us to be the best that we can be for Jesus. We are being sanctified by the Lord, "that He might present to Himself the church in all her glory, having no spot or wrinkle or any such thing; but that she should be holy and blameless" (Eph.5:27). "Christ also loved the church and gave Himself up for her" (Eph. 5:25). The glorification of the believers and the church, is intended in the sanctification of the believers and the church. The great Bible passage in Romans, outlining our victory in Christ, goes straight from justification to glorification without mentioning sanctification (Rom. 8:30). "He who began a good work in you will perfect it" (Phil. 1:6). The Bible tells us that "Thine eyes have seen my unformed substance; and in Thy book they were all written, the days that were ordained for me, when as yet there was not one of them" (Ps. 139:16). "How precious also are Thy thoughts to me, O God!" (Ps.139:17). God has intimate knowledge of us from the beginning, and even before time began. God began His work when we were not yet having one day of it. God is carrying out the work today that is necessary for our salvation and sanctification. God will complete the work of perfecting us until the day of Christ Jesus (Phil. 1:6). It is all a very good work. Amen. Before we existed, God's purposes were being attended to in the size and shape of our bodies and the nature of our faculties. We were in the mind of God in the way of foreknowledge and predestination. A lot was being done also in other people's lives that would be necessary to accomplish for us what God had for them. Only the Lord could weave this kind of web. He has the wisdom, power and knowledge to carry out His grace in all the goodness destined to be in His glory. The Lord knows the ones that belong to Him.

The Lord knows that when we are alive, how and when we will be joined to Christ, and when and how we will grow in grace and knowledge. God draws us at the right time to come to Jesus and works out all the details for the glory of His church and His Son. At one time, we may have been in a lost area in our spiritual lives, but the goodness in the power of God found us and fashioned us into a bride for the Lord Jesus. These ideas may be hard for some folks to accept. When I was a lot younger, I did not think much about what was in the Bible and spiritual life. When I got older, the Lord blest me to read and understand the Bible, and to grow by His grace in faith in Jesus. Today, I believe that nothing is impossible with God (Luke 1:37). The grace of God is necessary to believe the truth of God in the Bible. We are saved by God; by grace through faith (Eph. 2:8) not to fall back on our own wisdom, but by grace through faith to know Jesus and the power of His resurrection (Phil. 3:10). A believer knows that he was lost in sin, and that he woke up hearing about Jesus in the Bible. A miracle took place in his heart "through the living and abiding word of God" (1 Pet. 1:23). He learns about "the righteousness that comes from God on the basis of faith" in Jesus Christ (Phil. 3:9). A believer knows that he still sins, but he is comforted and enriched by knowing spiritually he has found the pearl of great value in Jesus (Matt. 13:45). We were poor and in great need, and He thought of us. That He thought of us at all makes it personal. That He already thought of us makes it providential. The goodness of God is perfect in love and His thoughts for us are called precious (Ps. 139:17). He sent me into His word, Christian, and changed my life in a way that made me glad. He gave me gifts of faith and knowledge and revealed to my heart His love and goodness. Amen.

The goodness of God instructs and comforts us over the course of our lives. "Even to your old age, I shall be the same, and even to your graying years I shall bear you! I have done it. And I shall carry you; and I shall bear you, and I shall deliver you" (Isa. 46:4). "Good and upright is the Lord; Therefore, He instructs sinners in the way" (Ps. 25:8). He counsels us with His eye upon us (Ps. 32:8). He brings us in the way of holiness and conformity to His image. He teaches us the doctrine and provides the enabling grace to walk in His way. He meets with us when we are straying. The eye of the providence of God sees everything and makes us understand that His power is in us, but the act is ours. Because the Lord is so good, Christian, penitent believers may expect forgiveness, but never demand it or think they deserve it. "For Thou, Lord art good, and ready to forgive, and abundant in lovingkindness to all who call upon Thee" (Ps. 86:5). God does not get tired of being good; His ears are open to every cry. If we knock, He opens the door. "Draw near to God and He will draw near to you" (James 4:8). He invites us to "draw near to the throne of grace that we may receive mercy and may find grace to help in time of need" (Heb. 4:16). This is all good. Those who keep waiting for the Lord, shall renew their strength (Isa. 40:31). "I'm the Lord your God, who upholds your right hand, who says to you, do not fear, I will help you" (Isa. 41:13). He is our comforter in affliction. The goodness of God is the ground of our assurance. The goodness of God is a stronghold in a time of trouble (Nahum 1:7).

It is part of our responsibility to be diligent and get a good understanding of God and meditate on it. When you read and think and study the Bible, Christian, you find out for yourself the truth about God. You find out that God is very good. The right sense of God's goodness reveals His lovingkindness and work to save your soul. What you find out about the Lord is important. What you will find is that God is holy, and He wants you to be holy also. You might agree that being holy is a good thing, but you might not be interested in that all the time in your life. Sadly, you might like your sin more than God. You might presume on His goodness which has some danger in it. On the other hand, a sense of God's goodness might be attractive, and make you more interested. You might pick the Bible up and read it and grow in faith. A sense of God's kindness makes you want to honor Him, be humble before Him and enter into worship. The correct sense of God's goodness will strike at the devil's temptations to sin in your soul. The correct sense of God's goodness assures you that God always has a good purpose for you, even during affliction. The correct sense of God's goodness is the desire to be forgiven of sin. The correct sense of God's goodness will make you patient with other people, and more interested in His plan for your life. The correct sense of God's goodness will make you grateful for what you have, and for what you do not have. The correct sense of God's goodness will make you seek His presence a lot more often. The truth of God's goodness will set you free to draw closer to Him. A sense of God's goodness will be reflected in your life, and in your testimony of Jesus. God's goodness comes with a good and clear conscience, bearing you witness in the Holy Spirit (Acts 23:1, Rom. 9:1). The sense of God's goodness, Christian, will appeal to your hearts main hopes and securities and become the main trust in your life. The full nature of God's goodness cannot be realized in this earthly life; but know this: the future will be bathed in the riches of Christ. At that time, we will have ushered into our hearts a profound and indescribable goodness. It will be a peaceful goodness and an eternal blessing. God's goodness will gladly, gratefully and rightly be understood, to be God's glory. Amen.

Faithfulness

*"The Lord's lovingkindnesses indeed never cease,
for His compassions never fail. They are new
every morning; Great is Thy faithfulness"*

(Lam. 3:22-23).

Dear Christian,

Faithfulness is God's attribute of perfect dependability. God's faithfulness, because He is true (John 14:6), means everything He says and does is trustworthy. He does not fail or forget. He does not change or disappoint. He confirms that which is true and keeps His promises. John tells us in the book of the Revelation that he "saw heaven opened and behold, a white horse, and He who sat upon it is called Faithful and True; and in righteousness He judges and wages war" (Rev. 19:11). "His name is called the Word of God" (Rev.19:13), "and on His robe and on His thigh, He has a name written, King of Kings and Lord of Lords" (Rev.19:16). A great victory is won, the beast and the false prophet are thrown alive into the lake of fire, and Satan is bound (Rev. 19:20, 20:1). This is a description by John of the second coming of Jesus Christ. When Jesus came the first time, John described His Deity and told us that the Word became flesh in the gospel of John. "In the beginning was the Word, and the Word was with God, and the Word was God" (John 1:1). "The Word became flesh and dwelt among us, and we beheld His glory, of the only begotten from the Father, full of grace and truth" (John 1:14). The names of Jesus listed in these passages

153

were; Faithful and True, Word of God, King of Kings and Lord of Lords. God is all-powerful and perfect in love, wisdom, patience, mercy, omniscient and self-existence. God is holy and cannot lie. He is Sovereign in the world He created and sustains it in justice. He has whatever it would take to be faithful to His promises. You can depend upon God. Amen. The gates of Hades cannot prevail against Him (Matt. 16:18).

The faithfulness of God is described as infinite (Ps. 36:5) and everlasting (Ps. 119:90), established (Ps. 89:2) and unfailing (Ps. 89:33). The nature of God is that His faithfulness will last forever. In a thousand years after eternity would have started, the Lord is not going to change His mind. The faithfulness of God is not like the faithfulness found upon the earth, where nothing is certain. God's nature is unchangeable, and this sure foundation will fill heaven forever. To be faithful is one of the eternal characteristics of God, and He cannot allow His faithfulness to fail (Ps. 89:33). God will never fail or forfeit His word. "God is not a man, that He should lie, nor a son of man that He should repent; has He said, and will He not do it? or has He spoken, and will He not make it good" (Num. 23:19). God cannot withdraw His promises. It is impossible for God to lie (Heb. 6:18). God does not change His mind, though He may change His way. I think this may apply in the case of the flood, where God was sorry that He made man, but Noah found grace in the eyes of God (Gen. 6:5-8). Man changed, but not God. Man became wicked and God remained faithful to His promise. The grace of God would still be secure for our redemption. From the standpoint of the gospel and God's choice, "the gift and the calling of God are irrevocable" (Rom. 11:29). Amen. God is faithful to His love (Isa. 46:4).

He had great mercy in store for the election of man. God chose the way of grace and mercy to keep His promises to man and keep His word of faithfulness to the covenant. That is, a Redeemer would come, and His words and Spirit would not depart from their mouth (Isa. 59:21). "For I, the Lord, do not change; therefore you, O sons of Jacob, are not consumed" (Mal. 3:6). God did not become unfaithful to the Abrahamic Covenant, but it was set aside for the New Testament Covenant, wherein God would call the Gentiles to Christ in Christianity. The conversion of the Gentiles is called a mystery (Eph. 3, 6, 9). In all of human history, God displays the glory of His mercy to sinners. Paul speaking to the Gentiles says, "For just as you were once disobedient to God, but now you have been shown mercy because of their disobedience, so these also now have been disobedient, in order that because of the mercy shown to you they also may be shown mercy. For God has shut up all in disobedience that He might show mercy to all" (Rom. 11: 30-32). Thus, both Jews and Gentiles were disobedient to God. By the Jews disobedience, the Gentiles came to know God's mercy. In the future, the Jews will come to know God's mercy from the Gentiles experience of God's mercy. The mercy from the Gentiles is the mercy of God in Christ. A day is coming when all the nations will come against Jerusalem, and God will pour out a Spirit of grace on the Jewish people, "and they will look on Me whom they have pierced; and they will mourn for Him and weep bitterly over Him" (Zech. 12:10). All men have been shut up under the sin of unbelief, that the promise by faith in Jesus Christ might be given to those who believe (Gal. 3:22). The purpose of God was, "that He might show mercy to all" (Rom. 11:32). It is in the unsearchable riches of God's grace, Christian, that He would show mercy to all men. Some men work so hard to establish their own righteousness, that they fail to see the righteousness that comes by faith (Rom. 3:22). The nature of God is to save by grace and to be merciful. The nature of God is to be faithful to His promises. It is impossible for God to lie, He will not change His purpose, and will save those folks throughout all generations (Ps. 119:90) who hope in Jesus. Know for a fact that God says what He means, and means what He says. Amen.

"The Lord's lovingkindnesses indeed never cease, for His compassions never fail. They are new every morning; great is Thy faithfulness" (Lam. 3: 22-23). Wherever God has life, Christian, He builds hope. The New covenant of love and faithfulness with God is a great comfort, because the compassion of the Lord cannot fail. Each day gives hope of God's mercy because He has a deep understanding of our weakness; He stays the course to reveal His promised compassion. We grow in grace and knowledge and behold His faithfulness. We have hope because God loves us and has helped us in the past. God's love for us, Christian, is by His choice, and His will is present to be faithful to us. We do not earn it and do not deserve it, yet He placed us in the new Covenant. Day after day and year after year, He remains faithful. He remains in our mind and heart and keeps us rejoicing in Jesus, especially when we read and study the word. God has been faithful throughout the years to build up my interest and heart for Jesus. God has never abandoned me only to myself, but He has stayed at the work of drawing me to Himself. Through failures, fears, and even sin, He has chosen to help me to repent and forgive me. "If we confess our sins, He is faithful and righteous to forgive us of our sins and to cleanse us from all unrighteousness" (1 John 1:9). Confession of sin results in the experience of divine forgiveness. As a new creature in Christ, we still sin and defile ourselves, but we learn the importance of confessing our sin. God is faithful at these times, to show His mercy and pardon and a restored fellowship. God chases away the guilt, not to sin again, but to value His faithful presence to lead us into paths of righteousness for His name's sake (Ps. 23:3).

When the truth is in you, Christian, you can live in truth, which means you will confess your sins. God shows a forgiving mercy, and is faithful to be patient with us. Amen. "Blessed are the poor in spirit for theirs is the kingdom of heaven" (Matt. 5:3). "Blessed are those who mourn for they shall be comforted" (Matt. 5:4). We are weak and mourn about our sin, and when we confess our sin, God gently releases forgiveness into our souls and we sense a cleansing. When we agree with God about our sin, and are sincere in seeking forgiveness, the Lord shows up to comfort us and provide proof of our fellowship with Himself. "If we walk in the light, as He Himself is in the light, we have fellowship with one another, and the blood of Jesus cleanses us from all sin" (1 John 1:7). The blood of Jesus discharges the guilt, and helps us procure future godly influences by which sin is subdued more and more. God is faithful. When you walk in the light, Christian, the Lord may use you in ways that you know, and maybe in some ways you cannot know (Eph 2:10, Matt 5:14-16). Today's mercies are for today's and tomorrow's troubles.

"O Lord, Thou art my God; I will exalt Thee, I will give thanks unto Thy name; for Thou hast worked wonders, plans formed long ago with faithfulness" (Isa.25:1). The wonders of God in our lives prove His goodness. In His wisdom, He devised to save sinners. In counsels from long ago He designed a way to comfort His people and to bring unto Himself the glory of His grace. All the operations of providence are according to His truth and faithfulness. He manifests His faithfulness in forgiving sins (1 John 1:9) and the carrying out of His purposes' (Jer. 51:29). "The Lord has fulfilled His word" (1 Kings 8:20). "Thou hast commanded Thy testimonies in righteousness and exceeding faithfulness" (Ps. 119:138). The word of God is the Lord's testimony. God is scrupulously faithful and true to all the details of His promises. "Know therefore that the Lord your God, He is God, the faithful God, who keeps His covenant and His lovingkindness to a thousandth generation with those who love Him, and keep His commandments" (Deut. 7:9).

God has many times faithfully dealt with man through covenants. Covenants are contracts between two partners. The Bible first describes major covenants with Adam (Gen. 2:16-17), Noah (Gen. 9:1-17) and then with Abraham (Gen. 12,15), as well as some others. The Abrahamic Covenant is found in Genesis 12:1-3 and the ceremony recorded in Genesis 15. In the Abrahamic covenant, God called out a special people for Himself that would bless the whole world. It also promised Abraham many descendants and a specific piece of land forever. One day, Israel will repent and be restored to God's favor (Zech. 12: 10-14, Rom. 11: 25-27) and possess the promised land. God will be faithful. Later, God sent Moses to rescue the people from Egyptian bondage, and establish the Mosaic covenant with the people. God gave them the Ten Commandments at Sinai (Ex. 19:5) and instituted animal sacrifices (Heb. 9:16). The covenant consisted of outward rites (Heb. 9:1-13) and was sealed by circumcision (Gen. 17:9-14). God promised to bless the people if they followed His commands, but curses if they disebeyed (Deut. 28). An extension of the Mosaic covenant can be seen in the Davidic covenant, when the Israelite king was the mediator between the Lord and the people. God promises David a royal kingdom in which the promises made to Abraham and Israel would be fulfilled through his lineage (2 Sam. 7). The Abrahamic, Mosaic and Davidic covenants were designed to lead us to Christ in the New Covenant (Gal. 3:17-25).

The New Covenant is the pinnacle and culmination of God's saving work for His people. The new covenant is fulfilled in the shedding of the blood of Jesus, our faithful Redeemer (Heb. 9:11-23). The new covenant is called everlasting (Heb.13:20) and is humbly remembered by Christians in the observance of the Lord's supper (1 Cor. 11:25). The new covenant is better, because God writes the laws on our hearts and puts His Spirit in us to empower us to love and obey His commands. In the beginning and after man sinned, God promised to save man through the seed of the women (Gen. 3:15). Along the way, God preserved the world in the flood with Noah and initiated redemption through the life of Abraham. God formed a special people in Israel and promised a Shepherd-King through David. God then fulfilled all the covenant promises in Jesus. The motive for the covenants made by God were to reveal to mankind His goodness, grace and love. Otherwise, no one would have ever known there even was a God. God would demonstrate His truth and faithfulness. God would fulfill a gracious promise to redeem man with grace and love. Man would be redeemed from the penalty, power and presence of sin. Throughout the history of mankind, the purpose of God was to bring us back to Himself (Luke 1 :68-79, Acts 2: 14-39, 3:11-36, 7 :2-50, 17:22-30). Diverse as the Bible may appear to us, Christian, all the historical covenants, including those of Adam, Noah, Abraham, Moses, David, and some minor covenants, and finally the New Covenant, are all effected by the blood of Jesus. The elect will be saved only by grace through faith, in the hoped for and accomplished work of the Messiah. Amen.

"The secret of the Lord is for those who fear Him, and He will make them know His covenant" (Ps. 25:14). Natural strength and wisdom cannot guess what the secrets of God are, and even some believers may stumble for words to sufficiently explain them. The intimate friendship of the Lord, Christian, is for those who fear Him. That is, by the grace of God, they know a reverential awe and profound respect for the Lord and a behavior that manifests this respect. The secrets are in the covenants and revealed to our hearts and minds for understanding. The secrets are felt and sealed up in the soul by the witness of the Holy Spirit. The secrets are written in the Bible. In the covenants are the grace and love of God. In the covenant is understanding: the righteousness of Christ, the mercy and patience of God, and the security and power of God. In the covenant are revealed the perfections of God, the providence of God and His faithfulness to many generations. "Jesus Christ is the same yesterday and today, yes and forever" (Heb. 13:8). "I'm the Alpha and the Omega, says the Lord God, who is and who was and who is to come, the Almighty" (Rev. 1:8). He is the same today as He was in eternity before time, as He will be in the new eternity to come. He planned our salvation, and is faithfully working through the New Covenant for our lives today. Christ was the same in the Old Testament days, as He is in our gospel day. Amen.

The new covenant or testament that we enter into with the Lord, Christian, is far superior than the old covenant. The old covenant was one of works, while the new covenant is one of grace. The grace of God was made available to us by the sacrifice of the Son of God and delivered to our hearts by the Holy Spirit. The Old Testament was established, with Moses as the mediator, between God and the people of Israel, after God freed them from Egypt (Ex. 7-15, 24:8). The ten commandments were laws to be obeyed by the people for their prosperity in the promised land. To deal with their sin, God set up animal sacrifices and installed Aaron as the high priest to intercede for the people. "Without the shedding of blood there is no forgiveness" (Heb. 9:22). The people built a temple and performed the animal sacrifices for hundreds of years. Then, God the Father sent His only begotten Son into the world to solve the sin problem once and for all (John 3:16). By dying on the cross, Jesus, without sin, became the lamb of God, whose shed blood was a perfect sacrifice to wash away the guilt of sin forever. Jesus became a new high priest (Heb. 4: 14-16), with the new and fulfilling promise of salvation and eternal life with God, by grace through faith (Eph. 2:8). Jesus, "came as light into the world, that everyone who believes in Him may not remain in darkness" (John 12:46). He is the only Savior, revealing God and exposing darkness and the ruin of sin.

The new covenant fulfills the faithfulness of God for all people everywhere, including Jews and Gentiles. Jesus is superior to Moses as a mediator and high priest, seated next to God in heaven. "By one offering He has perfected for all time those who are sanctified" (Heb. 10:14). Both the Old and New Testaments, Christian, are the revelation of the same God of love and light, and of mercy and faithfulness, who gives people the freedom to choose. The Old Testament was primarily for a specific people, while the New Testament extends to all people in the whole world to come back to God by choosing Jesus Christ. Today, people are saved by grace through faith and not of works (Eph. 2:8). Grace works by God's love (1 John 4:19). "For God so loved the world, that He gave His only begotten Son, that whoever believes in Him should not perish, but have everlasting life" (John 3:16). We are "standing on the promises of Christ my King "(R. Kelso Carter, 1886).

Faithfulness, an attribute of the Spirit (Gal. 5:22), is a truth about God. When He makes a promise, He keeps it. Being faithful is who God is. God is faithful to keep His word, and this means He is trustworthy. Being made in God's image (Gen. 1:26), and rich by His Spirit, we should reflect His faithfulness in our lives. God gives the gift of faith to us and empowers its use in our lives (Eph. 2:8, James 1:3, 2 Tim. 2:1). God's grace is the good will toward us, and the willingness to work in us (Phil. 2:13). "Let love and faithfulness never leave you; bind them around your neck, write them on the tablet of your heart" (Prov. 3:3). Be loyal to the Lord and faithful to the commands He gives you. "Faithful is He who calls you, and He also will bring it to pass" (1 Thess. 5:24). The love of God has called you and the faithfulness of God will preserve you. The faithfulness of God will accomplish all the good pleasure He has prepared for you. We need God's grace to be faithful, for sure; we also need to be responsible by picking up the Bible to read and study it for faith to flourish and reflect the Lord (Rom. 10:17). We need God's grace to be faithful stewards of God's manifold grace (1 Pet. 4:10). Freely you have received, freely give (Matt. 10:8). Amen.

Faith and faithfulness clearly are important topics in the New Testament. "Faith is the assurance of things hoped for and the conviction of things not seen" (Heb. 11:1). The Bible tells us that we have been saved by grace through faith; it is a gift of God (Eph. 2:8). The Bible tells us that we have been born again by the word of God (1 Pet. 1:23). Faith tells us the Bible is the word of God (2 Tim. 3:16), and that faith comes to us by reading the word of God (Rom. 10:17). The word of God tells us we have been chosen by God (Eph. 1:3-4). The word of God tells us that God loved us before we loved Him (1 John 4:19). Do I fully understand what it means to be chosen by God, being born again, and being first loved by God? The answer would have to be no, but I know the Bible is true and that God cannot lie (Titus 1:2). My life has been changed by the word of God. Amen.

God is a God of all manifold grace (1 Pet. 4:10, 5:10). Grace is the essence of God's being and the basis of His action. We were made in God's image. God is faithful. He would have us value and exercise, to a very high degree, the gift of faith in the love of His Son. In this world, we are to reflect our love for Jesus in the way of our faithfulness to God. It is impossible to please God without faith (Heb. 11:6). Faith means trusting God in the promises made to us because of Christ. Faith means trusting God in everything. Faith trusts Jesus Christ for salvation and the Holy Spirit for the power to live a Christian life. Faith increases in the heart of believers, by the grace of God, leading to the obedience of faith (Rom. 16:26). The obedience of faith is produced through the grace of faith. The true faith, Christian, works obedience into your life. When we come to Jesus and receive Him into our hearts, we are born again by the will of God (John 1:12). God defines faith as a receiving of Christ. He draws us (John 6:44). We receive a new heart and a new spirit and God's Spirit to help us walk by God's commandments

(Ezek. 36:26-27). This is the divine nature that sanctifies God in our hearts. He sanctifies our hearts to live for His glory by His grace. Amen. God works an inward change, Christian, in order to our walking in newness of life. We gain a new heart with a real spiritual sense of true faith in the choice of Jesus. A new heart will be conscious of spiritual pains and pleasures, the conflict of two natures (Rom. 7:14-25) and living by faith.

The gift of faith, by God's grace, will endow you to be inclined and enabled to do your duty with the Lord. The Holy Spirit works in you as a teacher, guide and sanctifier. With the gift of faith, the sense of spiritual life goes up an order of magnitude, and sends you into the Bible to learn the beginning of wisdom, that is, to discover the true meaning of the fear of the Lord. The renewing grace of God works your will to bring about His intended plans, purpose of life and fulfill the promises in His love for you. We understand His will better, and by His grace, do His commandments (Ps. 111:10). "For we are His workmanship, created in Christ Jesus for good works, which God prepared beforehand, that we should walk in them" (Eph. 2:10). By the grace of God, we behold salvation in our minds and in our bodies. The sum of the covenant of grace is, "You will be my people, and I will be your God" (Ezek. 36:28). He chose us and loved us, and the gifts of forgiveness of sin and salvation from God are proven true. The presence of God, Christian, is confirmed by the peace and joy and obedience He gives us, that passes our understanding.

His faithfulness to the covenant is realized by His work in us. This becomes known in spite of our failures and weakness. God works both sides of the covenant. He carries out His side of the agreement without a hitch, and He carries out our side of the agreement with His patience, mercy and grace. "See how great a love the Father has bestowed upon us, that we should be called children of God; and such we are" (1 John 3:1). We were lost in a mystery and did not know it, but He did. We were buried under ourselves and could not get free, and He knew it. He chose us before we were born, and was faithful to draw us into life (John 6:44). He was faithful to us after we were born to bring us to an abundant life in Jesus (John 10:10). The Father adopts all the children of the Son. Though by nature heirs of guilt and sin, He confers upon them the dignity of the sons of God. Nothing can stand in the way of God's love. The foundation or cornerstone of a believer's happiness is Jesus, "in whom you also are being built together into a dwelling of God in the Spirit" (Eph. 2:22).

The normal path for a Christian to think and walk is by faith in God. In the gospel, "the righteousness of God is revealed from faith to faith; as it is written, but the righteous man shall live by faith" (Rom. 1:17). "Christ lives in me; and the life that I now live in the flesh I live by faith in the Son of God, who loved me, and delivered Himself up for me" (Gal. 2:20). The reality of the war between the law of God and the law of sin (Rom. 7:14-23), is one in which we joyfully concur with the law of God in the inner man (Rom. 7:22). The practice of living for Jesus in our bodies, proving the obedience of faith, however, can be difficult and take some time, because we indeed have been defiled by sin. Faith establishes a daily relationship, Christian, where we are to look to Jesus for help as the One whom we trust and believe. Sometimes, we look far too much to ourselves for what we think is the best plan for our lives. We are to walk after the purpose of God and not our feelings of comfort for ourself. We are to be dead to the world and the law of sin, and alive in the spirit of the Lord Jesus. We are to be alive to the will of God. We are to be like Job; when he said, "though He slay me, I will hope in Him" (Job 13:15). We progress in the Christian life not by our feelings, but because of a deeper union of our hearts and will with God. God is at work to establish you as a spiritual man, and what matters is obeying God. Sin is defiling. Nothing selfish should be done; you have been crucified with Christ (Gal. 2:2). "Do you not know that your body is a temple of the Holy Spirit who is in you, whom you have from God, and that you are not your own? For you have been bought with a price: therefore, glorify God in your body (1 Cor. 6:19-20). When you choose and gain the Lord, you will have rest and joy, and know a purity of life. The Lord can use you, and you will seek ways to be used by Him. The ear will be attentive to His voice, and though sometimes you would rather be alone with the Lord, that may not always be your calling and duty. Our pleasure becomes His pleasure for us. The obedience of faith is produced by the grace of faith, and is indeed, humbling. To God be the glory.

The faithfulness of God cannot be defeated. "I know that Thou canst do all things, and that no purpose of Thine can be thwarted" (Job 42:2). God has unlimited knowledge, power and sovereignty, and the highest authority to rule. God will be faithful. "Delight yourself in the Lord, and He will give you the desires of your heart (Ps. 37:4). He gives you the desires of your new heart, not the old and selfish heart. Though the devil cannot touch God, Christian, he can disturb you. He tries to rob you of your comfort and peace in Jesus and make your life a burden. He gets you to focus more on your sins and troubles than the Savior. Though saved, we are still not free from the temptation and presence of sin. Sin can still defile us. When we are not faithful, the flower of faith can fade a little, and rob us of the sense of the assurance of our salvation. We are free from the condemnation of sin (Rom. 8:1), but a poor choice in the conflict with sin, reminds us that we are not our own. We still have some learning and growing in grace to experience. We must confess the error of our ways for cleansing (1 John 1:9). The promise from our faithful God is that "sin shall not be master over you, for you are not under law, but under grace" (Rom. 6:14). God, by grace, accepts the willing mind and sincerity as our gospel perfection. God's grace leaves room for repentance. God's grace will be sufficient (2 Cor. 12:9). We are called to be holy (1 Pet. 1:16). The Bible tells us that we will be impartially judged, according to our work. The world will discover who we are by our works whether we belong to Jesus. Therefore, we are obliged to faith, holiness, obedience and the fear of the Lord during the time of our stay on earth (1 Pet. 1:1:17). Living by faith in Jesus will be our victory (1 John 5:4). Amen.

Jesus paid our debt, and we are made the righteousness of God in Him (2 Cor. 5:21). When we sin, we can have doubts about our love and sincerity for Christ. The doubts and questions about our weakness and why we still sin, can stab at us and try to undermine the truth about the assurance of our salvation. Let me be clear. Assurance is not faith; it is an effect of faith. Assurance flows from faith. The assurance of salvation and pardon of sin comes from the witness of the Holy Spirit that we are children of God (Eph. 1:13, Rom. 8:14-16). We are already sons by faith in Christ Jesus (Gal. 4:6). We are first engrafted into Christ by faith before we have assurance of salvation. Assurance of salvation is a fruit of faith. A Christian can have faith, with or without assurance. A Christian cannot lose true faith, but assurance can come and go, based mostly on the feelings about the nature of our behavior. "God is not mocked; whatever a man sows, this he will also reap" (Gal. 6:7). If you cannot act like a Christian, do not expect your Father in heaven to let you think that He is pleased with some choices you make. The devil wants you to think that without assurance, you are not saved, and that is a lie. Assurance can be a delight in the soul, no doubt; and some Christians can have a lot of assurance, while others seem to have very little.

Be patient, and be prepared to grow gradually in spiritual graces, both qualitatively and quantitatively. "The path of the righteous is like the light of dawn, that shines brighter and brighter until the full day" (Prov. 4:18). "You will go forth and skip about like calves from the stall" (Mal. 4:2). You will be rich in some graces and weak in others. Not all men will be rich and weak in the same graces. The truth of God will make you want to leap for joy. Christ came as a shining light (John 12:46) into our lives, that shines more and more every day. We grow by degrees in life; from babies to children to adults and finally seniors. We slowly waded into deeper and deeper water for sin, and we usually end up slowly wading back out of the water to get away from sin. Growing in grace and knowledge and holiness can be slow, but should be steady. It is the duty, the work and the glory of a Christian to seek, strive and struggle in the endeavors to grow rich in grace. The righteousness of God is revealed to us in His time. We grow from faith to faith (Rom. 1:17), grace upon grace (John 1:16) and glory to glory (2 Cor. 3:18) in our Christian life. The path of the just, by the way of righteousness, is guided by the word of God, and faithfully worked into our heart by the Holy Spirit. The light of God shines brighter on our way. We grow to know more holiness, joy, and comfort by the grace of God. We grow more confident "that all things are working together for good to those who love God and are called according to His purpose" (Rom. 8:28). The riches in Christ become more known and unsearchable at the same time (Eph. 3:8).

Grace received is evidence of the good will of God toward us, and the faithful work of God in us. There is faith justifying us, by God's grace, and there is faith maintaining us, by God's grace, for the beginning and in the progress of our Christian life. We are being changed or transformed from one degree of glorious grace to another by the Spirit into the image of our Savior, Jesus Christ. To be what God intended and purposed for us to accomplish, no matter how small, will be glory. We are changed, Christian, by seeing the glory of God in Christ. The change from glory to glory is gradual. As we gaze upon Christ in faith, His power falls upon us, and we grow from glory to glory. To be like Christ is a process and takes a lifetime. Add to your faith: moral excellence, knowledge, self-control, perseverance, godliness, kindness and love, and you will be fruitful in your knowledge of Christ (2 Pet. 1:5-8). We are to labor to be rich in faith (Jude 20). Faith is called precious (2 Pet. 1:4) and a shield (Eph. 6:16). Faith spiritually protects your soul from evil attacks, and makes you desire to be obedient to the Lord, which becomes precious. Jesus gives us a sense of the importance of faith, when He wonders whether it will be found on earth when He comes again (Luke 18:8).

The thoughts about faith in Jesus will become the most important consideration and experience in your heart. The idea that God the Holy Spirit is reminding you of the Father's love and the Son's sacrifice about your eternal good is a point in time to be grateful and praise the Lord. You are being "protected by the power of God through faith for a salvation ready to be revealed in the last time" (1 Pet. 1:5). The work of protection and preservation by the Lord of those born again, from their own infirmities and the strong temptations in this life to seek sin, is the gracious effect of divine power. Our responsibility is to desire salvation by a strict reliance upon Christ, and to bring forth a diligent care that we respect Him. We are always under the assistance of God's grace. Amen. Faith is like a window to see the Lord; to see His precious promises, abiding love and patience. Faith is like a door; we open the door to walk into God's presence, and the influence of His grace comes along side of us to comfort and bless us. This is especially true in times of service and in church during the taking of the Lord's Supper. The faithful testimony of the Spirit of God attending by us in ministries that He has chosen for us, and in Bible study settles into our hearts a conviction that Jesus is coming again. The Lord is faithful to raise our spirits and seal our pardon when we worship Him in spirit and in truth (John 4:24). He shows up every day to talk to us, walk with us, and confirm His interest and love for us. Thank You, Lord. Amen.

The main object of the faith that God gives to us is in the person of Christ. Christ becomes the most precious to us, because He is the perfect and glorious righteousness that we, as descendants, become heirs to (Rom. 4:13). He alone is worthy (Rev. 5:1-5), and of great value and our most important treasure. He is the One that died, that we might live. It is because of Jesus that we are forgiven of our sin and inherit eternal life. Our faith works, because He was faithful, even unto death (Phil. 2:8-9). Faith for us brings Christ up close, filling us with assurance of the things we hoped for. Faith for us makes His riches, His favors and His glory the evidence of things not seen. Faith sets our soul upon fighting against sin, trembling at sin and grieving for sin. Faith sets us upon repentance, which cleanses and purifies our hearts, and gives strength for the next battle (Acts 15:9, 1 John 1:9). Faith is not leaves but fruit, and it is not just words but work (James 2:17). Faith will profit your soul by sending you into your prayers. Faith is important for obeying the Lord and not disputing with Him. Faith will put you in a place of waiting on the Lord for help and direction. Faith is the vehicle He has chosen for us to obtain the conviction of things not seen (Heb. 11:1). Faith is His sovereign gift to us to discover Christ, and not by works that we could boast about it (Eph. 2:

8-9). He chose faith as the way of salvation for us, before a great performance of miracles we could see with our eyes. The power of faith about Christ in the soul is God's work (John 6:29). Amen.

The gift of faith overcomes the world and ourselves by presenting Jesus as most excellent, glorious and all good. A strong faith will make you resist and conquer sin and trust God in every situation. A strong faith will prefer a spiritual life rather than a worldly or secular existence. A man with weak faith is still united to Christ and saved by Christ, because He has received Christ (John 1:12). A man is saved upon the account of the truth of his faith, not the strength of his faith. A weak faith will know the precious things of eternity. A weak faith can grow (Rom. 10:17, Heb. 12:2). He that has begun the good work will perfect it (Phil. 1:6). He that believes will be saved and know a glorious resurrection (John 3:16). The person of weak faith may not be able to stop the mouth of the lion or resist strong temptations for reasons that are between him and the Lord. Grace is the Lord's to give according to His own pleasure. A man may struggle to improve his interest in Christ; nevertheless, the Lord is faithful and will look after every soul that has true grace. Jesus Christ is a mighty and all-sufficient Savior. "He is able to save forever those who draw near to God through Him since He always lives to make intercession for them" (Heb. 7:25). The Lord lives with a purpose of working on our behalf, Christian, as an Advocate, Defender, and Mediator to see you brought all the way into heaven. The work of His intercession sustains the believer and guarantees a complete sanctification. Our life as a Christian, progressively grows in grace and knowledge to a faithful conclusion that honors and glorifies God the Father, the Son and the Holy Spirit. Amen.

By His death, Christ provided all that you would need for salvation. By the interceding work Christ is doing now, He meets us and applies the provision He made for us in His death. The faithful intercession of Christ helps keep the believer right now from sin in the world (Rom. 8:34). By avoiding sin, the believer remains in a sustained fellowship with the Lord. When we sin, we know it was the wrong choice, and the Holy Spirit pleads with us to confess the sin to restore peace in the soul by staying in close fellowship with the Lord (1 John 1:9). "He Himself is the propitiation for our sins" (1 John 2:2). The word "propitiation" refers to a sacrifice that turns away the wrath of God and makes God merciful and ready to forgive. "Let us hold fast the confession of our sin without wavering, for He who promised is faithful" (Heb.10:23). God is faithful, through whom you were called into fellowship with His Son, Jesus Christ our Lord (1 Cor, 1:9). God has promised to His Son a certain people for His inheritance, to deliver them from sin and to give them eternal life in glory. God is also faithful to discipline and afflict His people (1 Cor. 11:30, Ps. 119:175). "Who He justified, He also glorified" (Rom. 8:30). Amen.

The work that God has done for our salvation is comprehensive. He demonstrates a broad commitment that fully supports the idea of His being faithful to us. He wakes up our conscience, convicts us of sin and overcomes our resistance to the Holy Spirit. The work of the Lord subdues our remaining corruptions, and in love and faithfulness, He carries us all the way to heaven. He is our only hope of complete forgiveness and salvation. Amen. You cannot spiritually wake up on your own and give yourself the gift of faith to believe in Jesus and trust the gospel. God's work for us may take a lifetime, but He steadfastly remains faithful to the task the whole time. He is our hope (1 Tim. 1:1). God took our salvation up into His own hands (Isa. 59:16), or else there would have been no salvation. He starts it, and faithfully continues the work until it is perfect (Phil. 1:6). It is God working in us to will and to do His good pleasure (Phil. 2:13). The source of our encouragement is His kindness, mercy, grace and power. Amen. Our hope is founded on His ability, promise and character. Our hope is founded on His goodness, patience, love and faithfulness. Amen.

Faith to believe in Jesus is both a gift from God (Eph. 2:8) and a work of God (John 6:29). The carnal man and the lost sinner are always trying to do something to be acceptable with God to save themselves. What God only requires of them is "that you believe in Him whom He has sent" (John 6:29). A man will stumble at this, because he believes he must do more than just believe (Acts 16:31).

Doing something panders to his pride and denies that he is without strength (Rom. 5:6). The only work that God accepts is what He has done through His Son. The work has already been done, and the victory over sin has been won. They struggle to abandon what they believe should be their responsibility. The power of the Spirit of God is absolutely necessary to lay hold of Jesus. A religious life of prayers, tears, tithes and church attendance does not get it done (Rom. 6:23). "By the works of the law no flesh will be justified in His sight; for through the law comes the knowledge of sin" (Rom. 3:20). The word of faith is near you, it is in your mouth by confession, and in your heart by believing God raised Jesus from the dead. This brings salvation (Rom. 10:8-10). Faith comes from hearing the gospel (Rom. 10:17), believing the gospel (Acts 15:7), preaching (John 17:20) and reading the scriptures (John 20:30-31). The objects of faith are God the Father and Jesus the Son (John 14:1). "The time is fulfilled, and the kingdom of God is at hand; repent and believe in the gospel" (Mark 1:15). Be assured, Christian, "that what God has promised, He is able to perform" (Rom. 4:21).

Our confidence and assurance are built on the omnipotence and kindness of God. The faith that believes is not just a lip service, but it is one that acts. The faith that believes does not just sit in the head as facts, but is in the heart, serving the Lord and being perfected (James 2:22). Faith is shared and encouraged among believers (Rom. 1:12). Faith can be small (Matt. 8:26, 14:28-31, 17:20). If you desire the benefits of Christ, Christian, you must venture to come to Him like Peter on the water (Matt. 14:29). Faith can be confirmed and gain strength by being exercised in a trial, test or affliction (Matt 14:33, James 1:3). You grow in faith by experience. You can be encouraged about faith when you remember your past, and recall and see the Lord working more clearly. "If Christ has not been raised, your faith is worthless; you are still in your sins" (1 Cor. 15:17). There are many examples of believers and their testimony of faith in both the Old and New Testaments (Acts, Hebrews 11). The truth of the testimony of your faith for Jesus is a gift in your own heart by the Holy Spirit, which confirms the veracity of the Lord. The source of doubting God's word and the resurrection of Jesus is from the devil. Faith in Christ is not in vain; He lives within us. Amen.

The goal of the gospel "is love from a pure heart and a good conscience and a sincere faith" (1 Tim. 1:5). The main teaching of the commandments of God is to love God (Matt. 22:37) and to love one another (John 13:34). The gospel was "written that you may believe that Jesus is the Christ, the Son of God, and that believing you may have life in His name" (John 20:31). "By this all men will know that you are My disciples, if you have love for one another" (John 13:35). By the grace of God, Christian, it is a love from a pure heart, because it has been purified by faith from corrupt affections. By the grace of God, Christian, it comes from a clear and good conscience in believing the truth from the word of God. We are born again by the word of God to a living hope, that the proof of our faith may be found to result in praise, honor and glory at the revelation of Jesus Christ (1 Pet. 1:3,7,23). We grow into a sincere and true confidence in God. We grow into a faith rooted in God, that believes, lives and rests in living with gratitude for His lovingkindness. By the grace of God, you have the light; "believe in the light, in order that you may become sons of light" (John 12:36).

The fruits of faith are spiritual life and fellowship with Jesus now and forever, and freedom from spiritual death and separation from God. The fruits of faith are remission of sins, being right with God and growing in grace and knowledge. The fruits of faith are justification and sanctification (Acts 10:43, 13:39, 15:9). The fruits of faith include freedom from judgment (John 3:18), safety with the Lord (John 10:29), and salvation (Mark 16:16). We receive an inheritance among those who have been sanctified by faith in Jesus (Acts 26:18). God sees us in Jesus, as if we never sinned and we have peace with God (Rom.5:1). The quarrel with God and the penalty from sin is taken away. By the will of God, this makes way for peace. By faith, we take hold of God's hand and His strength, and come to know a healing in our heart from past sins, and a lovingkindness from Him for our future. This was in accordance with the manifold wisdom of God, and the eternal purpose which He carried out in Christ Jesus our Lord (Eph. 3:10-11). The purpose of God was to bring the light of the unfathomable riches of Christ into our hearts. The purpose of God was to make known, through the church, the manifold wisdom of God to the rulers and authorities in the heavenly places. It is through Jesus Christ that "we have a boldness and confident access through faith to God" (Eph. 3:12). We have a boldness to open our minds and hearts to God, as a father. We have acceptance with God by faith, believing by God's grace we have a mediator. We are humbled, and at the same time, made comfortable. We understand and rejoice in the Father's purpose of love, mercy and grace for our souls to rest in Jesus. We have permission with some liberty, and persuasion that the curse is gone. We can be honest about what is going on in our hearts and mind with Him. He already knows what we think we need and want, and what He knows we need and will do for us. Amen. God is faithful and able, with His power rooted in love, "to do exceeding abundantly beyond all that we ask or think, according to the power that works within us, to Him be the glory" (Eph. 3:20).

"Be on the alert, stand firm in the faith, act like men, be strong. Let all that you do be done in love" (1 Cor. 16:13-14). "The righteous shall live by faith" (Rom. 1:17). We are to grow strong in faith, giving glory to God (Rom. 4:20). We are to "continue in the faith firmly established and steadfast, and not moved away from the hope of the gospel that you have heard, which was proclaimed in all creation under heaven" (Col.1:23). This is God's work and His glory. We will abide in Jesus, and remain in expectation of the future as real evidence we are serious about our hopes to persevere in Him. If you walk away from God after tasting of His goodness, and fall into sin, and remain in it, you may not have had real faith to begin with (Heb. 6:4-8). However, if Christ remains your greatest joy, and your hope in Him remains sincere and strong, He will not let you go. Thank you, Jesus.

We resist evil by taking up the shield of faith (Eph. 6:16). We overcome the world and abide forever by having the word of God in us and doing the will of God (1 John 2:14,17). "For whatever is born of God overcomes the world; and this is the victory that overcomes the world-our faith" (1 John 5:4). By faith we cleave to Christ, and faith works in us by the love of God, and the Holy Spirit withdraws us from loving the world. Faith sanctifies our hearts and gives us strength to conquer the world. By faith, the Spirit of grace sees into the future, and beholds the glory of God, and prepares us for His glorious presence. Faith convinces us that the Lord is able to guard and protect every grace and purpose granted us in Christ Jesus from all eternity. Faith convinces us that everything in our soul that has been entrusted to Him will be guarded (2 Tim. 1:9,12). Faith convinces us to pray, believing we shall receive grace to live and serve the Lord. Faith is enough, Christian, because it is God's chosen way with us, and His power and gladness for us. To God be the glory. Many have died in faith without receiving the promises, but the Lord gave their hearts enough to know that He still would be keeping the promises (Heb. 11:13). They looked for heaven and believed God, that on earth they were exiles and that His presence was their home. I'm confident that they prayed: "not My will, but Thine be done" (Luke 22:42). Their hearts were in such a way that "God was not ashamed to be called their God; for He has prepared a city for them" (Heb. 11:16). By faith, they knew the profound victory of finding their life by losing their life for Christ (Matt. 11:39). To God be the glory. Amen.

Faithfulness is making faith a living reality in your life. This may become manifest in a number of ways. The Bible speaks of this in the way of being ready for the second coming of Jesus (Matt. 24:42-51). We are to "be on the alert, for you do not know which day the Lord is coming" (Matt. 24:42). The Lord is soon coming back to earth. If we die before He comes back, then that will be our experience of seeing the Lord. To be absent from the body is to be present with the Lord (2 Cor. 5:8). Meanwhile, we are stewards of our souls. Every one of us has a "house" to keep, which can be thought as taking care of our soul and heart. We are to "watch over our heart with all diligence, for from it flow the springs of life" (Prov. 4:23). We must keep our hearts from being defiled by sin and a conscience void of offence. We must keep out bad thoughts, and keep the good thoughts. We must make a covenant with our eyes and tongues to be careful about what we look at and speak about. Your life will be a lot more peaceful, Christian, if you faithfully protect your heart for Jesus. If we are asleep and not keeping our heart, the thief will break into your house and steal from you. On the other hand, a good man will be ready and guard the treasure of knowing Jesus by putting on the armor of God (Eph. 6:11).

"Who then is the faithful and sensible slave whom His master put in charge of his household to give them their food at the proper time? Blessed is that slave whom his master finds so doing when he comes" (Matt. 24:45-46). Some folks think this passage refers only to church ministers, but we are all stewards, and have been bought with a price (1 Cor. 6:20). We are servants of Christ and stewards of the mysteries of God. It is required of stewards that they are trustworthy (1 Cor. 4:1-2). A faithful believer of Jesus works for his master's honor and delivers the whole counsel of God, adheres to it himself and does not respect persons. It will not go well for the lazy slave, who will be assigned a place with the hypocrites (Matt. 45:51). Both wisdom and honesty are required of a good servant to be blessed and put in charge of his master's goods. A good steward will be an honest witness (Prov. 14:5), keep a secret (Pro. 11:13) and "act faithfully in whatever you accomplish for the brethren, and especially when they are strangers (3 John 5). He who is faithful in a very little thing is "faithful also in much" (Luke 16:10). How one does with what is little, is an indicator of how one will do with much. The riches of this world are the little thing, while God's grace is the greater thing. The riches of the world are not our own, Christian, but the spiritual riches of Christ are our own and, by the grace of God, they will not be taken away. A truly rich man is rich in faith, rich in Christ, towards God and with the promise of heaven. A man who faithfully serves God with the one talent that he does have, will very likely serve God and be entrusted with the more valuable talents of wisdom and grace from God.

The Bible has many illustrations of the lives of God's people who were faithful. By faith, Abel offered to God a better sacrifice than Cain (Heb. 11:4). By faith, Noah prepared an ark for the salvation of his household (Heb. 11:7). By faith, Abraham when he was called, left his home and when he was tested, offered up Isaac (Heb.11:11, 17). The list goes on, Christian, including: Joseph (Gen. 39:22-23), Moses (Num. 12:7), David (2 Sam. 22:22-25), Jeremiah (Jer. 26:1-5) and Daniel (Dan. 6:10). In the New Testament, we read about the faith of John the Baptist (Luke 3:7-20), Peter (Acts 4:8-12) and Paul (Acts 17:16-17). All these men of faith, worshipped, walked, worked and lived by faith. They suffered by faith and died by faith (Acts 7:54-55). They were made strong in weakness (2 Cor. 12:9). They were more than conquerors by faith (Rom. 8:37). They were never alone. The spoils of this kind of war will make you rich in honor, peace and glory with a crown of righteousness (James 1:12). They were persuaded or "convinced that neither death, nor life, nor angels, nor principalities, nor things present, nor things to come, nor powers, nor height, nor depth, nor any other created thing, shall be able to separate us from the love of God, which is in Christ Jesus our Lord" (Rom. 8:38-39). They "fixed their eyes on Jesus, the author and perfector of faith, who for the joy set before Him endured the cross" (Heb. 12:2). The faith of the saints, both dead and alive, Christian, should inspire you, but mainly, we look to Jesus as our example of faith. He is the object, author and purchaser of the spirit of faith. He is the perfector of faith; releasing the joy of faith and the power of faith in the souls of His people to overcome the world. Amen. Jesus "was faithful to Him who appointed Him" (Heb.3:2). The example of our Lord Jesus Christ is the gospel pattern proposed for our imitation (Phil. 5:1-2). Though He existed in the form of a man, emptied Himself, taking the form of a bond-servant. He humbled Himself by becoming obedient to the point of death, even death on a cross (Phil. 2:5-8). "Great is Thy faithfulness, O God my Father, there is no shadow of turning with Thee; Thou change not, Thy compassions they fail not; as Thou hast been Thou forever will be. Great is Thy faithfulness! Great is Thy faithfulness! Morning by morning new mercies I see; All I have needed Thy hand hath provided-Great is Thy faithfulness, Lord unto me!" (Great is Thy faithfulness, Thomas Chisholm and William Runyon, 1923). Amen.

Heart

Dear Christian,

The meaning of the word heart encompasses the whole man, with all his attributes; physical, intellectual and psychological. It is the heart that governs a man and his actions. The word heart is used figuratively as the central core or disposition of our inner life. The heart may be used more as a symbol or metaphor to describe something the mind cannot explain. It is the being of you and incapable of description. God gives us a heart to know Him (Jer. 31:33-34). The soul and the spirit can be pierced and divided by a sword as the word of God (Heb. 4:12). No mention is made of the heart somehow being divided. I think of the heart, figuratively speaking, as the sum of who I am. You are to "watch over your heart with all diligence, for from it flow the springs of life" (Prov. 4:23). Your character, personality, will and mind and emotions are today's terms which reflect something of the meaning of "heart" in the Bible. "You shall love the Lord your God with all your heart, and with all your soul, and with all your mind, and with all your strength" (Mark 12:30). He becomes our God by amazing acts of grace in creation (Gen. 2), and in recreation when we are born again in Jesus (John 3:3). We are to love God with all our thoughts, words and actions, that is, with our whole being. We can only really love God with the quality He deserves by depending upon the Holy Spirit after we are born again. We must receive Jesus, and be born of God to become a child of God (John 1:12-13). We love Him because He first loved us (1 John 4:19). We do not try hard to get God to love us. He first loves us by waking us up to His presence, and drawing us to Himself (John 6:44).

God has a heart, and for us, it is perfectly amazing. He provides the grace for us to learn that we are loved by Him. In return, His love for us is the incentive and moral cause of our love to Him. God was first in the work of love for us, even when "we were yet sinners, Christ died for us" (Rom. 5:8). We are saved from God's wrath and reconciled to God through the death of His Son (Rom. 5:9-10). "Behold, what manner of love the Father hath bestowed upon us, that we should be called the sons of God" (1 John 3:1). He seeks our love at the expense of His own Son's blood. He calls us according to His purpose and causes all things to work together for good to those who love God (Rom. 8:28). The heart that we love God with includes our emotions, the real me loves God more than my sins. The Spirit of God has stamped my spirit and soul or my self-conscious life with the love of God. By nature, we are disobedient and heirs of sin; but God has bestowed on us the dignity of being His children. By the grace of God, there is a new strength and a sincere desire to be with the Lord. The spiritual life from God is alive, Christian, and He has made me eager for more of Himself. "My soul thirsts for God" (Ps. 42:2). Amen. We are to love the Lord with all our mind. The mind means my intelligence and thought life. We destroy speculations against the knowledge of God and take all our thoughts captive to the obedience of Christ (2 Cor. 10:5). We are to love the Lord with all our strength. The strength means my will and body are being presented as a living sacrifice, acceptable to God as a spiritual service of worship (Rom.

12:1). The heart of a natural man is stony and does not submit to the will of God. God promises a heart of flesh and a new spirit to help us walk in His statutes (Ezek. 11:19-20). This is God's work and a gift. We will be His people, and He shall be our God (Jer. 32:38). Our old heart must first be broken and humbled as a part of receiving a new heart from God (Ps. 51: 1, 10 17).

"Blessed are the pure in heart; for they shall see God" (Matt. 5:8). To be pure in heart does not mean sinless perfection. "If we say we have no sin, we are deceiving ourselves, and the truth is not in us" (1 John 1:8). The saints have stumbled. What about the lives of Noah, Abraham, Job, Elijah, Moses, Peter and Paul? What about your own weakness at times with the Lord, when you acted against your knowledge? The idea of a pure heart is that we have a clear conscience. We are aware of the impurity and disobedience of sin that still dwells in us. The Lord looks at the inner man where He makes us know wisdom about sin (Ps. 51:6). The Lord looks on the heart (1 Sam. 16:7) and sees our infirmities. He sees the knowledge, affections, will and conscience at work for sin in a natural man. The heart of fallen man is totally depraved, deceitful and wicked (Jer. 17:9). The heart of a natural man is stony and hard and cannot seek God (Rom. 3:11), unless the Father draws him to Jesus (John 6:44). We need a new heart, but we are unable to change our own hearts. A change of heart towards God requires a miracle, a supernatural work by God, called being born again (John 3:3). Being born again is being born from above. God sprinkles clean water on us, gives us a new heart and a new spirit and His Spirit to cause us to walk in His statutes (Ezek. 36:25-27). God gives a new and excellent disposition of mind that is different than what it was before. The clean water signifies the blood of Christ and the grace of the Spirit, to remove guilt, and purify us from our corrupt inclinations. The new birth, Christian, bestows a saving faith (Eph. 2:8), purges our conscience from dead works (Heb. 9:14) and breaks the power of sin that controlled our heart. The promise of God's grace enables us to do our duty. Our responsibility and duty is to work carefully, with fear and trembling (Phil. 2:12), to discover what God has put into us. This sends us back to God for more strength and grace. Never forget, that without God's grace, we can do nothing. Amen.

The new heart sends us into the Bible for more precious faith (Rom. 10:17). We find the word of God is captivating and we sense a new satisfaction by looking into it. The Bible becomes a whole lot more interesting. We find that the word of God is living and active, causing a division between the soul and spirit "and able to judge the thoughts and intentions of the heart" (Heb. 4:12). Whereas once we were mostly aware of only natural thoughts in our soul, the word of God, as the sword of the Spirit, pierces deeply and divides your soul and spirit, cutting off the desire and practices of sinful habits. It releases understanding in your mind freeing you from prejudice and ignorance. It provides strength and a freedom in your will to follow obedience and reject rebellion. The sword cuts off the lusts of the flesh in the mind. The sword lets you see what the motives might be in your heart. The sword lets you see where once you were blind and hear where once you were deaf (Prov. 20:12). The sword convinces and convicts you of God's truth compared to the world's viewpoints and opinions. It allows the setting up of the kingdom of Jesus Christ in your heart, where the kingdom of self and Satan previously reigned. You will begin to be governed by the Lord and not your sin, and you will know the difference. The fog in your mind is gone, and your conscience is awake and sensitive. The Spirit of God has given you clarity in the gift of faith. It is a spiritual gift that testifies for Jesus in your heart and comforts you every day. Faith is an attitude whereby a man abandons all reliance on himself to be holy. Faith takes a man out of himself and puts him into Christ. We cleave to the Savior, who has words of forgiveness of sin and eternal life in heaven. Faith is trusting another Person for righteousness, and that person is Jesus Christ. We hear Jesus in our heart, and the joy and pleasure in the experience of gaining eternal life. The words we hear from God about judgment in the heart become life and not death (John 5:24). The gift of faith, Christian, grows in grace and knowledge and becomes a superb blessing, because God is powerful and faithful and at work, and cannot lie.

The new heart has a sincere desire to not sin against God in word or deed, but rather to please the Lord in all things. We are not perfect, but we know our heart's desire is to be holy. The Bible tells us that along with faith we have received the first fruits of the Spirit (Rom. 8:23). We know we have been changed, because we have deep desires to deny ourselves, confess our sins (1 John 1:9) and walk in paths of righteousness. We come to realize that we are being transformed by the renewing of our mind in God's time and in God's way. Our hearts become sincere with the Lord with undivided affections. We get free from feeling like a hypocrite. A pure heart will see Jesus more clearly and hear from the Holy Spirit more distinctly. A pure heart becomes more conscious of and grieves more quickly over foul thoughts, pride, and impatience. A pure heart will remember and repent over previous occasions in their lives that were not particularly gracious. He mourns about a lot of this in secret, and longs for another day when only the love of God will be shining. We know God today from a new heart filled with true knowledge. We know God today more clearly in communion and in the study and sharing of His word. We know and enjoy God more today by living in the changing behaviors He has wrought for us as we walk with Him. David in the Psalms said, "As for me, I shall behold Thy face in righteousness; I will be satisfied with Thy likeness when I awake" (Ps. 17:15). We cannot help but be satisfied, Christian, when we come into heaven and see Jesus, the Lamb of God (John 1:29). Our hearts will be thrilled. We will know that the assurances of all the things we hoped for and the conviction of all the things we did not see was indeed the work of the Lord our God. It will be joy unspeakable and full of glory (1 Pet. 1:8). Here we have a small taste and see shadows; in heaven we will awaken with His likeness. Amen.

"The virgin shall bear a Son, and they shall call His name Immanuel, which translated means, God with us" (Isa. 7:14, Matt. 1:23). The light of the gospel, Christian, is God with us. God is near us at every stage of our spiritual growth. He fills our hearts with peace and comfort. "Even though I walk through the valley of the shadow of death, I fear no evil; for Thou art with me; Thy rod and Thy staff, they comfort me" (Ps. 23:4). "I'm with you always, even to the end of the age" (Matt. 28:20). Some folks only see God up in heaven, while others see God against them; believers see God in their hearts working out a holy joy. We see the Lord now only by faith and have joy. Can you imagine how much greater that joy and delight will be when we see Him. Our crown will not fade away. "In Thy presence is fullness of joy; in Thy right hand are pleasures forever" (Ps. 16:11). The God who made us knows how to show us the path to life in Jesus. He starts on the inside by giving us a new heart. The heaven He prepares for us (John 14:2) will have joys without measure, mixture or end. I remember that the work of grace in my heart started many years ago; though it for the most part, it has grown slowly, it has been steady. When I consider the quality of grace over this same time, I greatly rejoice. The future is in the Lord's hands, Christian; I know the best is yet to come. He lives in our hearts. Amen.

"May the God of peace Himself sanctify you entirely; and may your spirit and soul and body be preserved complete, without blame at the coming of our Lord Jesus Christ" (1 Thess. 5:23). The verse supports the idea that man is composed of three parts: spirit, soul and body. "God formed man from the dust of the ground, and breathed into his nostrils the breath of life; and man became a living being (Gen. 2:7). The breath of life from God is man's spirit and the principle of his life (John 6:63). The body was formed from the dust of the ground. The difference between man and beast may be indicated in the way they received life from God. The beasts arose with life and a soul at the creative word of God with no mention of the spirit (Gen, 1:24-25, 2:19). For man, God breathed directly into the nostrils of man, which was the foundation of his preeminence and likeness to God, and man became a living soul (Gen. 2:7). In man, the spirit and soul were probably created together through the inspiration of God. The soul of man is of a different nature and higher origin than the soul of beasts. In the new creation of the soul, Christ breathed on His disciples to receive the Holy Spirit (John 20:22). A man became a much more rational creature with the potential to worship God. Our soul should breathe after Him who gave it. Amen.

The soul is unique and belongs to the self and reveals our personality. The soul is composed of the mind, will and emotions. The experiences of the soul are thoughts, intellect, love, ideals, hate, desire, choice, feelings and decision making. We are to "love the Lord our God with all our heart, and with all our soul, and with all our mind and with all our strength" (Mark 12:30). The main meaning is that we are to love the Lord our God with our entire being. The heart is the figurative center of man's character. "The good man out of the treasure of his mouth brings forth what is good, and the evil man out of the evil treasure brings forth what is evil; for the mouth speaks from that which fills the heart" (Luke 6:45). The heart is connected with thinking (Prov. 23:7) and will (2 Cor. 9:7) and desires (Rom. 1:24). David was called a man after God's heart, because he would do all of God's will (Acts 13:22). Our heart, soul and mind should be chasing after the will of God, with all our strength.

The heart is spoken of as important in our moral and spiritual life. Apparently, the Hebrew language had no word for "conscience", so the word "heart" was used to express the idea of conscience (Job 27:6, 1 Sam. 23:31). The word heart can also appear in the way of conscience in the New Testament (1 John 3:19-21). The heart may include a seat for conscience and moral character. David's heart troubled him after he had numbered the people (2 Sam. 24:10). God spoke to Abimelech, regarding Abraham's treachery, about the integrity of his heart (Gen. 20:5-6). The Bible tells us that the heart can be depraved and deceitful (Jer. 17:9) and that out of it comes evil thoughts, theft, adultery and false witness (Matt. 15:19). Though we can certainly be influenced and triggered by what goes on around us, our defilement comes from within our own hearts. "Each one is tempted when he is carried away and enticed by his own lust" (James 1:14). Lust conceives sin and sin brings forth death (James 1:15). Since the heart is a big part of our inner problem, the heart is where God goes to work. God does His work; a great and indispensable work, in our hearts for salvation. Amen.

"This is the covenant that I will make with them, I will put my laws upon their heart and upon their mind will I write them" (Heb. 10:16). Our conscience bears witness to the fact that the law is written on our hearts, because our thoughts alternately accuse or defend us (Rom. 2:15). God will have these thoughts to use when He judges our secrets. Our heart is where the seed of God is sown (Matt. 13:19, Luke 8:15). God promises to give us a new heart of flesh and remove the one of stone (Ezek. 36:26). "God gave us the Spirit as a pledge in our hearts for eternal life" (2 Cor. 1:22). The Bible mentions a heart that does not doubt (Mark 12:23), and an unbelieving heart that falls away from the living God (Heb. 3:12). The Bible tells us that "if you confess with your mouth Jesus as Lord, and believe in your heart that God raised Him from the dead, you shall be saved; for with the heart man believes, resulting in righteousness" (Rom. 10:9-10). The Bible also tells us that "the love of God has been poured out within our hearts through the Holy Spirit who was given to us" (Rom. 5:5) at the time of our justification with God. Paul prays "that Christ may dwell in our hearts by faith" (Eph. 3:17). In Romans, we are told that the Father searches our hearts to know what the mind of the Spirit is" (Rom. 8:27).

The heart is not only a center of spiritual activity, Christian, but also the operations of our personal life. The heart in the natural man is naturally wicked (Gen. 8:21), where it essentially contaminates the whole man's life and character. The conscience of a natural man is considered dead toward God (Heb. 9:14). The "natural man does not accept the things of the Spirit of God; for they are foolishness to him, and he cannot understand them, because they are spiritually appraised" (1 Cor. 2:14). Therefore, the heart must be changed; we must be born again (John 3:5) and receive a clean heart (Ps. 51:10). We must have a heart of flesh (Ezek. 11:19). We must be sprinkled by clean water and be given a new heart and a new spirit and a heart of flesh in place of a heart of stone (Ezek. 36:25-26). The change is from the loving heart of God that "He may guide us in paths of righteousness for His name's sake" (Ps. 23:3). "It is God who is at work in you, both to will and work for His good pleasure" (Phil. 2:13). We begin to know salvation in our heart by the power, wisdom, will and grace of God, drawing us to believe the testimony of Jesus. Amen. The natural man is a fallen creature who loves sin, and he must be changed to obey God. "No man may come to Me, unless the Father who sent Me draws him" (John 6:44). "Everyone who has heard and learned from the Father, comes to Me" (John 6:45). He who believes on Me has eternal life" (John 6:47). We need a new heart to believe. The fact that you believe, means you have the evidence of Divine life within you. This may be distasteful to some folks, but it is God's word. The new birth, Christian, is being "born not of blood, nor of the will of the flesh, nor of the will of man, but of God" (John 1:13). This means: your parents, yourself, a pastor or friend cannot perform this miracle, but only God. Amen. Others may be a conduit, but only God saves a man. We seek Christ because, God in His sovereign grace puts forth a power in us that overcomes our natural ways and life of depravity. It is God being God. We are humbled, and only God is glorified.

The new heart and spirit, with the aid of the Holy Spirit, all contribute to the emergence of the new man in you. The new man has a heart of flesh and is spiritually alive, compared to the heart of stone which was spiritually dead. The stony heart was hard and unresponsive to God, whereas the heart of flesh is soft and responsive to God and trusts Him. The heart of flesh is warm and yielding toward God, whereas the heart of stone is cold and unyielding to God. With a heart of flesh, we desire to draw near to God and live a life that is pleasing to Him. We desire to shed our selfish and sinful ways, put on the armor of God and listen for the Holy Spirit's voice. With a heart of stone, we refuse to listen or read the word of God and prefer to live a life that is pleasing to us. We remain ignorant and fear the Holy Spirit's voice, and as a result do not know or follow the will of God. The man with a heart of stone remains insensitive to the consequences for eternal life. The soul in the new man was defiled from the choices to sin before salvation and needs cleansing. By the grace of God, the soul of the new spiritual man will grow in grace to know more about Jesus.

He will strive to live an obedient lifestyle, and serve and work in the local church on the way to discover his purpose in life. This occurs because he is saved, not to be saved. The soul in the new man will be cleansed through a process called sanctification. This separation unto God or holiness, will increase over the remainder of his life to prepare him to come into the presence of God with great joy after he dies. The new man will grow deeper into the experience of eternal life by knowing and walking more with Jesus (John 17:3). Amen.

We are to love the Lord with all our heart, soul and mind (Mark 12:30). This means we are to love Him with everything we have. We speak of belief in the heart (Rom. 10:9, Luke 8:12, Mark 16:14), or the mind (Rom. 12:2, 2 Cor. 4:4) and the soul (Acts 14:22). The heart is where a person, with an understanding heart, discerns the difference between right and wrong (1 Kings 3:9). This passage speaks about the ability of the conscience, which is an important function of the spirit. The Holy Spirit awakens the conscience and convicts the soul of sin, righteousness and judgment (John 16:8). The light of the gospel comes on and the man sees the meaning of the shed blood of Jesus. The conscience of the man hears the Spirit speaking for God's will, and he wants to be saved. He may be saved but does not have assurance because of his ignorance of God's word and the forces to sin against his will. God is faithful and patient and sends us into His word for faith and grace and knowledge. Our own heart begins to experience a peace about Jesus and our conscience begins to know the pleasure of freedom from guilt.

We gain a sense of goodness about the Lord in our minds, and for the future of our souls, and our hearts get glad. "You shall know the truth, and the truth shall set you free" (John 8:32). "Therefore, we do not lose heart, but though our outer man is decaying, yet our inner man is being renewed day by day" (2 Cor. 4:6). Our conscience becomes our guide, and a place of faith where we can distinguish between obedience to the Lord or the seeking of something else. God examines our motives from the movements in our heart and conscience. This activity shows us where we are, how sincere we are and to whom we are serving. I believe our conscience reveals to us our commitment to Jesus. I have lived at times, Christian, with a weak conscience. A weak conscience has made my heart hurt and cry out for help. A weak conscience will carry regret and guilt from the choices we make. My own heart has smote me (2 Sam. 24:10). I have learned that God is patient and merciful, and that the promise of cleansing after confession of sin is true (1 John 1:9). The work God does in our heart can be very difficult for us, for sure, but I hesitate to think where I would be without His kindness. I'm grateful to God for Jesus. Amen. The sense of forgiveness from God in the heart, Christian, given how undeserving I have been, puts in me in a sense of awe and fear of the Lord (Ps. 130:4). Amen.

The heart, figuratively speaking, can mean the innermost or hidden part. The heart is the source of motives, the place of conscience and the will, and the seat of thought and passions. The heart is the site of good and evil. The heart is the seat of adultery (Matt. 5:28), doubt (Mark 11:23), hatred (Lev. 19:17)), lust (Rom. 1:24), evil (Ps. 28:3), pride (Prov. 16:5), and rebellion (Jer. 5:23) and more. The heart is the seat of desire (Rom. 10:1), gladness (Acts 2:26), love (Mark 12:30), obedience (Rom. 6:17), purpose (2 Cor. 9:11), reason (Mark 2:8), sorrow (John 14:1), thought (Matt. 9:4) and more. The word for heart in the Old and New Testaments in Hebrew and Greek, respectively, have wide psychological and spiritual meaning. The word "heart" is meant to include the workings of the mind, the will and the emotions. The heart can and will respond to what God has said with determination in the mind and emotions. You will know your heart is choosing obedience to Christ. You will know the Holy Spirit has moved in your conscience. The self interest in your heart has chosen holiness over sin. You are not sorry about doing the right thing, and your soul and body will know the blessing. God's word is not returning to Him void, without accomplishing what He desires (Isa. 55:11). God does not fix what we are or heal what we have, Christian, but He gives us a new heart. By the grace of God, we receive this new heart when we accept Jesus as

Savior. We become a new creation for which He will be Lord (2 Cor. 5:17). To God be the glory.

There appears to be a lot of similarities in the Bible for the immaterial parts of man that describe the heart and soul and spirit. At the same time, there also appears to be some distinctions. The overlapping abilities and duties between them can make it difficult to grasp the distinctions. When you die, the spirit goes back to God who gave it (Eccl. 12:7) and the soul goes to be with Jesus (2 Cor. 5:8). The body returns to the earth (Eccl. 12:7). Figuratively speaking, I think the heart would go with the immaterial soul as part of the description of the spiritual nature of man. The Christian is to watch over his heart with all diligence (Prov. 4:23). A Christian is to know a heart-felt obedience to Christ. The word of God is able to touch the heart and reveal your thoughts to you, which were already known to God. "Behold, this child is appointed for the fall and rise of many in Israel, and for a sign to be opposed, and a sword will pierce your own soul, to the end that thoughts from many hearts may be revealed" (Luke 2:34-35). There is either a secret yearning for righteousness with Jesus or a bitterness against Him. In this passage, Mary's soul was pierced and the emotional thoughts of her heart revealed. The word of God is able to divide between the soul and spirit, of both "joints and marrow" and able to judge the thoughts of the heart (Heb. 4:12). The soul and the spirit are both immaterial, but God's word is able to split them apart so that sometimes we can see our innermost being. A nonbeliever does not know the word of God and therefore cannot discriminate between the soul and spirit. He lives by his soul and the spirit is considered dead. The heart has been mentioned more in regards to belief (Rom. 10:9-10) and behavior (James 2:18-26). The heart will be accountable for its thoughts and desires (Jer. 17:10; Rom. 14:12; 2 Cor. 5:10; 1Cor. 4:5). The Holy Spirit has a penetrating quality to expose what is in our hearts and discover the ignorance and self-delusions in our minds. God's word can discriminate between your thoughts and intentions. Be diligent to study the word, let your heart out to the Lord to be bathed in God's truth, and plumb yourself for His work inside you. You cannot know your heart perfectly, or the future, but you can learn a lot and by the grace of God trust the Lord to know what to do. Amen.

Paul prayed "that the eyes of our heart may be enlightened" (Eph. 1:18), and that "God would strengthen us with power through His Spirit in the inner man; so that Christ may dwell in our hearts through faith" (Eph. 3:16-17). In the conflict of the two natures, "Paul joyfully concurred with the law of God in the inner man" (Rom. 7:22). We must watch closely our eyes and ears to be diligent in guarding our heart. Be assured that the Lord has the power to help us; He was the one who gave us the seeing eye and the hearing ear (Prov. 20:12). The heart is you, Christian; it is where you desire, deliberate and decide. It encompasses your mind, emotions and will and sense of right and wrong. The heart is a comprehensive term that includes your values, motives, understanding and conscience, and the place to which the Lord turns to speak to you. God searches our hearts (Rom. 8:27). When we are born again, we get a new heart and spirit (Ezek. 36:26). The means of adding more faith to our new life and heart is in reading the word of God. "For you have been born again not of seed which is perishable but imperishable, that is, through the living and abiding word of God" (1 Pet. 1:23).

The word of God is preached to you, shared by others with you and read by you. The word of God is where you and the Lord will meet up together. The word of God consists of the doctrine and directions for you on how to discover and live an abundant life (John 10:10). The word "of the Lord is perfect, restoring the soul; the testimony of the Lord is sure, making wise the simple. The precepts of the Lord are right, rejoicing the heart; the commandment of the Lord is pure, enlightening the eyes" (Ps. 19:7-8). The instructions from the Lord are inspiring and profitable for us (2 Tim. 3:16). They are to be followed and obeyed out of a heart of love for God. The instructions are righteous and fit for the reason of man. The gospel is good news. Free grace yields a heart of joy. The change in our heart brings peace. Peace and joy are the consequences of forgiveness of sin and acceptance with God. Peace and joy fill the hungry heart and calls it into action. There is true fear of the Lord resulting in greater trust, confidence and love, followed by greater obedience and service. The fear of the Lord is the beginning of wisdom (Prov. 1:7) and a worship of the Lord in spirit and in truth (John 4:24). "Thy words were found and I ate them, and Thy words became for me a joy and the delight of my heart" (Jer. 15:16).

Sometimes we think everything, including all are actions and thoughts are hidden, but guess what? "God knows the secrets of the heart" (Ps. 44:21). God is fully acquainted with all the inner workings of your mind. He knows how much you know and really care about Him, and whether you are sincere about a relationship with Him. Jesus is the truth (John 14:6), and He is truthful with us, He cannot lie (Heb. 6:18). The hypocrite cannot hide. A godly man knows in his heart that God cannot be deceived or excluded by our secrecy; God is omniscient (1 Sam 2;3). We can know that we are of the truth, Christian, "in whatever our heart condemns us; for God is greater than our heart, and knows all things" (1 John 3:20). "The Lord searches all hearts, and understands every intent of the thoughts. If you seek Him, He will let you find Him (1 Chron. 28:9). We are weak in prayer and the Spirit knows it, and intercedes for us with the Father with groanings too deep for words. The Father, in searching our hearts, knows what the mind of the Spirit is (Rom. 8:26-27). God does not just sit back and watch what is going on in your life; He searches your heart and learns what is going on and knows what to do to help you.

"God causes all things to work together for good to those who love God, to those who are called according to His purpose" (Rom. 8:28). The Lord opens our heart to respond to the things we hear from the Bible (Acts 16:14). God works in our hearts to will and to do what is His good pleasure (Phil. 2:13). He faithfully persuades us to embrace Christ. God shines "in our hearts to give the light of the glory of God in the face of Christ" (2 Cor. 4:6). There is power in the gospel to light up the mind. Our conscience is convinced, the will is engaged and the soul converted. The presence of this good power rejoices the heart, and we know that what is happening is from God and not ourselves. We know that the Lord knows us, and has given grace for our hearts to continue to reach out for Him in prayer. He knows our hearts better than we do ourselves; His knowledge of us is exact. We need this miracle of grace to keep us coming back to Jesus and spending time with Him to see His love, and develop the obedience of faith. The Christian life can be despairing because of slow growth in holiness and knowing the Lord. Our motives might be selfish. God will not be known as our sugar daddy. Let your heart take courage and wait for the Lord. He may seem to be late on something at times, or cut it pretty fine, but He always knows what He is doing. Any waiting your heart is called to do will be worth the time. God's grace will be a priceless wonder. God's goal or long- range plan is to establish our hearts in Jesus. His purpose is that we become a chaste bride, unblameable in holiness at the coming of our Lord Jesus (1 Thess. 3:13). The more you grow in the graces of love and holiness, the more you will know that you belong to the Lord. The more you grow in love with Jesus, the more you will realize you are safely tucked inside His heart. First, our hearts must be turned to God, and then to perfecting holiness in the fear of God. Finally, the hopes, desires and joy that comes to our hearts, by the grace of God, will be more of His presence now and for His coming again. Amen.

Jesus told us a parable to reveal to us the nature of the human heart and its response to the word of God (Matt. 13:1-23). It is called the Parable of the Sower. In it, He likened the human heart to soil and the seed to the word of God. Man's heart is like soil, capable of providing nourishment to the seed or the words of God for our growing in grace and knowledge. The seed fell on four types of soil or hearts, revealing four different types of growth responses. The first heart was called a hard heart, where the seeds fell beside the road and the birds came and ate them up. This is like the word entered the ear and sailed right through and out the other ear, without any understanding what the word was about. The evil one, in the form of birds, snatched the seed away and it leaves no impression. They are mindless and careless hearers of the word who pay no attention to what they heard. Another kind of heart was called the shallow heart, where the seed fell on stony ground which lacked sufficient soil to sustain growth. These folks hear the word of God and receive it with joy, but without developing a good root, the good effect is only temporary. When the sun came out or when there was some kind of affliction or persecution, the good effect falls away. No root means little resolution in the will, affection from the heart, and principles in the life that could establish a perseverance of faith in Jesus. The third kind of heart is called a crowded heart, where the seed fell among the thorns and weeds. This type of heart has some good gain by the word, but is overcome by the things of the world. Worry and the deceitfulness of riches choke the word, and it becomes unfruitful. They lose interest because of the cares of the world. They get distracted by power and money and develop confidence in them instead of Christ. Finally, there is the fruitful heart where the seed falls on good ground and produces a good crop. This man hears and receives the word, understands it, grows in God's grace, and bears fruit. The good ground is made ready by the grace of God.

"A man can receive nothing, unless it has been given him from heaven" (John 3:27). Some Christians will be more fruitful than others, because we are all under the pleasure of God's grace. Bearing fruit glorifies the Father and proves we are His disciples (John 15:8). Our responsibilities lie in exercising the means to make our heart ready, that is, prayer, Bible study and working out our salvation with fear and trembling (Phil. 2:12). The hard heart must be broken; the shallow heart given depth; and the worldly heart taught that the world is temporary. "What does it profit a man to gain the whole world, and forfeit his soul? (Mark 8:36). Eternal death will be a bitter experience. At times, Christian, throughout my life, I think my heart has been hard, shallow, crowded and fruitful. God was patient and by His grace, I endured. Endurance required time, patience, Bible study, prayer and service, but mostly the grace of God. It was God who was at work, nourishing my life with grace into the faith of obedience with a heart of joy. Thank you, Jesus.

Regeneration is God making a person spiritually alive, as a result of faith in Jesus Christ. Additional terms for regeneration include being "born again" and experiencing a "new birth". It is a radical change that involves receiving a new heart and a new spirit. God removes the heart of stone and gives you a heart of flesh (Ezek. 36:26). The Bible also says that He will put His Spirit within you and cause you to walk in His statutes (Ezek. 36:26). We are born the first time in this world as a natural man and do not accept the things of the Spirit of God; they are foolishness to us and we fail to understand the Lord's ways in our heart (1 Cor. 2:14). After we are born again, we begin to hear and see and seek divine things from the Bible. Our new spirit and the Holy Spirit are fueled by this word, which influences our soul for a fellowship with Jesus. In this way, Christ is being formed in our hearts, and we seek Him by a desire to live by faith with obedience and holiness which we know pleases Him (Eph. 2:1, 8, 19-20; 2 Cor. 5:17-20). The gift of a new heart is a huge and indispensable "game-changer". The process of sanctification is confirmed, by the grace of God, with welcomed changes showing up more frequently in our thoughts and lifestyle. The goal of the process of sanctification is to prepare us for our earthly purpose, and then to come safely into the Lord's presence after we die. Amen.

In the Bible, regeneration is spoken of as a kind of circumcision "of the heart, by the Spirit" (Rom. 2:29). God is not concerned with circumcision of the flesh, Christian, but He is concerned about what goes on inside you, that is, your heart. Circumcision refers to having a pure heart; a cutting off of old sinful and defiling ways of life and being separated unto God. "Blessed are the pure in heart, for they shall see God (Matt. 5:8). The Spirit gives life (John 6:63). God's plan is for us to know what love is; and to love and follow Him in Jesus. The Holy Spirit performs this kind of spiritual surgery on our heart. It cuts off disobedience to God. Circumcision changes the inspiration in our thoughts and deeds. "You have been made complete in Him, and in Him you were also circumcised with the circumcision made without hands, in the removal of the body of the flesh by the circumcision of Christ" (Col. 2:10-11). The pure heart is not free of sin, and is well aware of sin in the conscience, and burdened with the impurity that it still indwells us. God cleanses our hearts by faith (Acts 15:9). He saves us by the washing of regeneration and renewing of the Holy Spirit (Titus 3:5). If we confess our sins, He promises cleansing (1 John 1:9). The experience of a pure heart is a continuing process of denying self, confession, and walking in paths of righteousness after we stumble (James 3:2). This is not our work to be saved, but works out of us because we are saved. The circumcision turns our will from rebellion to obedience, our affections from self to God, and our walking away from darkness into His light. The power of God for salvation comes to us with His gift of a new heart. The glory is all belonging to God, as a result of the obedience and merits of Jesus Christ. Amen.

"The sacrifices of God are a broken spirit; a broken and contrite heart" (Ps. 51:17). We "give thanks to God with uprightness of heart" (Ps. 119:17), a heart that is steadfast (Ps. 57:7) and enlightened (2 Cor. 4:6). "You did not choose Me, but I chose you, and appointed you, that you should go and bear fruit" (John 15:16). By His providence and Spirit, He chose us to receive a new heart, and grace and glory, that we might bring forth fruit from a labor that will not be in vain. The new heart that God creates in you will thrill and rejoice (Isa. 60:5) and exult in the Lord (1 Sam. 2:1). The new heart carries a good treasure that brings forth what is good and sincere (Matt. 12:35; Acts 2:46). The new heart releases integrity (Ps. 101:2) and prayers for family and friends from an enlarged heart (Ps. 119:32). A new heart makes your mind wise (Prov.10:8) and your conscience tender (Acts 24:16). The conscience will take notice of every thought and deed, whether small or large, and will have it fall under the influence of the Lord. The heart will be compassionate and gracious, slow to anger and abounding in lovingkindness and truth, like the Lord. (Ex. 34:6). He calls us to be changed into the image of His Son; and in mercy equips us with a new heart that enables us to follow Jesus. He is pleased to put us under His mercy and grace that we might know the obedience of faith, and see Him in the future (Heb. 12:14). We have every reason now to acknowledge God's goodness to us, and to strongly believe that He will be gracious to us in the future. The heart of God will be an unimaginable sight of greatness in glory. Let this God be your God. Amen.

The response we have to God, from our regeneration with a new heart, is to love the Lord with all our heart, soul, mind and strength (Matt. 22:37). What we believe in our heart (Rom. 10:10), results in a watchfulness with diligence (Prov. 23), that makes us want to walk before Him from His truth in our inner man. Peter encouraged us to "sanctify Christ as Lord in your heart" (1 Pet. 3:15). We sanctify Christ in our hearts, Christian; when we adore Him, trust in His faithfulness, study the Bible to discover His wisdom and give Him all the glory for our salvation. We sanctify Christ when we worship Him above anything the world has to offer. He is our Creator, Savior, Lord and judge; hallowed be His name. Our hearts are His sanctuary. Our souls are His sanctuary. We are to be careful to do what God commands us to do with all our heart and all our soul (Deut. 26:16). Do God's will from the heart, with good will render service, as to the Lord, and not to men (Eph. 6:6-7). The King of Kings commands us to obedience, motivated and empowered by an internal desire to please Him. God has promised us this kind of heart. "The Lord Thy God will circumcise your heart, and the heart of your descendants, to love the Lord thy God with all your heart and with all your soul, in order that you may live" (Deut. 30:6). This is our spiritual circumcision that places us in the gospel covenant. By transforming our hearts, Christian, He replaced our natural and selfish ways with humility and repentance, purifying for Himself a people that would love and obey Him. Amen. "He leads us in paths of righteousness for His name's sake" (Ps. 23:3). He leads us to "trust in the Lord with all your heart" (Prov. 3:5). An uncircumcised ear cannot hear and respond to the Lord (Jer. 6:10). The Lord has opened your heart (Acts 16:14) and eyes and ears (Deut. 29:4; Prov. 20:12). To God be the glory. Amen.

There is another kind of heart described in the Bible called wicked. Wicked is defined as morally bad, evil, sinful, vile and dangerous. The person committing the wickedness may be guilty of harming others, because it is done with malice and indicates the depravity of the individual. "If I regard wickedness in my heart, the Lord will not hear" (Ps. 66:18). Even a Christian can regard iniquity or wickedness in their heart in secret. They may entertain desires for sin and reflect upon the past enjoyments of sin. A true Christian will be contrite about past sins, the backwardness found in his heart, the power of corruption, and carry a deep sense of unworthiness before the Lord. Through the fear of the consequences of sin, of God's honor and even their own conscience, they dare not be wicked. It is hard to pray if we regard iniquity in our heart. The sins of others and even some of the ways of our nation should bother our hearts. We must be willing to say like David; "search me, O God and know my heart; try me and know my anxious thoughts; and see if there be any hurtful way in me, and lead me in the everlasting way" (Ps. 139:23-24). Thank you, Lord for not turning your mercies away from me. Amen. The wicked heart is described as hard (Eph. 4:18), dark (Rom. 1:21), greedy (2 Pet. 2:14), and full of evil (Gen. 6:5). It is also described as lustful (Prov. 6:25), arrogant (Jer. 49:16), rebellious (Jer. 5:23), unrepentant (Rom. 2:5) and uncircumcised (Acts 7:51). Where would we be without Jesus and the promises of God, and the gift of a new heart? We are not perfect now, but we are promised a freedom from evil in the future (2 Cor 3:17, John 8:36, Gal. 5:1, Rom. 6:22, Rev. 21:4). Some of the wicked and evil spirits are so bad that God has them in a holding prison ahead of the coming judgment day (Rev. 20:12-15).

Meanwhile, Christian "put on the whole armor of God, that you may be able to stand firm against the schemes of the devil. For our struggle is not against flesh and blood but against the rulers, against the powers, against the world forces of wickedness in the heavenly places" (Eph. 6:11-12). The armor of God protects your heart and soul from sin. The armor of God is made up of God's truth, righteousness, faith, salvation and His word. They are spiritual weapons of war that cannot be defeated. Amen. The devil is wicked and wants you to focus on the flesh. He wants you to try to defeat him by your own hard effort to be holy. The devil wants you to be ignorant and stay away from the Bible and seeking the Lord for help. The devil's heart is against you, but God's heart is for you. "What then shall we say to these things? If God is for us, who is against us? (Rom. 8:31). If the devil had his way, you would have never heard the call of Jesus, and woken up to eternal life with the Lord. If the devil had his heart's way, you would still be lost in some addiction and bearing the penalty for your sins. The devil's heart for wickedness against you, knows no bounds. The truth is: nothing can separate us from the love of God, which is in Christ Jesus our Lord (Rom. 8:39). Amen.

The grace of God is the greatest blessing in your heart. It is His grace and mercy that saves your soul and allows you to keep your heart (Prov. 4:23). We are to hide the word of God in our heart that we might not sin against God (Ps. 119:11). The word must be known and prized. The word must occupy your understanding and affection in order for it to be treasured or hidden. When the word is hidden in the heart, the life shall be hidden from sin (Charles Spurgeon). To teach us to watch after our hearts is a gracious and saving work of God. To give up your heart to God is a saving work of God. To have a trust and rest that relies on Jesus is a saving work of God. To keep your heart from ignorance and pride is a saving work of God. To get a good understanding and a clear conscience is a saving work of God. The man that acts with faith to purpose is living with a saving work of God in his heart. It is a difficult task to keep your heart. When we find ourselves daily watching and working our hearts for Jesus, by the grace of God, we are in a blessed state.

We have sinned and our hearts have been defiled, but God's grace is greater than our sin (Rom. 5:20-21). Amen. The man of God exerts himself against sin, but cannot and does not just trust himself. "How can a young man keep his way pure? By keeping to Thy word" (Ps.119:9). God's way for us to have a clean heart is to believe, trust and walk with Jesus by faith. Faith comes by hearing the word of God (Rom. 10:17). God has magnified His word according to all His name (Ps. 138:2). It is the Lord, our God, that sends us into His word; to read and study, to meditate, rejoice and delight in His teaching and presence. This is the pathway ordained by God, to keep our hearts with all diligence. We will never be perfect, but we can be accepted. "For if the willingness is there, it is acceptable according to what a man has, not according to what he does not have" (2 Cor. 8:12). God looks at the heart, which means the quality not quantity, for its readiness and sincere endeavors. God's word is laid up in our heart, Christian, the place of love and life as our greatest treasure. The word of God keeps the conscience alive from the desires to sin against God and ourselves. I'm afraid of sin, and I consider temptation a thorn in my flesh. To prevent this fear; read the Bible and hide the words in your heart, go to church, pray, and serve the Lord. Always be drawing near to God, and He will be drawing near to you (James 4:8). Amen.

A Christian knows some of the riches of God's grace. He knows the riches of forgiveness of sin by justification. He knows the growth of grace in the consolations that come along with sanctification. The goodness and power of God's grace to save draws our heart closer to Him in gratitude. The Christian is being weaned away from earthly possessions. "If riches increase, do not set your heart upon them" (Ps. 62:10). If you set your heart upon something other than the Lord, He will remove it in His time. We are to "lay up for ourselves treasures in heaven, where neither moth or rust destroys, and where thieves do not break in or steal; for where your treasure is, there will your heart be also" (Matt. 6:20-21). God knows how to fill your heart. He lets you see and know your Christian family connection, and that He is preparing a place for you with an inheritance (John 14:1-3). God takes us to a place where our assurance is built upon the greatness of our Savior and what He has done and will do for us as His bride. Seeing, knowing and realizing that God has become the greatest experience of your life is a great spring of delight and comfort in your life. He has become our portion (Ps. 119:57, Lam. 3:24)). There is no possession like Jesus. God is all sufficient, Christian; get Him and you have everything. When you are tempted to sin, remind yourself that the Lord is your portion. He has infinite love to care and comfort you, and infinite power to protect and save you.

God will be our eternal good portion. Our being in a state

of grace is a high and noble privilege from God that heals our hearts with a foretaste of heaven. God gives assurance to us in the gift of peace, which confirms His gracious ways with us. The Holy Spirit, as a comforter pours this love into our hearts (Rom. 5:5). We "have received a spirit of adoption as sons by which we cry out, Abba Father!" (Rom. 8:15). "The Spirit Himself bears witness that we are children of God" (Rom. 8:16). From bondage to freedom from sin, from orphan to adoption as a son, and from fatherless to a Father in heaven. The Holy Spirit, working as the comforter speaks words of acceptance and peace with God to the heart of a believer during sanctification. "For all who are being led by the Spirit of God, these are the sons of God" (Rom. 8:14). The Holy Spirit leads you to understand the scriptures. The Holy Spirit convicts you that Jesus is the way, the truth and the life with God (John 14:6). The new life becomes a wonder in the heart that leads you to depend more and more on God, whom you have not seen except by understanding your faith. The Holy Spirit gives you reproofs for sin, encourages prayer, and draws you to works of love and service. The consequences of a spiritual life with Jesus convicts you of passing from death to life. A state of grace from God starts out with a gift of living hope and faith in Jesus (1 Pet. 1:3). It grows into a vision in your heart, that believes in your mind that Jesus saves. No matter what you thought before, now you believe: you believe in Jesus. Amen.

By the grace of God, you will behold and enjoy your salvation in your mind (Isa. 62:11). Faith (2 Pet. 1:1), hope (Col. 1:17), a good conscience (2 Cor. 1:12) and loving the brothers and sisters (1 John 3:14), all contribute to building the grace of assurance in our hearts. By God's building up the trust of Jesus in your heart, Christian, you are being given notice of your salvation. The redemption worked out by God, and the proclaiming of the gospel of grace in Jesus' name, will be offered to the ends of the earth. The work of deliverance in the hearts of believers shall be done by God. "Behold His reward is with Him, and His work before Him" (Isa. 62:11). God's work is wrought in us to be a holy person, and our reward is to know the Redeemer. Jesus Christ is our Savior and the reward of salvation Himself. "Behold, God is my salvation, I will trust and not be afraid; for the Lord God is my strength and song and He has become my salvation" (Isa. 12:2). He gives us songs in the night. Those that have God as their strength also have God as their song. We have the comfort in our hearts, and He gets the glory released from our hearts. Amen.

We are called saints (1 Cor. 1:2), chosen and called to salvation through sanctification (2 Thess. 2:13). We shall be called the redeemed of the Lord (Rom. 3:24, Eph. 1:7). God seeks us out (Isa. 62:12). We are called, and God works on our broken heart, humiliation and repentance, to prepare us to be a holy people. The Lord builds into our hearts comfort, peace and the assurance of our salvation. Take heart, Christian, folks are being delivered and saved in spite of the opposition in the world and the powers of darkness. God gives grace to folks, and they experience the reasons to praise Him. Their hearts will be rich with gratitude, and they know that God deserves the glory. By Jesus Christ, Christian, any anger that God could have directed toward us for sin has been turned away. He is our peace (Eph. 2:14). We are safe in Jesus. We have hearts that gladly come to Him. We freely trust Him to prepare, preserve and guide us "in paths of righteousness for His name's sake" (Ps. 23:3).

We still have a lot of heart work to be done. We have thorns and temptations in the flesh to resist in gaining the knowledge that His grace always will be sufficient for us (2 Cor. 12:9). We are responsible to work out our salvation with fear and trembling (Phil. 2:12). "For it is God who is at work in you, both to will and to work for His good pleasure" (Phil. 2:13). We have been called and justified by God (Rom. 8:30). "God has chosen you from the beginning for salvation through sanctification by the Spirit and faith in the truth" (2 Thess. 2:13). We are called by God to be holy (1 Pet. 1:15-16). Our hearts are changed when we act responsibly alongside God's sovereignty. We do our best to cooperate with the workings of the Holy Spirit, and in this way, discover in our heart the work of God. Our cooperation does not earn eternal life, but discovers the love and goodness of God for our soul. We love, because He first loved us (1 John 4:19). We must be set apart and grow to be holy in God's way. It is the pleasure of God to do this by His grace, and not our effort. We work and wait in prayer and study on the Lord. We are saved by grace through faith (Eph. 2:8).

Faith is most realized when we are made to know our weaknesses. In a bible passage, the Lord tells Paul that "My grace is sufficient for you, for My power is perfected in weakness" (2 Cor. 12:9). In the same passage, Paul tells us that he would rather boast about his weaknesses, that the power of Christ may dwell in him. We are to boast in the Lord (1 Cor. 1:31). "For when I am weak, then I am strong" (2 Cor. 12:10). This may sound odd, Christian, but we need more of God's power and grace and not more of our own power. We first try to manage our sin and weakness without God and fail. Our weakness humbly leads us to call upon God, and to meet with Him for help. Read your Bible (Rom. 10:17). Promises from God strengthen our faith and hope. Faith is assurance of hope and conviction of things not seen (Heb. 11:1). Faith pleases God (Heb. 11:6). The presence of Christ alive in your heart is eternal life (John 17:3). Amen. When the grace of faith from trust and endurance is built up in your heart, in the Lord's time it spiritually releases an important strength to combat sin, and gives great pleasure in looking forward to being with Jesus. Amen.

To Jesus we owe the peace in our heart from the freedom of guilt for sin, and He deserves our service. To those that are being sanctified by Christ, the Lord sends them into the word for heart surgery. The Lord will send them to a local church to worship and to associate and serve with fellow saints. The people of God's church have been bought with a price and are saved sinners. People from all over the world, and over a long period of time, will be gathered and become one holy nation in glory. The beauty of the church is Jesus alive in the heart of the saint. The church is a house of faith and miracles. The church is a place of growth in grace and knowledge. Praise God; the Father, Son and Holy Spirit, that He changed our hearts. "Therefore, we will joyously draw water from the springs of salvation" (Isa. 12:3). To God be the glory. The best is yet to come.

Assurance in the heart is a gift from God and a personal conviction. You can be persuaded that nothing can separate you from the love of God (Rom. 8:38). The blind man once said "Whether He is a sinner I do not know; one thing I do know, that, whereas I was blind, now I see" (John 9:25). The new heart comes with spiritual light for spiritual realities. You know there is life after death (John 5:24), and there will be a future judgment (Acts 24:25). You know the miracle of being saved, and that you did not work for it or deserve it (Eph. 2:8-9). You know that when Jesus appears you will be like Him (1 John 3:2). You know that all things are working together for your good (Rom. 8:28). You will know that it was by the grace of God, you are what you are (1 Cor. 5:10, Ps. 57:2). It was always God who was at work in you (Phil. 2:13).

God's love and interest in you, Christian, can be realized by taking notice of what is happening in your heart. You are not the man you used to be. You will know the increase in the grace of God in your life, by His power to act that enables you to walk with Jesus. Amen. God remembers and fully understands our hearts regarding the covenant He made with us in Jesus. God cannot be defeated and will not throw away His choice of you to be found in Jesus. The ability of God to keep His side of the covenant was never in doubt. It is sealed. However, our side of the covenant needs His help to be sealed. We need the Lord to seal His promises even for our side of the covenant to Himself. We need the grace of God to protect and secure our hearts for Himself. He seals our pardon with the grace of obedience in our new man. He lessens the space between Christ and ourselves and strengthens our souls against temptation. We get ripe for holiness and longing for God's presence. We want to have a more complete vision of God. We want to hear from the Holy Spirit more clearly and frequently. It is a not my will be done, but Thy will be done. It is not something I demand or deserve but rather a place where I can be grateful for His love. We get thirsty for God, and live with fear and trembling for the wonder He has become in our hearts.

We come to know the scriptures in a way that we can feel them breathe. We enjoy the fact that Jesus has been registered in our hearts as a matchless portion. "The Lord is my portion, says my soul, therefore I have hope in Him" (Lam. 3:24). My heart knows that the answer to this life, and the future, is the glory of God. The portion with Jesus that we have come to lean upon, is forever. My soul, heart, spirit, and mind all agree; "the Lord is my portion" (Ps. 119:57). "My flesh and my heart may fail, but God is the strength of my heart and my portion forever" (Ps. 73:26). In relation to salvation, Christian, God is and will ever be the only necessary portion. By God's will and pleasure, He becomes our most blessed portion. Because of the magnitude and importance of this dignity, "be all the more diligent to make certain about His calling and choosing you" (2 Pet. 1:10). God is infinitely above any and all other notions we may have about Him. Amen.

"Let not your heart be troubled; believe in God, believe also in Me. I go to prepare a place for you. I will come again and receive you to Myself; that where I'm, there you may be also" (John 14:1,3). He is "a very present help in trouble" (Ps. 46:1). The night before Jesus was arrested and condemned to die on the cross, He spent the time comforting His disciples. We are to believe in God. We are to believe in His wonderous love, infinite wisdom, faithfulness and absolute sovereignty. God has enough ability and power to stabilize any believing heart. He personally will receive us unto Himself and take us to a place He prepared for us. Jesus Himself, Christian, is coming again. This thought should clear your heart of any troubling thoughts. The Lord is near us. "Be anxious for nothing, but in everything by prayer and supplication, let your requests be made known to God. And the peace of God, which surpasses all comprehension, shall guard your hearts and your minds in Christ Jesus" (Phil. 4:6-7). We must ease our minds with prayer and thanksgiving. The peace of God is a cure, because we keep the sense of being reconciled to God as His child. The peace keeps us from sinking under the weight of trouble. "The steadfast of mind, Thou wilt keep in perfect peace" (Isa. 26:3). The promise is that God will abundantly supply the way into the eternal kingdom of Jesus Christ (2 Pet. 1:11). In your faith for a peaceful heart, supply moral excellence, knowledge, self-control, perseverance, godliness, brotherly kindness and love (2 Pet. 1:5-7). The truth here, Christian, is that, when you discover or realize that God has a hold of your heart, and become your portion, you will know Him as your Healer, Redeemer and the Savior of your soul. God builds assurance about Jesus in your heart. Amen.

No man can always know the heart of God towards him by the circumstances he may find himself in. God knows our hearts and what He is doing for our good. We know His hand may be seen as against us, when His heart is for us from the example of Job's life (Job 1). The Lord's hand was against Saul and for David (1 Sam. 15-16, Ps.118:22). The Lord favored Abel over Cain (Gen. 4:1-7) and Moses over Pharaoh (Ex. 7,8). The Lord told Moses that "I will be gracious to whom I will be gracious, and will show compassion on whom I will show compassion" (Ex. 33:19). Sometimes folks are left to themselves and fall into wickedness and bondage before their conversion and the kind mercy of God rescues them. This brings God more glory in their salvation. The mercy of God changed Saul from ignorance and unbelief into Paul, and the service of the gospel on the road to Damascus (Acts 9, 1 Tim. 1:12-13). The mercy of God changed me from selfish disobedience into an obedience of faith (Rom. 16:26). I was in misery one time and the heart of God showed me mercy. I once thought that God did not love me, because I did not keep His commandments (John 14:15). I was wrong and deceived. I admit that I did not know the Lord well enough with a good Bible understanding to love Him with a full obedience, but He still loved me (Eph. 2:3-5, Rom. 5:8). God was at work in my trouble to accomplish a purpose that I was not fully aware of at times. Amen.

An ignorant heart is a heart in the dark (Prov. 19:2). In the dark, a person may practice sin without serious consideration of the negative consequences. They might be lost, or be a hypocrite, or a weak Christian serving two masters. At one time in some ways, I served two masters and looked like a hypocrite. The truth was, I was not following the knowledge I had of the truth with an undivided heart. I was suffering in a conflict that I was ill equipped to fight. Satan presents the bait and hides the hook. We are enticed and carried away by our own lust, which gives birth to sin (James 1:14-15). I was responsible for defiling my own heart. My own heart, the world and Satan were drawing me to sin, and in part, I thought it would make me happy. The world is lost, and along with Satan, encourages folks to not believe or trust what the "old Bible" has to say. They think they are enlightened about truth, and instead, have chosen what they want to believe, and reject the truth, the Bible and Jesus. They would prefer that you would quit going to church, and not talk to them about sin, righteousness, judgment (John16:8), forgiveness and Jesus. They ridicule you for tithing your income. The devil wants to destroy you (John 10:10) and kill your heart for Jesus. Other folks will blame you about the ideas of judgment, which they do not want to hear, not realizing that they are the words of love from God. Nonbelievers may feel threatened by the truth, and get angry about how you may think about them. They may feel you judged them as not saved. Let them alone; they are really still angry at God, and will not change by your arguing with them. You know that they need the miracle of God drawing them to Jesus to be born again. You know that they need a new heart. You know that they need to read the Bible to get the truth. You know they need prayer. You know they need the Lord to go to work for them and change their heart, because that is what He did for you. Amen.

What is going on in your heart, Christian, is new to you, but not to God. No one else really knows your spiritual struggles except you. It is all right that other people do not understand you. What is important is that you are moving forward with the Lord. God's wisdom in Jesus "was predestined to our glory; if the rulers of that age had understood it, they would not have crucified the Lord of glory" (1 Cor. 2:7-8). The words "to our glory", Christian, speaks to our future glorification, which God determined would be a spectacular view of His grace and mercy and love. Indeed, all the glory belongs to God. Amen. "We exult in hope of the glory of God" (Rom. 5:2). Exult is an emotion that I think comes out of the heart of a man. It is an expression of great delight and great confidence in what God has done and will do for us. It is not self-confidence, but a complete joy released unto a great and good God.

All men are sinful and guilty before God, and we are only justified, by grace through faith, based on the redemptive work of Jesus Christ on the cross (Rom. 5:1). God's grace is only realized through Jesus, and ministered to us by the Holy Spirit, who indwells and gives us power to live for Jesus. We cannot obey God's commands by reliance on our natural strength, instead we learn to rely on the Holy Spirit, the Spirit of grace. We stand on firm ground "freely bestowed on us in the Beloved" (Eph. 1:6). Do not frustrate the grace of God by not letting God work in you (Gal. 2:21). The heart must believe and consent to be loved by God; to testify of His goodness, to not trust the flesh and to be certain of God's kindness now and for the future. We are always standing in God's grace. "God is able to keep you from stumbling, and to make you stand in the presence of His glory blameless with great joy" (Jude 24). To abide in Christ as a branch, where Jesus is the true vine (John 15:1-5), is to stand and be alive in an environment of His grace. Our state of peace in Jesus is on firm ground. Our hearts are persuaded of His love. "I know whom I have believed and I'm convinced that He is able to guard what I have entrusted to Him until that day" (2 Tim. 1:12). He holds us. Our heart can stand, Christian, only because it stands in the Son of God. Amen.

The grace of God makes you afraid to trust your own heart. The grace of God makes you think about your own heart, and to examine it and watch over it. You become careful about what goes into it and what comes out of it. True grace will work your heart to stay close to Jesus. I'd rather have Jesus than silver or gold or be a king in a vast domain (I'd rather have Jesus, Rhea Miller, 1922). I want and need Jesus in my heart to do the right thing. The grace of God gives our hearts a good rest when we spend time with Jesus, that the world cannot compete with. Amen. The way of holiness is reasonable and enabled by the Holy Spirit. The way of godliness is called the Highway of Holiness (Isa. 35:8). When God comes to save us, Christian, He chalks out the way by the gospel. The way to heaven has been appointed by God, and directed by divine providence. The redeemed children of God will walk on this road. The Holy Spirit will lead them. The way is broad that leads to destruction, but the way is narrow that leads to life (Matt. 7:13-14). The end of the narrow way, for the ransomed of the Lord, will be a heart of gladness and everlasting joy (Isa. 35:10). Jesus has the words and power to forgive our sins and grant eternal life (John 6:68). He saved us to walk on the narrow road with Himself.

Since we have been given all things by Christ, Christian, He becomes all things to us. He owns me; I have been bought with a price: therefore, I will glorify God (1 Cor. 6:20). My heart, soul, mind and body belong to Him. He patiently keeps us on the road. I hope that the Lord will use me for His pleasure, according to His good and perfect will, and for His glory. The road with Jesus to heaven may be filled with some rough spots or affliction that troubles our heart, but remember those whom the Lord loves He disciplines (Heb. 12:6). In any affliction, if your heart is drawn out to Christ and to be closer to Him, then you can have confidence that God's grace has a loving purpose. If under trials and temptation, you study the Bible and pray for help, this honors God. God knows best about how we surrender our hearts to Himself. If your soul becomes more holy from your affliction, then the trial has come to your life in God's love. We may be distressed by various trials, that the proof of your faith may be found to result in praise and glory at the revelation of Jesus Christ (1 Pet. 1:6-7). "The God of all grace, will Himself perfect, confirm and strengthen and establish you (1 Pet. 5:10). Amen.

The best is yet to come. The best is reserved until heaven. Our hearts will be melted and poured out when we see Jesus. Our faith and our hopes will be facts, and His love will be forevermore. We will have "an inheritance which is imperishable and undefiled and will not fade away, reserved in heaven" (1 Pet. 1:4). This inheritance is secured by the promise, power and the blood of Jesus. The inheritance is pure and perfect; it will completely satisfy the soul and fill the heart. The Christian life in this world has been a place of warfare and struggle with a believing hope in Jesus. In our new home, we will know peace and rest. Our living in this world is passing away, we are going to die. In this world, our hearts can be disappointed and our souls troubled. We work too hard for too long for too little without enough rest. By the grace of God, we know some rest in this world in Jesus, but our creator has designs and plans for the hearts of believers to know an incomprehensible rest in Jesus. When believers get to heaven, they shall have a much clearer vision of God. Now we see and know Him in part, but in heaven we shall have a much greater apprehension of God, as it were, face to face (1 Cor. 13:12). We will see God and His glory. We will gain more knowledge and understanding of the mysteries of spiritual life. We will know more about the Trinity, heaven, creation, redemption and the victory of Jesus in our life, as well as the gospel in the whole world. We will know the mysteries of providence in saving our souls. We will know immortality in our glorified bodies and the perfections of God's grace. Our hearts will know the superlative joys of salvation. We will know a presence of God that will fill and inflame our hearts with delight. We will know the depth of God's love. The God who made us and knows us, will have prepared a perfect place that fits us. Our hearts and minds will be completely satisfied with Thy likeness when we come into eternal life.

"For now, we see in a mirror dimly, but then face to face; now I know in part, but then I shall know fully just as I also have been fully known" (1 Cor. 13:12). "If anyone loves God, he is known by Him" (1 Cor. 8:3). God knows us before He gives us a new heart, and God knows us after He gives us a new heart. In the new heart abides the gifts of "faith, hope and love, these three, but the greatest of these is love" (1 Cor. 13:13). The Lord knows those who are His (2 Tim. 2:19) and that "we love, because He first loved us" (1 John 4:19). God recognizes our love for Him, Christian, because it is a love that He imparted and grew within us. It is important to know the doctrine of Christ. The evidence of true doctrine and true spiritual life with Jesus can be realized by how much you love other Christians. Our love for God becomes known by our love for others. The quality of love may be noticed in your feelings, but is an action initiated in your will. It is a love that flows naturally with ease and is fulfilling and peaceful. It flows with strangers and folks with difficult personalities as well as people you already get along with. The grace of love in our heart is a gift that first flowed from God (1 John 4:9). The fruit of this love in us opens our eyes and ears to help others for God's glory. The result is not self-love. God becomes such a great knowledge of life to us, that we enjoy His presence and desire He get all the glory all the time. God's glory becomes our happiness, and we seek that His will be done (Luke 22:42). What I once thought was best for me has changed. I now regard, His good and perfect will, as my best good.

God says, "give Me your heart My son, and let your eyes delight in My ways" (Prov. 23:26). God calls for and requires all of us to give Him our hearts. We must set our love upon Him. We must not divide our heart between God and the world. We must love the Lord, our God, with all our heart (Matt. 22:37). "No man can serve two masters; for either he will hate the one and love the other" (Matt. 6:24). You cannot serve God and yourself. You cannot lay up treasures on earth and in heaven at the same time, they will come into conflict. "Where your treasure is, there will be your heart also (Matt. 6:21). I know that you cannot serve two masters; Christian, I tried and failed. By the grace of God, I hate sin and love Jesus. Amen. The grace of godliness that is active in my heart is because He first loved me. Eternal life (John 3:16) and glory for me (1 Cor. 2:7) can be seen as serving a self-interest; but the fact is, my interest in these things originated and grew from the fruit of His love for me in being born again. We are first drawn to God by His love, and in Him we learn to love Him back. From this love, we learn to love others and even ourselves. God will always know our heart. The Bible reveals a lot about the heart of God. In heaven, we will know more. Even in heaven, there will be a whole lot more we cannot know, because we will always be children compared to God.

"Though you have not seen Him, you love Him, and though you do not see Him now, but believe in Him, you greatly rejoice with joy inexpressible and full of glory, obtaining as the outcome of your faith the salvation of your souls" (1Pet. 1:8-9). True faith produces true love for Jesus. This love becomes sincere and affectionate, with a mind rich in understanding and assurance, and a will delighted to be in His service. True faith develops a heart of love for God and rejoices in His heart of mercy and grace. Being made in God's image and rich in His Spirit, we should reflect His heart of love in our life for others. A heart of love has peace and joy inside it. Peace and joy come from our deep sense of love and acceptance from God. The well-being, that abides in our heart, is a gift of grace from God's heart, letting us know we are His children. Amen. To God be the glory.

Freedom

*"It was for freedom that Christ set us free;
therefore, keep standing firm and do not
be subject again to a yoke of slavery"*
(Gal. 5:1).

Dear Christian,

We owe our freedom from the penalty and practice of sin to Jesus Christ. He was anointed to preach the gospel to the poor in spirit, recover sight to the blind, and to set free those who are in bondage and downtrodden (Luke 4:18). The gospel is a proclamation of freedom to give rest to those who are under the burden of guilt and corruption. He came in God's name to heal the broken-hearted. We are not set free to do whatever we want to do. We are set free to be in a relationship with our Creator and discover the purpose He has chosen for us in this life. We are set free from the law and the curse of sin by the power of God, according to His good will and perfect way. The broken and surrendered believer knows freedom when he yields to the guidance of the indwelling Holy Spirit. The believer knows freedom when he walks with Jesus and worships the Lord from his heart in spirit and truth (John 4:24). The believer discovers God's love in a relationship with Jesus. The believer discovers the work of the Holy Spirit in a call to holiness and over time, by the grace of God, discovers the freedom that Jesus died for us to experience. The ways of freedom in Jesus strongly influence us, those around us, and even our country.

We are born as natural men, without freedom and under the bondage of sin (1 Cor. 2:14). We are bound to instincts for sin and captive to impulses of sin; therefore, we sin. "All have sinned and fall short of the glory of God" (Rom. 3:23). "For the wages of sin is death, but the free gift of God is eternal life in Christ Jesus our Lord" (Rom. 6:23). We live under a death sentence from which Jesus sets us free. Sin, shame and guilt is bondage not freedom; when Jesus sets us free, we become free indeed. Jesus said, "The thief comes only to steal, kill, and destroy; I came that they may have life, and might have it abundantly" (John 10:10). When you remember that you are saved by grace, Christian, it helps you live by grace. The truth of being in Jesus brings about a deep spiritual sense of peace and freedom. Your heart works with the Lord out of gratitude and love, and not trying to win God's approval. This is freedom. Guilt cannot survive here, because God's grace is always greater than our sin and weakness. We are encouraged to stand firm in this gospel. The sense of freedom and being right with God, Christian, is the greatest freedom of all. Amen. Be diligent to understand the grace principle and attentive to the voice of God. The great blessings of grace are peace and assurance with God, and freedom and joy to walk with Him.

The shed blood of Jesus gives us freedom from the power of sin. The blood of Jesus washes away the defilement from sin that has lodged in our conscience. Sin and temptations are great thorns in our lives. We are weak and need God's grace to know freedom. God's grace leads us into confessing our sins for cleansing from a defiled conscience (1 John 1:9). God's grace is greater than our sin (Rom. 5:20). The Bible says, "As sin reigned in death, even so grace might reign through righteousness to eternal life through Jesus Christ our Lord" (Rom. 5:21). To know that this grace has a hold on you means belonging to the Lord God and the building up of freedom in your heart. We are His workmanship (Eph. 2:10). God makes us holy when He redeems us through the blood of the Lamb, His Son, Jesus Christ. We hear a call to trust and receive Jesus as a

Savior to forgive us of our sin and save us from the penalty of sin. The call from God is an invitation and instruction on how to be saved. The call is not a gamble; it has authority. Some folks do not understand or recognize this voice and choose to ignore it. Some folks delay, because they are not ready, while other folks gladly receive the call. The call is to be born again, "not of blood, nor of the will of the flesh, nor of the will of man, but of God" (John 1:12). When we hear the call and receive the invitation from God, He gives us a new spirit and heart (Ezek. 36:26) with the gifts of faith, hope, and love for Jesus. The result is the creation of a new man (2 Cor. 5:17). Only the new man can know freedom. The power of God penetrates a dead man's heart and gives him a new heart that will learn to love Him. God loves us enough to desire to save us, but it cannot take place the way we were. We are sinners and God hates sin (Prov. 6:16-19). The great condemnation of sin was revealed by the death of a Savior. "For God so loved the world, that He gave His only begotten Son, that whoever believes in Him should not perish, but have eternal life" (John 3:16). Amen.

We cannot get freedom and save ourselves by our own wisdom and power. We cannot cleanse our own conscience, remove guilt or do anything as a work to know, earn or obtain freedom. Dead men cannot hear without a miracle of God's grace in their hearts. God, the creator, established the way to freedom. Man is humbled and God is glorified. "He made Him who knew no sin to be sin on our behalf, that we might become the righteousness of God in Him" (2 Cor. 5:21). We are born in sin, and naturally enjoy sin because, according to the Bible, we are a natural man. We are dominated by our soul which brings forth sin and bondage. A giant cloud hangs on our hearts called guilt. We are captives to sin by our own choices, and blind and ignorant about the truth and how to get freedom. God's plan was for us to be born again and receive a new spiritual heart. God's plan was for His Son Jesus to die in order to pay the price of our penalty for sin and provide for our cleansing. Christ must become a man and die to satisfy the holiness and justice of God for sin. At the same time, God's mercy would be satisfied in the saving of guilty sinners. Thus, Jesus paid the price for us and removed the penalty. This is by the grace of God, Christian, that we will celebrate throughout eternity. "Without the shedding of blood there is no forgiveness" (Heb. 9:22). We must be changed to know and have true freedom. God gives the learning senses of the eye and the ear to hear His voice and to see the beauty of His holiness (Prov. 20:12). Jesus is God's only remedy for freedom from sin.

On the road to freedom, the Lord opens our understanding of Jesus in the gospel. The veil is removed. The Bible says that "Whenever a man turns to the Lord, the veil is taken away" (2 Cor. 3:16). Living under the law and as a natural man, there is a veil over the heart. When a man is converted to God, Christian, the veil of ignorance and blindness of the mind and the hardness of the heart is taken away. Amen. We are God's workmanship (Eph. 2:10). There is a division between the soul and the spirit and, by the grace of God, your rebellion and carnality are more clearly exposed to your understanding. By the word of God and the sword of the Spirit, they are cut off (Heb. 4:12). The word of God, that is the Bible, is alive. It cuts at the roots of sin in your life, draining away the desires to sin. Whereas, once your soul had trouble even knowing a spiritual life, the word of God pierces through and separates the soul and the spirit. The word of God seizes upon your conscience and frees it to hear the alarm bell of repentance. The new spirit is rooting out the old sinful habits and releasing your will from bondage into the freedom of choice. The new man is waxing stronger while the old man is waning out of your heart. We more clearly see and welcome the cleansing flood of holiness from a God who, indeed, loves us in Jesus. We are made willing to be clean by the sacrifice of Christ.

The Bible becomes a great treasure chest to look into and see how to grow in grace and knowledge. We learn that if He washes me, I will be whiter than snow (Ps. 51:7). I clearly sense the strength that I am freer to choose to not sin, and follow through with my decision. My decision is informed and strengthened in my new man by the Holy Spirit. Freedom comes into your soul; it fills the heart and clears the conscience. I was healed by being broken of myself or the old man. Freedom is a cleansing gift that is real and of eternal value. It comes from the God who created you to be a living stone, precious in His sight (1 Pet. 2:4). "You are a chosen race, a royal priesthood, a holy nation, a people for God's own possession, that you may proclaim the excellencies of Him who has called you out of darkness into His marvelous light" (1 Pet. 2:9). Jesus "was pierced through for our iniquities, and by His scourging we are healed" (Isa. 53:5). "Because He poured out Himself to death, He was allotted a portion with the great" (Isa. 53:12). The God who calls us out of the bondage of darkness, Christian, makes Jesus great and strong in our souls. "For we are His workmanship, created in Jesus for good works, which God prepared beforehand, that we should walk in them" (Eph. 2:10). Praise the Lord, Amen.

"Faithful is He who calls you, and He also will bring it to pass" (1 Thess. 5:24). "For I am confident of this very thing, that He who began a good work in you will perfect it until the day of Christ Jesus" (Phil. 1:6). "God is at work in you, both to will and to work for His good pleasure" (Phil. 2:13). "I will cry to God most high, to God who accomplishes all things for me" (Ps.57:2). "May the God of peace sanctify you entirely" (1 Thess. 5:23). Our salvation, Christian, involves both our responsibility and God's sovereignty. God does the spiritual heavy lifting. We must fight by putting on the armor of God (Eph. 6:11-18). Be diligent to study the Bible, pray and serve the Lord in the local church. We work out what God has put into us. He saves us and deserves all the glory. In God's time, we grow in the strength of His grace and knowledge. We are always His workmanship. In God's time, we experience a freedom in Jesus Christ that is both peaceful and enjoyable. The new man breathes deeply in this freedom, without sin, for God's presence and will to be done for us in his life. He freed me from bondage, Christian, and I long to use my freedom for Him. Amen.

The blessing of living with freedom in my soul strongly encourages me to deeply trust in the Lord. It supports my prayer life and sends me more and more into His word to have more of His life in me. "He must increase, but I must decrease" (John 3:30). True freedom lies in your surrender to Jesus. What looks like a defeat to the world is a victory in Jesus. I think David said this best in the Psalms. "The Lord is my shepherd; I shall not want. He makes me lie down in green pastures; He leads me beside quiet waters. He restores my soul; He guides me in the paths of righteousness for His name's sake" (Ps. 23:1-3). The greatness of this Psalm to me, Christian, lies in the freedom it describes we come to know after we surrender to Jesus. Freedom, that is, spiritual freedom is a gift of God. We come to know we belong to Him by His work in us. We belong to the Lord; we are the sheep of His pasture. He is the guardian of our souls. He cares for us, watches over us, preserves us and has plans for our welfare and not calamity to give us a future and a hope (Jer. 29:11). He is our refuge (Ps. 46:1-5). "I am the good shepherd" (John 10:11). God is all-sufficient for anything from our past, in the present, and for the future. Our freedom is born out of our relationship to Him. We can hear His voice (John 10:3), we can know His voice (John 10:4), we can follow Him (John 10:27) and find pasture (John 10:9). The thought that He "makes me" lie down in green pastures is not troublesome, but highly comforting. God's word is my green pasture. His goodness has led me beside still waters. I'm reminded of the story of Jesus and a man walking in the sand making 4 footprints, and then it goes to two footprints. The fellow wants to know what happened. The answer from Jesus is that the two footprints were the times I was carrying you. Thank you, Jesus for being my shepherd.

To be guided by God into paths of righteousness is a great thing. To be saved from the wrath of God has great value indeed, and to be saved from sin and led into paths of holiness has great value. The work that God does for us will be thorough and complete, that is, the grace of God will make us free from the power and presence of sin. "He who began a good work in you will perfect it until the day of Christ Jesus" (Phil. 1:9). It is to the honor of Jesus that we should be a holy people. It is for His name's sake. Being led away from bondage and into freedom on paths of righteousness, in spite of my weakness, is a deliverance that proves He is a good shepherd. His name will be magnified. I trust God leading me in any path that lifts up the name of Jesus. He restores my soul by giving me the gift of repentance. The paths of righteousness, Christian, are watered with fountains of consolation. God brings us back when we fall into errors or wander away. Our baggage does not hold us back. It is a path that leads to Himself. The manner that He saves us brings honor to the Lord. It reveals His character and perfections, especially the love and faithfulness that He provides as our safe and certain Guide.

In the nature of our sanctification, the sense of freedom will seem to come and go according to our choices about sin. The thing to do is talk to the Lord. "If we confess our sins, He is faithful and righteous to forgive us our sins and to cleanse us from all unrighteousness" (1 John 1:9). This important verse of scripture speaks about God's covenant faithfulness to us, justice for His Son and Himself, and His glory in the justification of sinners. Further, not only is forgiveness proclaimed, but a cleansing of all unrighteousness. We still may sin, and though we are already forgiven, we still confess it for freedom, forgiveness and a new beginning. Amen. When we sin, the guilt of unrighteousness shows up in our conscience. A new man will confess his sin. The battle against sin is on-going. We acknowledge we are unworthy, and we agree with the Lord and experience contrition. We are humbled in our weakness and desire to be cleansed and not to sin again. We are serious and sincere in confession of sin and seek forgiveness. Confession is the evidence that we are forgiven. It is important that we agree with a holy God. The work of Jesus Christ on the cross for us has already been done and was a perfect sacrifice. Our soul by confession, in a way, is vomiting out the filth of sin. If you have a repeated sin, your life will feel like a waste because of your foolishness. It is like an act of unbelief, and you will suffer for it. Nevertheless, you are His son. You will humbly return to God and confess your sin. I believe that God forgives sin when we agree with Him, and He takes it away and will remember it no more (Heb. 8:12). It is the grace of God being merciful about our unrighteousness for the sake of Jesus. Sin is being defeated and our hearts made stronger when we seek His forgiveness. In God's time, Christian, the child of God comes to know that the faith that endures becomes more precious and praiseworthy (1 Pet. 1:7). The child of God is developing a history with the Lord that works to confirm, strengthen and establish his faith (1 Pet.1:10). The gifts in the call to believe and persevere in Jesus, from the God of all grace, will be in the crown of your glory (1 Pet. 5:4, James 1:12 and 1 Cor. 2:7). A heart of gratitude for the freedom attained by the grace and work of God in this life is the proof of future freedom in the life to come. Amen.

"Therefore, having been justified by faith, we have peace with God through our Lord Jesus Christ" (Rom. 5:1). Justification takes away the guilt of sin and makes the way for peace. We have been pardoned of sin and saved by the grace of God. It is like we never sinned. It is not of our work that no one should boast (Eph. 2: 8-9). We experience peace and freedom and stand forever in His grace rejoicing in the hope of future glory (Rom. 5:1-2). However, we still will sin and therefore are in need of continued pardon. Sin will rob us of the sense of freedom from slavery. We must mature and experience God. We must learn our sincerity, and know the love of God. The Lord our God goes to work building a weight of glory for Christ and His children. The process of sanctification, by the grace of God, works an experience of God into our hearts through the Holy Spirit. This involves tribulation, perseverance, proven character, hope, and the love of God (Rom. 5:2-5). We must sense the love of God. Amen. Our continued pardon includes the responsibility to confess our sins. Confession is an important part of our Christian faith. Confession is about cleansing us from all unrighteousness (1 John 1:9). Cleansing from the defilement of sin is a miracle of God's grace that brings back the sense of freedom after we have sinned. God purges away the unrighteous nature that still lurks in our hearts. We experience a holy lovingkindness. In His time, we are delivered from the power and practice of sin. This may occur shortly after we truly desire, in our hearts, to be delivered from sin. God gets the glory. We are never perfect (1 John 1:8,10), Christian, but we have been changed. The fact that we grow in grace by this kind of miracle is undeniable to a real Christian. A clear conscience is a great place of freedom. The Lord cleans us up in the soul or on the inside first, and the work in the flesh usually follows shortly after. A pure heart is the enduring work of God. Amen.

"Beloved, now we are children of God, and it has not appeared as yet what we shall be. We know that, when He appears, we shall be like Him, because we shall see Him just as He is. And everyone who has this hope fixed on Him purifies himself, just as He is pure" (1 John 3:2-3). "Draw near to God and He will draw near to you" (James 4:8). Draw near to God in prayer, Bible study and worship and He will draw near to you in mercy. Draw near to God, Christian, in faith, trust and obedience and He will draw near to you in love, comforts and hope. Without holiness, no one will see the Lord (Heb. 12:14). "Now may the God of hope fill you with all joy and peace in believing, that you may abound in hope by the power of the Holy Spirit" (Rom. 15:13). God's work in us is always drawing us to be like Christ. He has put in place the greatest gifts and most love for those that honor the Son. God sets the truth in our hearts, Christian, that the best concept of freedom will only be known and secured in the hearts of individuals that seek Jesus.

"If you abide in My word, then you are truly disciples of Mine; and you shall know the truth, and the truth shall set you free" (John 8:31-32). The evidence of salvation and true freedom is abiding in the word. Some folks might think they are free and do not know the word of God. I would submit to you that they do not know the depths of freedom that Jesus spoke about. To walk and serve with Jesus is more important than to know just what is true. Demons believe in God's existence and power, but since their belief was without sincere works in their soul and body, it was considered dead (James 2:19). It brings them no salvation, peace or freedom except to shudder before God (Matt. 25:41). To know the Truth is to know Jesus. Jesus said, "I am the way, the truth and the life" (John 14:6). "If therefore the Son shall make you free, you shall be free indeed" (John 8:36). The truth gives spiritual liberty, Christian; it sets you free from the power of sin and the darkness of spiritual death (Eph. 4:18). The man of the world thinks that being a Christian and going to church and tithing limits his freedom. The man of the world as a natural man is blind, ignorant and unconscious of his bondage and spiritual trouble. He is not free to choose Jesus until he is drawn by God (John 6:44). The believer is the Lord's freeman and servant (1 Cor. 7:22). "Though you were slaves of sin, you became obedient from the heart to that form of teaching to which you were committed, and having been freed from sin, you became slaves of righteousness" (Rom. 6:17-18). "Having been slaves of sin and freed to God, you derive your benefit, resulting in sanctification, and the outcome, eternal life" (Rom. 6:22). Conversion is a freedom from the service of sin. We are delivered out of Egypt and brought into the bond of the covenant. Freedom is not serving two masters. Amen.

We end up with the same great hopes in our thoughts and prayers for sanctification, that the Lord wants to work in us. There is a pleading with the Lord for more freedom from sin and self and greater desires for a sense of His presence with us. He makes, leads, restores and guides us in paths of righteousness for His name's sake (Ps. 23:2-3). To God be the glory. This gracious work of the love of God for our spiritual needs, develops in us a love and delight for obedience. The precious gift of holiness or sanctification is a great blessing of grace and privilege for us, and honor for Jesus. He accomplishes all this for "His name's sake" and for His adopted children. The joy and desire for freedom from sin and for the Lord, is from the Lord Himself. The peace in freedom is from the Lord. The way of righteousness is in the gift of freedom from God. Freedom is not to do whatever we think is right or fun. Our prayers become "Make me walk in the path of Thy commandments, for I delight in it" (Ps. 119:35). "Revive me through Thy righteousness" (Ps. 119:40). The Lord teaches us the path of life, and by His love makes us go in it. God's teaching enlightens the mind, provides understanding, and bolsters the weakness of our hearts and will against the power of our corrupt inclinations. Amen.

"The gate is small, and the way is narrow that leads to life, and few are those who find it" (Matt. 7:14). The way of the world is broad, Christian, and leads to destruction, and many are those who enter by it. By God's grace, I want the narrow path, and by

God's grace I will walk in it. "It is God who is at work in you, both to will and to work for His good pleasure" (Phil. 2:13). "We are His workmanship" (Eph. 2:13). I pray that God will "incline my heart to Thy testimonies" (Ps. 119:36). I pray that God will "Turn my eyes from looking at vanity, and revive me in Thy ways" (Ps. 119:37). Help me to pray. Help me to read more and meditate on your word. Help me to have more of your life in the way of righteousness. Amen. "Create in me a clean heart, O God" and "make me to hear joy and gladness" (Ps. 51:8,10). The old natural man is being "put off" and the new spiritual man created in Christ Jesus is "put on" (Eph. 4:22-24). God has provided for us a sure salvation, free from death and hell with Himself in Heaven. God has sealed for us a sure salvation by the presence of the Holy Spirit of adoption. When you "hear" this acceptance, it means that you are alive and free to be joyful and glad. The word of God is alive and describes for our hearts and minds the true meaning of freedom. To God be the glory.

"Now the Lord is the Spirit; and where the Spirit of the Lord is, there is liberty" (2 Cor. 3:17). The Spirit of the Lord our God, Christian, is in the Gospel, and when He works, there is liberty. That is, freedom from danger and the law and sin; freedom to come to the throne of grace and freedom to pray. Our hearts are set free to learn about God and live in the ways of His commandments. God Himself cannot be accurately described by men's words. The Bible does express to us though that God is a mystery as a Trinity, comprised of the Father, Son and Holy Spirit. They are one in essence, yet three distinct personalities. I think in the above passage, that the Lord is Jesus Christ (2 Cor. 3:16) and the Spirit of the Lord is the Holy Spirit. The Bible also tells us that "The law of the Spirit of life in Christ Jesus has set you free from the law of sin and of death" (Rom. 8:2). The Spirit of Christ is God liberating us from sin and death, and transforming us into the same image from glory to glory (2 Cor. 3:18). Amen. When the Gospel is received into your heart, then the Spirit of the Lord is given. Wherever the Spirit lives, there is liberty. We are being led by the Spirit of God (Rom. 8:14) and have received a spirit of adoption (Rom. 8:15). We are called children of God (Rom. 8:16). The Father searches our hearts to know what the mind of the Spirit is and then intercedes for us according to the will of God (Rom. 8:27). Sanctification is the fruit of Justification. All the members of the Trinity are at work interceding for us and bringing about our spiritual freedom. Our salvation is designed, but what is chiefly designed is the honor of Jesus Christ. All the providences of God are working to bring us closer to God, to restore our affections for Him, bless us with freedom and secure our salvation, all to honor the Lord Jesus.

"We know that God is causing all things to work together for good to those who love God, to those who are called according to His purpose" (Rom. 8:28). Only God can cause all things to work together. Even sin is permitted to work for our good. The privileges we have, Christian, were freely given to us by the grace of God. Our freedom was predestinated. "For whom He foreknew, He also predestinated to become conformed to the image of His Son, that He might be the first-born among many brethren; and whom He predestined, these He also called; and whom He called, these He also justified; and whom He justified, these He also glorified" (Rom. 8:29-30). This is the counsel of God, conveyed to us through Jesus Christ, in the Gospel Covenant. Amen. This is the word of God. Though not specifically mentioned here, it takes in the whole of our sanctification. "It was for freedom that Christ set us free" (Gal. 5:1). It was the good pleasure of the Father to secure Him a remnant as a gift for His labors. "We are chosen according to the foreknowledge of God the Father, by the sanctifying work of the Spirit, that you obey Jesus Christ and be sprinkled with His blood" (1 Pet. 1:2). Our freedom is from the everlasting love and affection of our Father. We do not conform ourselves to Christ, Christian, to be saved. We were given to the Son by the Father and can only be certain of the freedom in our election by our conformity to Christ. We should always give thanks to God, "because God has chosen you from the beginning for salvation through sanctification by the Spirit and faith in the truth" (2 Thess. 2:13). Every crown will be cast before the throne. This is God's perfect work. He laid the foundation and will be building upon it your whole life to His glory and your great benefit. Salvation is all of grace. In the ages to come, God will show the surpassing riches of His grace in kindness toward us in Christ Jesus (Eph. 2:7). Amen.

Our important responsibility is to "work out our salvation with fear and trembling" what He is working into us (Phil. 2:12). The encouragement to work out your salvation is meant as an incentive to act in ways that please the Lord. Do not abuse your freedom and the grace of God by willfully continuing in sin. We are to guard our hearts and minds by putting on the armor of God (Eph. 6:11-18). It is not a work that saves you; God has already done that. As you do your part, Christian, you will see and realize the Holy Spirit is doing His part to help you to be free and holy. Do not trust your own heart but lean upon Jesus. He who began a good work in you will finish the job (Phil. 1:6). With fear and trembling is meant humility and vigilance, respectively. Work with an anxious care in a serious, difficult and important manner. Realize how tremendously precious eternity will be, and live for the One who secured it for you. "But to this one I will look, to him who is humble and contrite of spirit, and who trembles at My word" (Isa. 66:2). We need to look upon the word with an awe of God's majesty and purity. We need to remember that we are but men facing the truth in judgment. We need to remember that we are a living temple where God dwells (1 Cor. 3:16). We are in heaven on earth. We have been bought with a price (1 Cor. 6:20). "Thy word is a lamp unto my feet, and a light to my path" (Ps. 119:105). To know the light, you must "walk" in the Bible. Jesus said, "I am the light of the world; he who follows me shall not walk in the darkness, but shall have the light of life" (John 8:12). When you walk with Jesus, Christian, you will know the gift and pleasures and power of freedom. Jesus did what He did in the power of the Holy Spirit (Luke 4:1,14,18; 5:17; Matt. 5:18). He is our example (1 John 2:6).

The law of the Spirit will accomplish what God has promised. The law of the Spirit is more powerful than the law of sin and death. The word for law used in this case is not a law like the Mosaic Law or commandments and requirements, but stands for a regulative principle or rule or standard of acting. It is a principle of operation. Our new man in Jesus has a new heart, a new spirit, a new life and new laws. Our new man has a supernatural energy in the influences of the Holy Spirit. Despite this, the Holy Spirit can be quenched (1 Thess. 5:19), grieved (Eph. 4:30) and resisted (Acts 7:51) by my free will. We are in a conflict of two natures (Rom. 7:14-24). The new man, because he is free, can exercise a desire and power to do God's will (Ezek. 36:27, Phil. 2:13). The source of this power in the new man is the Holy Spirit, through which we are set free because of the work of Jesus (Rom. 7:24-25). The freedom in Christ does not mean you can do whatever you think is right or want, but rather to please God by doing what you learn is right from Him. Our freedom is not a license to sin. The New Testament uses the word law with regard to the law of love (Rom. 13:10), the law of faith (Rom. 3:27) and the law of liberty (James 1:25, 2:12) as it does for the law of the Spirit of life in Christ (Rom. 8:2). Along with the laws appearing in the New Testament, the Holy Spirit provides for us precious promises. These include freedom (Rom. 8:2), strength (Rom. 8:11), victory over sin (Rom. 8:13), leading us (Rom. 8:14), adoption (Rom. 8:15-16) and helping us in prayer (Rom. 8:26). The new man is a spiritual man. He has been changed or freed from bondage to sin and self on the inside, in the heart first. The actions of the body or the outside follows being redirected by our renewed will in Jesus. What follows from spiritual freedom is the privilege of holy living, by the grace of God, with a faith that produces obedience (Rom. 1:5). Amen.

"It is the Spirit who gives life; the flesh profits nothing; the words that I have spoken to you are spirit and life" (John 6:63). Our freedom is a gift of God. It is amazing to me how many people think they must earn their new life in Christ. The flesh has no part in the work of God except to follow the soul led by the spirit. Dead men can only be made alive by God. The natural man thinks he should or must contribute something in the way of obedience to be saved. God has made it otherwise, so that no flesh will boast or glory in itself (Eph. 2:9). Some men fight this battle of error their whole life believing that God will save them, because they are not bad enough to be lost. This is not the scripture. The scripture is that, "All men have sinned and fallen short of the glory of God" (Rom. 3:23), and "the wages of sin is death, but the free gift of God is eternal life in Christ Jesus" (Rom. 6:23). "For just as the Father raises the dead and gives them life, even so the Son also gives live to whom He wishes" (John 5:21). The Bible tells us that our regeneration is the work of all three persons of the Trinity (John 3:5; 5:21; 6:44, 63). The Bible tells us that the resurrection of Jesus was the work of all three persons of the Trinity (John 10:18, Rom. 8:11, Eph. 1:20). We are drawn to Jesus by the work of the Father (John 6:65). We have been born again by the Spirit (John 3:5) and "through the living and abiding word of God" (1 Pet. 1:23).

Being born again and gaining freedom is a mysterious combination of God's sovereignty and man's responsibility. God gets all the glory. We are to discover what God has put into us about believing in Christ, being sincere, and having desires to read the Bible. We discover being quickened by the Holy Spirit. A great sense of freedom and security emerges from the heart of the person who only trusts in Christ. "The Lord is my strength and song, and has become my salvation" (Ps. 118:14). The security means a freedom from fear about what might happen in life and death. We discover that God rewards those who seek Him (Heb. 11:6). "To him who orders his way aright I shall show the salvation of God" (Ps. 50:23). "With long life I will satisfy him and let him behold My salvation" (Ps. 91:16). God blesses you with a great foretaste of eternal freedom when He lets you see and behold your salvation. Amen. The song of a redeemed man, Christian, is music in the ear of God. It brings forth praise and gratitude and honors God. A holy life honors God. God blesses a man with a sincerity that rises to heaven. The work of following Jesus from your heart is a miracle. I pray that God will give you grace to order your life right. To behold your salvation is to know that, He loved you before you set your love on Him. To behold your salvation is to understand your freedom from sin because of Jesus.

Who is like our God, Christian? He gives us a conquering grace, and then He rewards us for it. He makes us content about leaving this life by knowing we will enter into a rest that will be all glorious. He gives an intelligent trust and warm affections by His grace and then prepares a place filled with peace and joy. He forgives us of all our sins and then fills our hearts with gratitude. We desert Him at times from weakness, but He never leaves us. To behold your salvation results in a great freedom. God gives us a freedom to believe in Jesus over and above anything else in this world. God gives us a freedom to be grateful and cherish the heart and work of God to save us. Amen. The powers of darkness tried to ruin me, but the Lord delivered me. I was reminded of the story of a righteous man named Simeon in the Bible who was promised by the Holy Spirit that he would not die until he had seen the Lord's Christ (Luke 2:26). When he saw Jesus in the Temple, He proclaimed that he was ready to depart in peace "for my eyes have seen Thy salvation" (Luke 2:30). When you "see" Jesus, your soul rejoices in freedom, because you have seen your salvation. Amen.

"If you abide in My word, then you are truly disciples of Mine; and you shall know the truth, and the truth shall make you free" (John 8:31-32). "If therefore the Son shall make you free, you shall be free indeed" (John 8:36). Justification makes you free from the guilt of sin and saves you from the wrath of God. Sanctification sets you apart and makes you free from the bondage of corruption. The Gospel frees you from the ceremonies of the Law, desires to sin, selfish behaviors, prejudices and lies that entangle the soul. The Gospel introduces you to Jesus, the grace of God and holiness. The Christian is an intelligent person whose thoughts, by the grace of God, are delivered into an obedience of faith in Christ (Rom. 16:25-26). We are always spiritual children with God, Christian, who has chosen us to learn about Christ and grow in grace. We start out rather ignorant and weak as natural men; in time, by the mercies of God, we grow in knowledge and gain strength as spiritual men with a testimony for Jesus. The word of God is something we continue to look into and hold on. We learn we are disciples. We learn that "The one who has endured to the end will be saved" (Matt. 10;22). We learn that the growth of faith came by reading the word of God (Rom. 10:17). We learn that it is the Truth in Jesus that gave us spiritual liberty from darkness, blindness and spiritual death (Eph. 4:18). Spiritual freedom in Jesus means eternal life. Amen.

Spiritual truth is much more important than the facts from the world, because they deal with the Lord and eternity. Jesus said, "I am the way, and the truth, and the life; no one comes to the Father, but through Me" (John 14:6). Truth is not found in the world's philosophy but can be found in a Person. Jesus is the full revelation of God (Heb. 1-3). When God calls a man and/or when His Spirit speaks to our hearts, Christian, it comes with a different authority than that found in the world. God 's word strikes more deeply and with more force than our feelings and desires. When God's word strikes, our conscience is alerted. The words we hear are more peaceful, profound and complete. The truth is setting you free. In Jesus are hid "all the treasures of wisdom and knowledge" (Col. 2:3). Jesus is the truth about God, the way to God, and the life with God (John 14:6). Jesus "came that you might have life, and might have it abundantly" (John 10:10). When we walk with Jesus, He becomes our freedom. It is impossible to know what freedom is and to have freedom without Jesus. It was for freedom that Jesus came to earth for us (Gal. 5:1). Freedom is being released when the power of sin and bondage and the wrath of God are diminished, and we become a slave of His righteousness (Rom. 6:18). The long-term benefits of freedom are a more complete sanctification and then glorification. The subjection of your heart to God's righteousness is the beginning of your growth into perfect liberty. Amen.

The gospel is called a law of liberty. "One who looks intently at the perfect law, the law of liberty, and abides by it, not having become a forgetful hearer but an effectual doer, this man shall be blessed in what he does" (James 1:25). "So speak and so act, as those who are to be judged by the law of liberty" (James 2:12). The gospel is about being liberated. It gives us a deliverance from sin and guilt, wrath and death and the Jewish ceremonial laws. The law, which stands for the word of God, is perfect because it comes from God and reveals His will. The Christian law is a law of love; we are free to love God and our neighbors. It is perfect, because it reveals the full revelation of God in Jesus (Heb. 1:1-3). The gospel is the perfect law of a gracious salvation, able to convert the soul. It is a perfect law, because it allows us to realize our God-given purpose and destiny. It is our responsibility to look intently into the word of God. We are to look carefully, inspect with interest and curiosity, meditate on it patiently yet diligently, and release our hearts into the study of the word of God.

Living by a faith in Christ works a transforming power that promotes and prompts a desire for obedience without compulsion. He saves us from ourselves. Amen. By the grace of God, we find ourselves abiding and persevering with a readiness to obey. We find ourselves falling in love with Jesus and being held captive to the truth of the gospel. We are running on the road to eternal freedom. The word of God takes root in the soul, Christian, to the extent that you know you have found the great treasure in the field and the pearl of great value (Matt. 13:44-46). From great joy, you sell all that you have and surrender everything you are, and go out and buy the field and the pearl. Amen. Hearing is good, but doing and experiencing the Christian life for yourself and with others is much better proof of God's grace. You will be blessed in your deeds, not for your deeds. "You see that faith was working with his works, and as a result of the works, faith was perfected" (James 2:22). Faith without works is dead (James 2:17). To know the perfection of faith, the Lord has told us we must be doers of the word and not hearers only. Doers of the word can know a special presence of God, especially when they help others. "Where the Spirit of the Lord is, there is liberty" (2 Cor. 3:17). Where the Spirit of the Lord is, it yields to us a sense of freedom in the heart, Christian, that becomes a nature of love in our soul for others. The service of the Lord is a perfect freedom. Amen.

We will be judged and are responsible to God about how we responded to the gospel from our heart. We will be judged by the law of liberty (James 2:12). We must be conscious of our duty and conversation. We are encouraged to be merciful since we are vessels of the mercy of God (Rom. 9:23). Mercy triumphs over judgment (James 2:13). Blessed are the merciful, for they shall obtain mercy (Matt. 5:7). We must have compassion for the souls of others. Those in a state of sin or want, and the ignorant and careless, may not yet know the love of God and the depths of freedom and forgiveness in Jesus. Mercy is giving them a part of your heart, rather than just a piece of your mind. They may need instruction and/or assistance and compassion in their misery. You do not always know what is going on in another man's heart, but God always does. The person may be suffering because of sin or the devil's hatred like Job did. Jesus can help them, heal them and bless them. They may need the testimony of Jesus for strength and encouragement. "The testimony of Jesus is the spirit of Prophecy" (Rev. 19:10). Jesus is coming again. To me, this is prophecy and a fact. A Bible prophecy was never made by an act of the human will but men moved by the Holy Spirit spoke from God (2 Pet. 1:21). The Bible has a lot of fulfilled prophecies, many about Jesus. God is good and gracious and all-powerful. He can meet any need in the most perfect way. To be merciful with other folks is godly, and I believe has the potential to present the opportunity for them to hope in God. In our newfound freedom, we reflect God's mercy. Showing mercy to others also has the promise to the merciful, that they shall obtain mercy from men, but especially God. The merciful will judge charitably and receive mercy in their time of need, by the mercy of God. The merciful remember that they themselves are unworthy recipients of God's merciful work for their freedom in Jesus. The merciful shall inherit the Kingdom of God (Matt. 25:34). To God be the glory that a Christian can be merciful. Amen.

We live in a country, by the grace of God, that was founded as a Christian nation. God has been merciful with us, and allowed us to share with the world the ideals of freedom and mercy. Although our nation has not been perfect, the Lord has used us to share the gospel in our world. Our Founders and the people had a passion for freedom. They escaped England and left for America primarily for religious freedom. They fought for freedom and established a country with 13 colonies with a Constitution and a Bill of Rights. The people were influenced by Jesus and by men like Luther,

Calvin and Knox. They were also influenced by men like Rousseau and Locke. The providential view of God's sovereignty traveled from the Reformers to the Founders of our nation. Our Founders established what is called a republic. The constitution protects the people from the will of the majority. The Bill of Rights is the first 10 amendments to the Constitution. It guarantees civil rights and liberties to the individual and protects the right of religious beliefs and practice. It prevents the government from creating or favoring a religion. The genius of America, in my opinion, is a secular government with a free and religious people. There is no statement in the Constitution or the Amendments about "separation of church and state". Those folks who want a godless country and godless leaders use this non-constitutional phrase to try to eliminate religious influence. Our government includes non-believers and believers in Jesus. The Founders believed that religion and serving God was living a good and moral life and was indispensable for a good society. They intended a secular state in which God's moral laws would play an important part. "We the people" means a great deal, and I believe that through the people God would bless the nation both spiritually and physically. In this spiritual environment, we would build our institutions on truth the best we could. Under the providence of God, we have achieved more freedom, both civil and religious, and prosperity in our country than the world has ever seen.

The framework of our republic is still present, but the spirit, which I believe is Christianity, has been suffocated. "Blessed is the nation whose God is the Lord; and the people whom He hath chosen for His own inheritance," (Ps. 33:12). God's chosen people are blessed by a spiritual religion, which includes the true understanding of freedom. God's grace rules the day. The Lord fashions our hearts and understands our works (Ps. 33:15). "Behold, the eye of the Lord is on those who fear Him, on those who hope for His lovingkindness" (Ps. 33:18). The fear or reverence of God promotes holiness and hope through grace in the person of Jesus. Today, we have generations of folks that have grown up that do not know or fear the Lord, Christian; they are doing what they think is right in their own eyes (Judges 17:6). Though the country started with the Bible as the foundation for character development, we are transitioning to godless secular methods of education and governance, which have marginalized our Christian heritage. A few folks have a voice with a big volume, but without wisdom. For various reasons, they want to change or destroy the American way of life. We the people choose and need free and fair elections. I sense that someone is trying to steal my freedom, and it is not a pleasing thought. "Righteousness exalts a nation, but sin is a disgrace to any people" (Prov. 14:34). A righteous administration of government and equity between all men is called justice. The general practice and protection of good men, charity and compassion to strangers and the poor exalt a nation. We need to be a nation of laws. On the other hand, vice reigning in a nation is a disgrace. Sin is a reproach to a city and a dishonor to people. America has never been perfect. The rejection of the Bible as the word of God dooms our nation as inglorious. The current direction of America and the world suggests difficult times are coming (2 Tim. 3:1-3). Pray for your nation. The only hope we have is Jesus. Amen. Can we change our ways? If we do, it will "not be by might nor by power, but by My Spirit, says the Lord of hosts" (Zech. 4:6).

The goodness and spiritual freedom we have in Jesus is a gift from God that builds our personal righteousness. Together with other believers, our testimony for God's righteousness must be protected, developed and maintained in our nation for our freedom. The devil means a war to steal, kill and destroy (John 10:10). "How blessed are the people whose God is the Lord" (Ps. 144:15). Freedom in any country requires power to defend it in order to keep it. Our freedom in Jesus was obtained by His power and will be maintained by His grace and power. We are responsible to exert our strength by cooperating with God in order to live in His freedom. Amen.

"Once you were not a people, but now you are the people of God; you had not received mercy, but now you have received mercy" (1 Pet. 2:10). While we were sinners in bondage, Christ in mercy for us, died for our freedom (Gal. 5:1, Rom. 5:8). "You are a chosen race, a royal priesthood, a holy nation, a people for God's own possession, that you may proclaim the excellencies of Him who called you out of darkness into His marvelous light" (1 Pet. 2:9). All true Christians have been shown great mercy in being chosen and cared for, and blessed with spiritual prosperity. All true Christians compose one holy nation, devoted to God and sanctified by the Holy Spirit. Our "citizenship is in heaven, from which we eagerly wait for a Savior, the Lord Jesus Christ who will transform the body of our humble state into conformity with the body of His glory" (Phil. 3:20-21). Our new body will be recognizable (Matt. 17:4) but with a complete change of our inward nature. On earth, we know that if we abide in His word, you shall know the truth, and the truth will set you free (John 8:32). In heaven, we will know perfect freedom. In heaven, we will be holy and completely free to follow and obey the Lord Jesus. Amen.

Holiness

"As obedient children, do not be conformed to the former lusts which were yours in your ignorance, but like the Holy One who called you, be holy yourselves in all your behavior; because it is written, you shall be holy for I'm holy"

(1 Pet. 1:14-16).

Dear Christian,

God is holy. The Bible says that God is holy, holy, holy (Isa. 6:3, Rev. 4:8). This repetition and emphasis support the idea that the thoughts of holiness are about a Triune God and are of utmost importance. The complete definition of the holiness of God is difficult for us to arrive at, because we cannot fully understand the essence of God's character. God is also love (1 John 4:8) and light (1 John 1:5). The word of God emphasizes the spiritual value of God's holiness by saying three times that God is holy. God the Father, the Son and the Holy Spirit are holy. We cannot fully describe God's holiness, but we can sense the importance, purity and beauty of holiness. It means a lot to God, Christian; He calls us to be holy and tells us that without holiness, we will not see Him (Heb. 12:14). The word "holiness" means "to be set apart". Holiness sets God apart from His creation, and will set us apart from the world. The Bible is called the Holy Bible; it is set apart from any other book, because it alone contains the word of God.

Israel is called the holy land; angels are called holy and the Sabbath is a holy day for worship. The land of Israel, angels and the Sabbath have been set apart by God. The Christian becomes separated from sin, by the grace of God, and grows to be more holy. God hates sin (Ps. 5:4-6, Prov. 6:16-19), and "cannot be tempted by evil, and He Himself does not tempt anyone" (James 1:13). Holiness is who God is, Christian, and holiness is what He has in our salvation and eternity. Holiness is an inherent perfection of God's being. He did not choose to be holy because He wanted to be, or just thought it was a good idea. Holiness gives moral beauty and purity to all the perfections of God. God's perfect wisdom, power, patience, goodness and faithfulness all operate and work with God's holiness. The Spirit of God is called the Holy Spirit (John 14:26, Acts 5:3-4). For our encouragement, Christian, God has told us He would send another Comforter, the Spirit of truth (John 14:16-17). The presence of the Holy Spirit "would teach you all things, and bring to your remembrance, whatsoever I have said to you" (John 14:26). Jesus would be speaking to us through the Holy Spirit, to plead His cause and do His work to make ready the Bride of Christ in holiness and truth. Amen.

The holiness of Christ was announced in the Psalms and by the Prophets. "For Thou wilt not abandon my soul to Hades; neither wilt Thou allow Thy Holy One to undergo decay" (Ps. 16:10). This verse is written about Christ and His resurrection. God would not abandon the soul of Jesus in Hades, the place of the dead. Because we are in Christ, we also will not be forsaken (Heb. 13:5) by God, but will know the holy faithfulness of God. Since Jesus bore our sin without becoming a sinner, He remained the Holy One. The Holy One refers to Jesus (Acts 2:27, 13:35), whose body did not decay or see corruption. We shall die, and because of sin see corruption, but we shall be separated, and rise to everlasting life because of Christ's resurrection. The resurrection of Jesus proved He was able to remove sin and its penalty. He proved His power over death, and His deity (1 Cor. 15:1-4). His resurrection is the cause and guarantee of the rising of all His people (1 Cor. 15:20-23, 1 Pet. 1:3). The holiness of Christ was proclaimed by the angel

Gabriel to Mary (Luke 1:35), by the centurion at His crucifixion (Luke 23:47) and demons (Mark 1:24). The holiness of Christ was proclaimed by Peter (Acts 4:27, 30), Paul (2 Cor. 5:21), John (1 John 2:1, 29) and Christ Himself (Rev. 3:7). "He appeared in order to take away sins; and in Him there is no sin (1 John 3:5). "For it was fitting that we should have such a High Priest, holy, innocent, undefiled, separated from sinners and exalted above the heavens" (Heb.7:26). To come to God, Christian, we needed a holy High Priest to encourage and enable us to do so (Luke 1:35). His nature was holy, and He loved His Father with all His heart. In living upon the earth, He was undefiled. He was made higher than the heavens which is the highest. Our praise of Jesus ought to know no bounds. Amen.

"Who is like Thee among the gods, O Lord? Who is like Thee, majestic in holiness, awesome in praises, working wonders?" (Ex. 15:11). This verse is from the Song of Moses which Israel sang after their deliverance from Egypt. It mirrors the glad deliverance of the church through the ages, and the working wonders for believers delivered from sin by the Lord. Holiness is a glorious perfection belonging to the nature of God. The holiness of God is His glory and a great title of honor. I shudder to think about the possibility of any evil in God. "He has made everything beautiful in its time (Eccl. 3:11). The holiness of God means a perfect freedom from evil. He loves truth and righteousness (Ps. 5:4). God can only be holy. God hates all sin, Christian: where the guilt and filth has been washed away by the Mediator, He loves their persons. "For the Lord is righteous; He loves righteousness; the upright will behold His face" (Ps. 11:7). "Pursue peace with all men, and the sanctification without which no one will see the Lord" (Heb. 12:14). Think hard and long about this last verse, Christian, and let it be a word of encouragement and victory for your heart in the battles against sin. The reward and the promise for being like Him, is to see Him. Also, "we know that when He appears, we shall be like Him, because we shall see Him just as He is. Everyone who has this hope fixed on Him purifies himself, just as He is pure" (1 John 3:2-3).

What you believe should and will motivate your behavior. We live holy lives, Christian, because we are children of God. We are not trying to be holy to prove we are children of God. The unbeliever sins against God and the law, while the believer sins against his Father and against love. What we do either proclaims the truth of Jesus or it does not. By the grace of God, the hope we have in Jesus "does not disappoint, because the love of God has been poured out within our hearts through the Holy Spirit who was given to us" (Rom. 5:5). It is our responsibility to "work out our salvation with fear and trembling" (Phil. 2:12). This means to be engaged in a life-long pursuit of holiness, striving to be like Christ. At the same time, Christian, we depend upon the power of the Holy Spirit to work within us according to His good pleasure (Phil. 2:13). We must and will be holy to see Jesus and inhabit heaven. Thank you, Jesus. Amen.

We were originally made in the image of God and after His likeness (Gen. 1:26-27). Man was made upright (Eccl. 7:29). This does not mean his posture, but rather, man was made like God with wisdom and goodness. God made man rational and without fault. Man fell from God and into himself, but God recovered man after His own image in Jesus. We have "laid aside the old self with its evil practices, and have put on the new self who is being renewed to a true knowledge according to the image of the One who created him" (Col. 3:9-10). The image of God is recovered by sanctifying grace. The holiness of God is seen in our redemption. "He who did not spare His own Son, but delivered Him up for us all" (Rom. 8:32), tells us what great value God puts upon holiness. His own Son suffered, died and felt forsaken (Ps. 22:1). The honor of God's holiness is preserved in our justification by the call for repentance and a faith that purifies the heart (Acts15:9). The honor of God's holiness is preserved in our sanctification "by perseverance in doing good" (Rom. 2:7). The rewards for holiness are heavenly and the punishments of evil are eternal. The powerful motive for good in the Son of God dying for us, tells us how much God detests evil and how much it took to satisfy the Divine perfection. The stress from the Lord for your salvation is laid upon your holy living, and God will let you know this truth. God will not be mocked (Gal. 6:7).

The importance of holiness in the believer's life also appears in the High Priestly Prayer of Jesus. He asks the Father to "sanctify them in the truth" (John 17:17). He was saying to the Father, make them holy. Paul expressed a similar hope for the believers to God, the Father. "Now may the God of peace Himself sanctify you entirely; and may your spirit and soul and body be preserved complete, without blame at the coming of our Lord Jesus Christ" (1 Thess. 5:23). They were asking God the Father to continue to work and confirm holiness in the believers. They wanted the Father to strengthen your faith and kindle their affections for a holy life. We have the Holy Spirit as a witness and a pledge that God will complete His purpose (2 Cor. 5:5). I believe that Jesus is currently interceding for our sanctification (Rom. 8:34). Apply your hopes, thoughts and prayers to God for holiness, Christian, because He delights to work holiness into your spirit. He starts the work in this life and will perfect it in the next. In holiness, we honor God and bless ourselves. God is all glorious in holiness (Ex. 15:11). His people will reflect His holiness.

The Bible tells us "Whom He foreknew, He also predestined to become conformed to the image of His Son" (Rom. 8:29). We "are chosen according to the foreknowledge of God the Father, by the sanctifying work of the Spirit, that you may obey Jesus Christ and be sprinkled with His blood" (1 Pet. 1:1-2). "He chose us in Him before the foundation of the world" (Eph. 1:4). "Whoever calls upon the name of the Lord will be saved" (Rom. 10:13). We acted according to the foreknowledge of God by our own volition. Amen. The full meaning of these passages is beyond our finite comprehension. We did not save ourselves. The doctrine of election is in the Bible, Christian; showing us that the necessary and powerful work for us, from the beginning to the end, is a gift of God. We are being conformed into the image of His Son. Our responsibility is to discover and receive His work of salvation into our lives "with fear and trembling" (Phil. 3:12). Amen. "God has chosen you from the beginning for salvation through sanctification by the Spirit and faith in the truth" (2 Thess. 2:13). The honor for our sanctification goes to Jesus; He is the first-born and the pattern, and will have the pre-eminence. I'm not perfect, Christian, but I'm being conformed to be like Him. Amen and thank you, Jesus. Again, we are not elected by God because we are holy, but that we might be holy. Faith and holiness go together. The call from God for you to be holy is clear in the gospel, and becomes effectual by the power of the Holy Spirit working in your heart. Amen.

"Therefore, gird your mind for action, fix your hope on the grace to be brought to you at the revelation of Jesus Christ" (1 Pet. 1:13) in your heart. "Like the Holy One who called you, be holy yourselves in all your behavior; because it is written, you shall be holy, for I'm holy" (1 Pet. 1;15-16). We are called to be holy, and by the grace of God, we are enabled to become holy. The Bible tells us that "God disciplines us for our good, that we may share His holiness" (Heb. 12:10). After God made our body, He breathed into us a spirit and man became a living soul (Gen. 2:7). God disciplines us to improve our graces, which reflect the image of God. The purpose of God in discipline or affliction is that we may run a more complete spiritual race. The purpose of God is to build a deeper faith with more patience, and the peaceful fruit of righteousness or holiness (Heb. 12:11). "Those whom the Lord loves He disciplines" (Heb. 12:6). It is for our eternal good. Discipline reveals what is really in your heart for God and quickens your prayer life. Christ "gave Himself for us, that He might redeem us from every lawless deed and purify for Himself a people for His own possession, zealous for good deeds" (Titus 2:14). God makes heaven more real and significant to us by faith. Affliction may be a pathway to your spiritual growth; however, Christian, the flesh may not be grateful under the difficulty of it. David said "before I was afflicted, I went astray, but now I keep Thy word" (Ps. 119:67). David learned to see the benefits of adversity. The Prodigal son's distress brought him to his senses and then back to his father (Luke 15:17-18). Amen. "For the grace of God has appeared, bringing salvation to all men, instructing us to deny ungodliness and worldly desires and to live sensibly, righteously and godly in the present age" (Titus 2:11-12). We are disciples of God's grace, Christian, which is not only a saving grace but a training grace. "We are disciplined by the Lord in order that we may not be condemned with the world" (1 Cor. 11:32). Amen.

"I urge you therefore, brethren, by the mercies of God that you present your bodies a living and holy sacrifice, acceptable to God, which is your spiritual service of worship. And do not be conformed to this world, but be transformed by the renewing of your mind" (Rom. 12:1-2). "Lay aside the old self that you may be renewed in the spirit of your mind and put on the new self, which in the likeness of God has been created in righteousness and holiness of the truth" (Eph. 4:22-24). Seek Jesus first, Christian, and as His power and presence become more intimate to you, the world and yourself will fall further away from your selfish interest. You cannot serve two masters (i.e., yourself and God). The pleasure of "the world is passing away, and also its lusts; but the one who does the will of God abides forever" (1 John 2:17). Your body should be listening to what your soul says, and your soul should be listening to what the love of the Lord says to your spirit. In the end, Christian, your life of faith, holiness, obedience and work will provide the evidence that you belong to Jesus and not the world. Your conscience will be your witness.

Godliness or holy living is not an option; looking for Jesus to appear as our blessed Savior is a responsibility that God's children grow into (Titus 2:12-13). "Godliness is profitable for all things, since it holds promise for the present life and also for the life to come" (1 Tim. 4:8). A crown of righteousness is being laid up for all those who have loved His appearing (2 Tim. 4:8). Godliness at first may seem to be a burden, but it turns out to be a great gain when accompanied by contentment (1 Tim. 6:6). As a man of God, pursue faith in Jesus, love, righteousness and gentleness. "Fight the good fight of faith; take hold of the eternal life to which you were called" (1 Tim. 6:12). Heaven will be a fight, Christian; you will fight against your sin and temptations, and you will need the Lord's help. It is a spiritual war and eternal life is the crown. Though you live in the flesh, you put on God's armor to protect your soul in battle (Eph. 6:11-18). Get a good knowledge of God from your Bible and allow the Holy Spirit to build up faith in your heart and conscience. Open your heart up to God when you read it that He might aid and bless your search with the truth of your believing and knowing your sincerity. It is God who is at work (Phil. 2:13) with power to enable you to "take every thought captive to the obedience of Christ" (2 Cor. 10:5). Herein lies the love of God. Amen. Having the promises of God, cleanse yourself from all defilement of flesh and spirit, perfecting holiness in the fear of God" (2 Cor. 7:1). Herein lies your responsibility in the working out of your salvation with fear and trembling (Phil.2:12). To God be the glory.

God is holy (Isa. 6:3). God is absolutely unique and has infinite value and excellence. God's intrinsic purity, which can only bring forth righteous actions, is His glory. The attribute of God's holiness brings forth from us a great confidence and worship experience. Jesus Himself referred to His Father as righteous when He revealed to the disciples that He was sent by the Father (John 17:25). The Bible tells us, "We have an Advocate with the Father, Jesus Christ the righteous" (1 John 2:1). We have an Advocate in the Holy Spirit called the Comforter that resides within us (John 14:6). He helps us intercede for ourselves (Rom. 8:26). In heaven, we have an Advocate with the Father; the mediator of our redemption, pleading the propitiation for our sins. "He made Him who knew no sin to be sin on our behalf, that we might become the righteousness of God in Him" (2 Cor. 5:21). In Jesus we are wrapped in a robe of His righteousness (Isa. 61:10), and bear the name, "The Lord our righteousness" (Jer. 33:16). Jesus always lives to make intercession for those who draw near to God through Him (Heb. 7:25). In Christ, "If we confess our sins, He is faithful and righteous to forgive us our sins and to cleanse us of all unrighteousness" (1 John 1:9). In Christ, we are new creatures reconciled to God with a new heart. We are justified freely by the grace of God. In Christ, God was not imputing or counting our trespasses against us for the sake of the merit of Jesus Christ. Therefore, we make mention of the righteousness of Jesus alone. We live, Christian, because He died for us. Amen. "If you live according to the flesh, you must die; but if by the Spirit you are putting to death the deeds of the body, you will live" (Rom. 8:13). God is at work in you, giving you the desire and power to kill sin (Phil. 2:13). Our responsibility is to die to self, surrender to the Spirit and follow Jesus in putting on the new self (Col. 3:1-5). The direction of your life should be with a strong willingness to be led by the Spirit (Rom. 6:19). We are in a war that "joyfully concurs with the law of God in the inner man" (Rom. 7:22).

The Bible tells us that sinners can only be justified and saved and made fit for heaven solely upon Christ's righteousness being imputed to them (Rom. 5:18-21, 2 Cor. 5:21, Phil. 3:7-10). A righteousness imputed means that the merit of Christ, as our mediator, is legally charged to our account. The righteousness of Christ as our substitute means that He becomes our Surety. This means our being saved by grace and not by our work (Eph. 2:8, Rom. 3:21-22, 1 Cor. 1:30). In salvation, Christian, there must be the merit of Christ's work imputed to us and the moral qualities of Christ's character imparted for us. The actual word "imparted" is not used in the Bible, but some folks use this term to define sanctification. Some other folks prefer to use the term "progressive sanctification" to describe our growth in grace and holiness. Both terms have been used to describe the work of the Holy Spirit to teach the sinner spiritual life. The graces of the Spirit of God, that is faith, repentance, love, humility and more, are received into the heart of God's elect. The mind, will and affections of the saved soul is greatly blessed by virtue of being one with Christ. The fruit and effect of Christ's work, Christian, will be the ground or the way you can realize or behold your salvation. It is true that we should grow in grace and knowledge after we are saved, if indeed we are saved. The Holy Spirit is imparted when you are born again to bring about His righteousness in your life. This is the grace of God in which you behold your salvation and not work to earn or prove it. You work out what God has already wrought in you. Amen.

Your sanctification follows your justification. Imputed righteousness can be viewed as justification, whereas imparted righteousness, where moral qualities of character are concerned, can be viewed as sanctification. The imputed nature of the righteousness of Jesus is absolutely necessary for salvation. God is holy and just, and does not save sinners by infusing good character into them or enabling the Holy Spirit to make them worthy of salvation. God has perfect satisfaction of His holiness and justice on what Christ has done alone for us to be righteous. A progressive growth in holiness is not necessary for your salvation. What you learn or have been enabled to do by the grace of God, makes no contribution to your being saved. If it did, it would be a works salvation. We are in Christ by His virtue, and not our faith, love and obedience. The Holy Spirit points us to Jesus and directs us to rest on Him alone. Amen. We aim for holiness. To grow in grace and knowledge and to be sanctified by the Spirit of Christ will give you more assurances you are saved. It may provide more opportunities to be useful for the Lord. We still run the race, with faith and love and seek to bear fruit and bring forth good works. Doing righteousness means we live in the light of the gospel (Heb. 12:1). Run the race with patience, looking unto Jesus, our Savior and Lord. Keep coming to Him every day in worship and gratitude. God's will be done. We belong to Him, and He will use us according to His good pleasure. He will take us home when He knows we are ready. The final aspect of our salvation, when sanctification will be perfected (Phil. 1:6), is called glorification. This will be a one-time event, when we see Jesus. "When He appears, we shall be like Him, because we shall see Him just as He is. And everyone who has this hope fixed on Him purifies himself, just as He is pure" (1 John 3:2-3). Amen.

To know the difference between right and wrong, we should and must start with God. God exists. He is truth and He is holy (Jer. 10:10, John 17:3, Rev. 4:8). The Lord is righteous (Ps. 11:7). God set the perfect standard based on His own perfect nature. We were made in the image of God (Gen. 1:26). Most believers treat man as being composed of a spirit, soul and body (1 Thess. 5:23). The spirit is thought to be where God speaks with us. Most believers treat the function of conscience as a part of man's spirit. Conscience reproves sin and approves of righteousness and the place where God expresses holiness. The conscience provides us with the sense of being morally right or wrong in your conduct, intentions and character. The thought that it is better to be good may come from the conscience. It is our inner judge of moral issues. The New Testament sees man's conscience as the instrument of judgment and a means of guidance. Some folks have used the metaphors of the "voice within" or the "inner light". John Calvin saw the conscience as a battleground, and Luther said that it was neither safe or right to go against conscience. The source of the conscience has been debatable. I have heard it is in the mind, spirit, heart, soul, self, brain and feelings. Some folks think it is a brain concept that arises from neurological complexity. I know this; it is very important and essential for the conscience to be educated and informed by the Holy Spirit. God speaks to us in our conscience. The conscience is to our souls what pain sensors are to our bodies. The conscience can inflict distress, especially in the form of guilt, whenever we violate what our hearts tell us is right (John MacArthur). The conscience is a witness to our inner value system. It is a trustworthy guide when it is informed and ruled by God and followed by you.

"The Lord God formed man of dust from the ground, and breathed into his nostrils the breath of life; and man became a living being." (Gen. 2:7). The breath of God formed the spirit of man, and he became a living soul with a mind, will and emotions. Man has a body that tells him how he feels and a mind to tell him what he thinks. Most importantly, man had a spirit; if it was illuminated by the Holy Spirit, it could know what God desires. "The spirit of man is the lamp of the Lord, searching all the innermost parts of his being" (Prov. 20:27). The Father of spirits is called the Father of lights (James 1:17, Heb.12:9). God lights the candle of conscience that gives us understanding of ourselves and others. God, figuratively speaking, lights the candle for Himself for the important purpose of intercession on our behalf (Rom. 8:26-27), and for the privilege and honor He gives us to worship Himself

(John 4:24). It is essential that the conscience be awakened from its essentially comatose state in the natural man and be properly educated by the Holy Spirit.

The conscience, Christian, is the organ of faith. The moral issues and questions about right and wrong are apprehended and informed in our conscience by the Holy Spirit. When we fall short of God's expectations, we can know the pains of selfish behavior and guilt. In the conscience, we can know the sense of being unfaithful to the Lord. When we follow God from our conscience, we can know the pleasures of being faithful. Thus, faith and conscience cannot be separated. When we are born again and walk by faith, the conscience has been "quickened", and we have been properly educated and informed to walk in newness of life (Rom. 6:4). The new spirit and heart we receive from God (Ezek. 36:26) makes it possible to hear from God. You are enlightened by the Holy Spirit so "that you may prove what the will of God is, that which is good and acceptable and perfect" (Rom. 12:2). The gift of faith from God is alive, and allows the born-again believer to be influenced by the Spirit of God. "For all who are being led by the Spirit of God, these are the sons of God" (Rom. 8:14). What follows is a good and clear conscience (1 Pet. 3:16). A conscience that hears the Holy Spirit can follow Jesus and become stout and glad.

As you grow in grace and knowledge, the witness of your conscience and the Holy Spirit will grow closer together. Read the Bible for faith (Rom. 10:17) to inform your conscience about what the Lord thinks. God is holy and allows stress about the lack of purity in your life to be realized in your conscience. "I'm telling the truth in Christ, I'm not lying, my conscience bearing me witness in the Holy Spirit" (Rom. 9:1). "The Spirit Himself bears witness with our spirit that we are children of God" (Rom. 8:16). "No one knows the thoughts of God except the Spirit of God. Now we have received, not the spirit of the world, but the Spirit who is from God, that we might know the things freely given us by God" (1 Cor. 2:11-12). By the gracious influences of the Holy Spirit, we can know the great privileges of the gospel. We have His voice in our conscience that speaks His will. The voice is usually a yes or no about right and wrong. After we have spent some time in the word, and grown in grace, our spirit will sense some things that are of the Lord, and some things that are not. The voice of conscience will not be put off by discussion from us, some rationalizations or mention of our good works. When we do not listen, Christian, God does not change His mind about us, but we can suffer with guilt and shame and lack peace. When we listen and obey our conscience, Christian, we have peace and assurance we belong to Jesus. The difference is immeasurable. When we walk with Jesus paying a sincere attention to our conscience, we begin to know and enjoy the "obedience of Faith" (Rom. 16:26). To God be the glory.

There are different types of consciences described in the word of God. Paul claimed, "I also do my best to maintain always a blameless conscience both before God and before men" (Acts 24:16). He said "I have lived my life with a perfectly good conscience before God up to this day" (Acts 23:1). A good, clear and blameless conscience does not mean one that has a "sinless" conscience. It means a person that is sensitive to avoid sin, is willing to obey the Lord, and confess their sin for cleansing (1 John 1:9). "If our heart does not condemn us, we have confidence before God" (1 John 3:21). The testimony of a clear conscience will help you be transparent when serving the Lord (2 Tim. 1:3). Sin must be forsaken before we can pray with confidence. We serve and pray with sincerity the best, from a good and clear conscience toward God (1 Pet. 3:21), and love from a pure heart with sincere faith (1 Tim. 1:5). Our conscience is where we learn God's standard of holiness. As our knowledge grows, the more our conscience will judge us. The conscience can be limited by a lack of knowledge, so it may be weak at times. A man with a weak conscience might follow his own ideas, instead of the word of God (1 Cor. 8:7). Be careful, we can sin against Christ by defiling the conscience of a weaker brother with less knowledge (1 Cor. 8:8-12). Do not be a stumbling block; sometimes we must deny ourselves for weaker brothers. The conscience should not be violated.

The Bible also speaks of a seared conscience in which the sense of the conscience has been deadened, because it was not listened to a lot of times. A seared conscience is numb, and it gets more difficult to be convicted about a God-given duty (1 Tim. 4:2). The Bible also mentions an evil conscience. "Let us draw near with a sincere heart in full assurance of faith, having our hearts sprinkled clean from an evil conscience" (Heb.10:22). All of us have sinned and come short of the glory of God (Rom. 3:23). We all have need of "the sanctifying work of the Spirit, that you may obey Jesus Christ and be sprinkled with His blood" (1 Pet. 1:2). The end of election is eternal life; but before this, we must be sanctified by the Spirit. By sanctification I mean being separated to God and reflect the image of God, mortifying our sins, and following Jesus in obedience. This is holiness. Our souls are purified when we obey the truth. The Lord produces fruits in the hearts of Christians (Gal. 5:22-23). The allusion to the sprinkling of the blood converts back to Jewish sacrificial language, but now and once and for all, faith in the sprinkling of Jesus' blood obtains forgiveness of sins (Rom. 3:25). The sprinkling of His blood alone justifies us before God (Rom. 5:9), seals the covenant (Luke 22:20), cleanses us from sin (1 John 1:7), and receives us into heaven (Heb. 10:19). Praise the Lord. The cleansing we receive leads us to the grace of "holding to the mystery of the faith with a clear conscience" (1 Tim. 3:9). This is the kind of conscience, Christian, that God builds into our hopes of seeing Jesus in heaven. Faith is a mystery that is held in our minds by the love of the Truth (John 14:6). God draws us to Himself by the power of His love (1 John 4:19). The cleansing of our conscience is a spiritual miracle in us by God. Only the Lord could do this kind of work, and only the Lord deserves all the glory. Amen.

It is from our conscience that God examines our motives, whether we really desire to obey Him or want to seek something else. We need His help to overcome ourselves. "God is greater than our heart, and knows all things" (1 John 3:20). If our conscience condemns us, then God probably does to, and if our conscience acquits us, then God probably does to. The spirit of man is the lamp of the Lord, searching all the innermost parts of his being (Prov. 20:27). The spirit works for God and helps us know our hearts. It is a gift from God that allows us to take notice of ourselves and to hear His judgments. We have been baptized into Christ, Christian, not to remove dirt, but to have a conscience that becomes enlightened. Baptism is a God-ordained symbolic appeal to God, a calling on the name of Jesus in the way of repentance, help and commitment to be saved. The true circumcision of the heart by the spirit (Rom. 2:29), and the grace of God, engages us to believe and hope in Jesus to be saved. The true circumcision of the heart is an "appeal to God for a good conscience-through the resurrection of Jesus Christ" (1 Pet. 3:21). In saving us, God places the foundation of faith and hope in Jesus in the conscience of our spirit. This gift is what makes us able to appeal to God for us to die to sin, and live with holiness and newness of life (Rom. 6:4). To God be the glory. By His love, Christian, we show we are of the truth; but if our heart condemns us, we take comfort that God knows our own heart better than we do. God's knowing us is perfect and infallible and a good thing for us. "There are ways that seem right to a man, but its end is the way of death" (Prov. 16:25). Be careful to not deceive yourself, or let your pride block you from thinking God knows best. Even in trials and trouble, God knows best, so turn your heart to Him. "For this finds favor, if for the sake of conscience toward God a man bears up under sorrows when suffering unjustly" (1 Pet. 2:19). God is the Supreme Court. We are not our own, but have been bought with a price (1 Cor. 6:19-20). We are clothed with the righteousness of His Son. I'm encouraged that God knows all things, Christian, and has chosen to be patient, merciful, kind and understanding, and to be reconciled to us as His children. Amen. He has implanted His love in your heart and works for your salvation (Phil. 2:13). In spite of our weakness, He has chosen to not forsake us (Heb. 13:5). His ability to judge my conscience with truth is much greater than mine. We are forgiven sinners.

The conscience bears witness in your heart, where your thoughts will alternately accuse you of being guilty, or defend you of not being guilty (Rom. 2:15). The conscience usually speaks to us in a yes or no manner. There is no discussion, whereas our minds will have thoughts of explanation, excuses and opinion to argue with the conscience. Whether Jew or Gentile, Christian, there will be no excuse or escape, except in the gospel of the grace of God. Whether it is instinct or nature or law; right and wrong are written on the heart and a wrong decision releases guilt upon the conscience. Conscience is like someone else inside you. Conscience is God's preacher in the bosom (Thomas Brooks). We sin by failing to do what our conscience tells us to do. A clean conscience brings freedom whereas a defiled conscience brings bondage. "To the pure, all things are pure; but to those who are defiled and unbelieving, nothing is pure, but both their mind and their conscience are defiled" (Titus 1:15). Being sound in faith with a clear conscience is what the Lord shows us is important and necessary. The work of the Lord in us makes the way of life highly desirable to us. All men have a conscience, or else God could not judge all men. The Christian conscience has the light of Jesus falling on it. Make conscience of hearkening to the voice of a conscience that is fed and corrected by the word of God.

The conscience is the moral nature or moral machinery of every man in the universe. It is set up as the judgment seat of God within us. God appeals to the human conscience within the heart of man. We are in a judgment every day, Christian, and a recording is being made of the activity going on in our conscience. We will stand in judgment someday with two witnesses; one will be God and the other will be our conscience. In this courtroom, the evidence that we belong to Jesus will be presented. The evidence will be presented that we received and walked with Jesus, and He saved us. In that day, Christ will be the judge, and the secrets of our hearts will be released. "Wait until the Lord comes who will bring to light the things hidden in the darkness and disclose the motives of men's hearts; and then each man's praise will come to him from God" (1 Cor. 4:5). My conscience tells me that we will give an account, and God and my conscience will be at least two of the witnesses. In that day, unforgiven sinners will be under terrors of conscience without a Savior, but the forgiven saints will have great comfort. The judgments of God will be final. God is faithful to His children in this life to let out His voice in their conscience about their sins. It will be to your wisdom and great joy to submit to this cry in your conscience while you are alive on the earth. Secret sins may make their way into public sins and great anguish. The Bible gives us the examples of Ananias and Sapphira (Acts 5:1-12), David (2 Sam. 12:9-12) and Achan (Joshua 7:16-26). Faith and the purpose in sinning cannot mix or stand together. One sin can eat all your lunch. Joy in your conscience will be your greatest joy and trouble in your conscience will be your greatest trouble. Let your confidence be in the testimony of your conscience, not in fleshly wisdom but in the grace of God (2 Cor. 1:12). A good conscience will be your best friend in good, bad, difficult and the worst of times. Keeping faith and a good conscience, by the grace of God, is a worthy triumph in life.

A clear conscience blesses us with freedom from guilt and access to God. We are introduced to a new way of living, which includes having a great priest to intercede for us. "Let us draw near with a sincere heart in full assurance of faith, having our hearts sprinkled clean from an evil conscience" (Heb. 10:22). You will enjoy the privilege of walking with Jesus. A clean conscience chases away fear and gives back safety. The individual with a clean conscience will draw near to God. We draw near to God by: conversion to Jesus, Bible study, holy conversation and living, and humble worship. We draw near in the full assurance of faith that we are justified by Christ's righteousness. We draw near with our hearts sprinkled with His blood having been cleansed from guilt and filth, and fear and ignorance by reasons of sin. Only Jesus can clean the conscience and then get a man moving for God. A clean conscience is necessary for love from a pure heart (1 Tim. 1:5), liberty in witnessing (1 Pet. 3:15-16) and confidence in prayer (1 John 3:21-22)).

A holy person will endeavor to listen to his conscience to hear from the Lord and to be like the Lord Jesus. He will "joyfully concur with the law of God in the inner man" (Rom. 7:22). He will seek and highly value the idea and the experience of the obedience of Faith (Rom. 1:5). He will seek to live by the spirit and not the flesh. The voice he hears, he recognizes, because it matches what the scripture has to say. He will know a love and kindness for fellow believers (Rom. 13:8). Since holy believers have known mercy, they will be merciful. They will pursue faith and study the Bible more and more to know the Lord. A holy person in Jesus will be inspired, mastered and live with the fruit of the spirit and especially love (Gal. 5:22-23). Their soul will cling to the Lord in all circumstances and trust that His goodness will always be with them (Ps. 63:8). They will seek, thirst and long for knowledge about the Lord and desire His presence. "Because Thy lovingkindness is better than life, my lips will praise Thee" (Ps. 63:3). God calls us to be holy (1 Pet. 1:15). The Bible tells us that "He died for all, that they who live should no longer live for themselves, but for Him who died and rose again on their behalf" (2 Cor. 5:15). Growing to be holy is evidence of saving faith and the gift of sincerity thriving in the conscience. Nothing unclean will enter heaven, Christian, "only those names who are written in the Lamb's book of life" (Rev. 21:27). Without holiness no one will see the Lord (Heb. 12:14).

A life of holiness is a journey, providentially and perfectly designed by the Lord, our God. Holiness in the heart becomes the greatest blessing of life. Being tired of sin, failure, and physical and mental disappointments, we wake up in a place of weakness where we know that we need the Lord. God takes us up into His own hands and presses out the impurities of a believer in His time and way. It is a great wonder, Christian; we get to a point in our lives when we think all we have is Jesus, and then we know that He is all we will ever need. The grace of God leads us to realize the difference between God's strength and ours. Divine strength and grace against afflictions, together with weakness in our life, is when Jesus becomes our boast (2 Cor. 12:9). Amen. In the sense of your need, God kindles the love of Jesus. In the sense of feeling lost, you are being found. In the sense of being empty, you are being filled. When you are weak, God's grace becomes your shield and Jesus your boasting song. The battle against sin can be fierce and wearisome, but faith is the victory (1 John 5:4). The battle for holiness requires God's strength. "By His doing you are in Christ Jesus, who became to us wisdom from God, and righteousness and sanctification, and redemption, that, just as it is written, let him who boasts, boast in the Lord" (1 Cor. 1:30-31). Open your heart to Jesus, Christian, that the pressure of His hand will make you humble. God gives grace to the humble (James 4:6). "In everything give thanks; for this is God's will for you in Christ Jesus" (1 Thess. 5:13). "Do not lose heart, but though our outer man is decaying, yet our inner man is being renewed day by day. For momentary light affliction is producing for us an eternal weight of glory far beyond all comparison, for the things which are seen are temporal, but the things which are not seen are eternal" (2 Cor. 4:16-18). By the grace of God, we will be holy. Thank you, Jesus.

We cannot attain holiness on our own, Christian, and we cannot maintain our new life without the Lord continuing to work on us with His enabling grace. I believe that God delights in this work and takes us as far as possible when we wait upon Him. We wait in Bible study, prayer and obedience. God moves us from the darkness of corruption into His marvelous light (1 Pet. 2:9). We are too lame to do it on our own. The stress we experience about holiness and our salvation is laid into our conscience by the voice of God. We must be drawn by God to Jesus and be born again. Being made in God's image (Gen. 1:26), and rich by His Spirit, we should reflect His holiness in our lives. We must have a new heart and spirit for the Holy Spirit to enlighten and instruct our conscience. In love, God inclines our desires, affections, hopes and a willingness to be holy (Phil. 2:13). He conforms us to the image of His purity that we may know the pleasures of holiness and have communion with Him, all to our great comfort. We pray, "Take my life, and let it be consecrated, Lord, to Thee. Take my moments and my days, let them flow in ceaseless praise" (Take my life, and let it be, Frances R. Havergal, 1874). God has such a high value for holiness that He designed our renewed nature and His glory to adorn it. His plan for us required that His only begotten Son would die that we might become holy. I pray for you, "Now may the God of peace Himself sanctify you entirely; and may your spirit and soul and body be preserved complete, without blame at the coming of our Lord Jesus Christ. Faithful is He who calls you, and He also will bring it to pass" (1 Thess. 5:23-24). To God be the glory of His grace. Amen.

Questions for Reflection

Do you think that God has the wisdom and power to be able to save you for eternal life?

Do you think that God providentially steps into your life to accomplish the purpose for which He created you?

Do you believe that the gift of faith comes from reading the word of God, and that God is patiently at work to finish your faith?

Do you think that God can only be perfectly good with you, or do you think that your struggles and afflictions in life show He is angry?

When you confessed your sin to God, was He faithful to forgive you and cleanse you from all unrighteousness?

Does your relationship with God involve fear and trembling, and are you growing from faith to faith?

Do you feel yourself falling in love with Jesus, and are you gaining the assurance that He loves you?

Does the sense of knowing the truth from the Bible make you feel free, and are you living with freedom in a Christian nation?

Do you pursue peace with all men and holiness with the Lord in a way that after you die you will see Jesus?

Invitation to Receive Jesus

There is only one way to be saved, and that is God's way; and God's way for us is to receive a person into our heart, and that person is His Son, the Lord Jesus Christ (John 14:6). The life and work of Jesus will save you from the penalty of sin by the sacrifice of Himself on the cross (Heb. 9:26). He took our place. He will save you from the power of sin (1 John 2:1-2, Heb. 9:24) and the presence of sin (Heb. 9:28). With an open heart please read, believe, and consider what is written below that He may bring salvation to your soul.

First, it is a fact that God loves you. "For God so loved the world that He gave His only begotten Son, that whosoever believes in Him should not perish, but have eternal life (John 3:16). There must be a sense of appreciation and gratitude to God, that even though you have sinned, He loves you and chose to save you and has a plan for your life.

Second, it is a fact though that you are a sinner dead in sin. "For all have sinned and come short of the glory of God" (Rom. 3:23). "For the wages of sin is death" (Rom. 6:23). There must be a sense that you are dead in sin and helpless to save yourself. You are lost and need help and only God can help you.

Third, it is a fact that Jesus Christ died to save you by paying the penalty for sin. "But God demonstrates His own love toward us, in that while we were yet sinners, Christ died for us" (Rom. 5:8). There must be a sense of surrender to Jesus as the only way I can be forgiven and saved. I must recognize that Jesus died for me and through Him, I can experience God's love.

Fourth, it is a fact that you can be saved by faith in the Lord

Jesus Christ. "What must I do to be saved? Believe in the Lord Jesus Christ and you shall be saved" (Acts 16:30-31). Say a prayer like the one shown below to receive Jesus into your heart. You can use your own words, but you must be sincere.

Dear Jesus, I confess that I have sinned against you. I did not keep my heart for you, but kept it for myself, because I wanted to sin. I was wrong. I'm sorry and I need you to help me; please forgive me and save me from the penalty of my sin. Thank you for dying on the cross for my sins. I accept what you have done for me and receive you as my Savior and Lord. I turn from myself and trust you to come into my heart. Thank you for forgiving me of my sins and giving me eternal life. Take control of my life and make me the kind of person you want me to be. In Jesus' name, thank you.

If you prayed this prayer sincerely, then Jesus Christ has come into your heart as He promised. You are a child of God and your sins have been forgiven. You have eternal life. "For by grace you have been saved through faith; and that not of yourselves, it is the gift of God; not as a result of works, that no one should boast" (Eph. 2:8-9). You have confessed with your mouth and believed in your heart for His righteousness to be saved (Rom. 10:9-10). God has given you a new heart and spirit and the Holy Spirit to help you grow in grace and knowledge. He will comfort you, and lead you into a holy and fruitful life. Read your Bible and pray, and find a local church to worship the Lord in and establish friendships with fellow believers. "The righteous man shall live by faith" (Rom. 1:17). Amen.

Further Reading

Brooks, T. (1861). The Works of Thomas Brooks (6 volumes). Banner of Truth Trust (1980). Carlisle, PA.

Charnock, S. (1853). The Existence and Attributes of God (2 volumes) Baker Book House (1979). Grand Rapids, MI.

Henry, M. (1706). Matthew Henry's Commentary on the Whole Bible (6 volumes). MacDonald Publishing Company (1983). Mclean, VI.

Nee, W. (1968). The Spiritual man (3 volumes). Christian Fellowship Publishers, Inc., New York, NY.

Pink, A. W. (1945). Exposition of the Gospel of John (3 Volumes). Zondervan Publishers (1975). Grand Rapids, MI.

Spurgeon, C. H. (1885). The treasury of David (3 Volumes). MacDonald Publishing Company (1990). Mclean, VI.

www.Preceptaustin.org (2017). Commentaries by verse.

Topical Index